BROADWAY'S PRIZE-WINNING MUSICALS: AN ANNOTATED GUIDE FOR LIBRARIES AND AUDIO COLLECTORS
Leo N. Miletich

AN ADVANCE REVIEW

"This valuable reference work provides everything you ever wanted to know about Broadway's prize-winning musicals. . . . This is no dry recitation of facts. The writing is breezy without being glib, informative without being dull. Miletich manages a world of compression that nevertheless includes all the bases. . . . This is a guide in the true sense of the word: explanatory, provocative, informative and opinionated."

Si Isenberg, Publisher, *Stages* magazine

Broadway's
Prize-Winning Musicals
An Annotated Guide
for Libraries and Audio Collectors

HAWORTH Library and Information Science
Peter Gellatly, Editor in Chief

New, Recent, and Forthcoming Titles:

The In-House Option: Professional Issues of Library Automation by T. D. Webb

British University Libraries by Toby Burrows

Women Online: Perspectives on Women's Studies in Online Databases edited by Steven D. Atkinson and Judith Hudson

Buyers and Borrowers: The Application of Consumer Theory to the Study of Library Use by Charles D. Emery

Broadway's Prize-Winning Musicals: An Annotated Guide for Libraries and Audio Collectors by Leo N. Miletich

Academic Libraries in Greece: The Present Situation and Future Prospects edited by Dean H. Keller

Introductory CD ROM Searching: The Key to Effective Ondisc Searching by Joseph Meloche

Broadway's Prize-Winning Musicals
An Annotated Guide for Libraries and Audio Collectors

Leo N. Miletich

The Haworth Press, Inc.
New York • London • Norwood (Australia)

The Haworth Press, Inc., 10 Alice Street, Binghamton, NY 13904-1580

Library of Congress Cataloging-in-Publication Data

Miletich, Leo N.
    Broadway's prize-winning musicals : an annotated guide for libraries and audio collectors / Leo N. Miletich.
        p.   cm.
    Includes bibliographical references (p.   ) and index.
    ISBN 1-56024-288-4 (alk. paper)
    1. Musicals—Discography.   I. Title.
ML156.4.M8M54   1992
016.7821'4'0266—dc20   92-4125
                                                                                          CIP
                                                                                          MN

This book is dedicated, with love and respect, to the memory of Irving Berlin, Leonard Bernstein, Dorothy Fields, George Gershwin, Ira Gershwin, Oscar Hammerstein, Lorenz Hart, Jerome Kern, Alan Jay Lerner, Frank Loesser, Frederick Loewe, Cole Porter, Richard Rodgers,

and to

the memory of I. T. Cohen who allowed me to program musicals for two happy years on KLOZ-FM in El Paso,

and to

the El Paso record-store clerk who, when asked if he had any Cole Porter music in stock, replied, "Who?"

and to

theater critics everywhere—without their thoughtful, insightful, balanced, and unbiased reviews, how would audiences ever know if they were having a good time?

ABOUT THE AUTHOR

Leo N. Miletich is a freelance writer living in El Paso, Texas. His diverse interests include a lifelong fascination with musical theater and years of collecting research recordings of musicals. Original cast recordings were the mainstay of his 13-year career in radio, which included a syndicated program of composer musicographies entitled "The American Musical Heritage Series." Mr. Miletich has published a wide variety of articles and essays in publications ranging from *Library Journal, Reason,* and *The Journal of Library Administration* to *The Humanist, Personnel Administrator, Playboy, Publishers Weekly, Administrative Management,* and *Collection Management.*

CONTENTS

Preface:
The Best Seat in the House

... I am of the idea that musicals are one of the greatest
achievements of the human race.

— British critic Rhoda Koenig,
Punch, August 17, 1990

Welcome to the theater!

Specifically, welcome to the musical theater as it is represented
through audio recordings, the theater of the mind. No big ticket
prices or sidewalk scalpers, no transportation or parking problems,
and the seats are as comfortable as the listeners care to make them.
Here you can build your own scenery, sew your own costumes, and
choreograph your own dances. Best of all, getting dressed up is not
required; sending out for pizza is encouraged.

The world of the recorded musical is one of catchy tunes, rhymes
both simple and tricky, rhythms that are bouncy or romantic,
starkly dramatic or danceable — from polkas to waltzes, square
dances to ballets, reels to rock. The musical world is peopled with
characters so filled with strong emotion — from love to hate and
everything in between — they just have to burst forth in song to tell
about it. It is a world where the best are honored with applause,
fame (however fleeting), and the occasional award.

As Ethel Merman once sang from the stage of New York's Imperial Theatre, "(There's No Business Like) Show Business!"

Thousands of musicals have appeared since the form began taking shape in the 1920s, and most since the 1940s have been recorded in one way or another. The amount of material available can
be staggering, intimidating to the nonexpert or novice fan. What to
get? What to listen to? Is this one a good show? Or that one? How
can I tell in advance? As with anything of a creative nature, these
are subjective questions not easily answered.

Everyone agrees that there are both good and bad shows. Some
superb shows played for over a thousand performances or went on

literally for years: *A Chorus Line* [Act One, 1976] presently holds the Broadway record at fifteen years; *The Fantasticks* [Act Five] has been playing continuously Off-Broadway for over *thirty* years. Then there are the shows that closed in a week, or a day, or out of town, regardless of the talent involved. Even the legendary giants of the theater have produced some unenchanted evenings. There are never any guarantees.

Professional critics often disagree over what is best or worst, which can be hilarious when the show being simultaneously praised and pummeled is not yours. All criticism, of course, is subjective. Two people seeing the same show at the same time can come away with diametrically opposed views concerning its merits and faults, for everything is being filtered through the individual's personal value system, prejudices and preferences, whatever degree of objectivity is claimed. Reviews often reveal more about the reviewer than the show in question. Observe:

Big River [Act One, 1985]

". . . almost totally uninvolving . . . commits the unpardonable sin of being dull."

Douglas Watt, New York *Daily News*,
April 26, 1985

". . . at last Broadway has a new musical of substance [that] touches feelings and thoughts worthy of civilized adults — and children."

Jack Kroll, *Newsweek*,
May 6, 1985

Cabaret [Act One, 1967]

". . . both brilliant and remarkable . . . a bright, handsome and steadily entertaining show."

Richard Watts, Jr., *New York Post*,
November 21, 1966

"'Cabaret' is schizoid, and schizophrenic theatre will not do."

Martin Gottfried, *Women's Wear Daily*,
November 21, 1966

City of Angels [Act One, 1990]

"I found it the most brilliant of musical comedies."
Doug Watt, New York *Daily News*,
December 22, 1989

". . . just because I didn't have a good time, why should I assume you won't?"
Howard Kissel, New York *Daily News*,
December 12, 1989

Fiddler on the Roof [Act One, 1965]

". . . one of the great works of the American musical theatre . . . touching, beautiful, warm, funny and inspiring. It is a work of art."
John Chapman, New York *Daily News*,
September 23, 1964

"It seemed to me there was an over-abundance of self-pity displayed."
John McClain, New York *Journal-American*,
September 23, 1964

Into the Woods [Act One, 1988]

". . . a seamless masterpiece . . . Once again, Sondheim takes the musical to new, dizzying heights."
Jim Hiley, *The Listener*,
October 4, 1990

"It's all childlike without being charming, silly without being funny . . . a muddle of trite sophistication and didactic homilies."
Rhoda Koenig, *Punch*,
October 5, 1990

Jesus Christ, Superstar [Act Five]

". . . so stunningly effective a theatrical experience that I am still finding it difficult to compose my thoughts about it. It is, in short, a triumph."
Douglas Watt, New York *Daily News*,
October 13, 1971

". . . it wasn't worthy of the furor, enthusiasm and ire that it has aroused . . . commonplace and never exciting or moving."

Richard Watts, *New York Post*,
October 13, 1971

The Mystery of Edwin Drood [Act One, 1986]

". . . one of the New York Shakespeare Festival's happiest hours and as pleasurable an evening as Broadway has seen in years."

Howard Kissel, *Women's Wear Daily*,
December 4, 1985

"The mystery . . . is how so much talent got to be lavished on such a well-meaning, tiresome project."

Linda Winer, *USA Today*,
December 3, 1985

The Rothschilds [Act Five]

"*The Rothschilds* is not a good play it's a great play . . . . a great play with satisfactory music. . . . Inspirational."

John Schubeck, WABC-TV,
October 19, 1970

"This lead-footed and overstuffed musical, oldest of old fashioned, only represents the vulgarity of money and the vulgarization of Jewishness. It also represents the vulgarization of musical theatre."

Martin Gottfried, *Women's Wear Daily*,
October 21, 1970

The Saint of Bleecker Street [Act Two, 1954-1955]

". . . to the end, and in spite of our fascination — we remain unmoved."

Walter Kerr, New York *Herald Tribune*,
December 28, 1954

"It is deeply moving."

Robert Coleman, New York *Daily Mirror*,
December 28, 1954

1776 [Act One, 1969]

"A magnificently staged and stunningly original musical
. . . it is funny, it is moving. . . . It is an artistic creation such
as we do not often find in our theater."

John Chapman, New York *Daily News*,
March 17, 1969

". . . has as much to do with present rebellion as a watermelon
at a race riot. . . . cardboard characters from summer historical
pageants, and the whole business is rather bizarre."

Martin Gottfried, *Women's Wear Daily*,
March 17, 1969

Some critics may even praise and damn a musical in a single
review, as when Walter Kerr filled his *New York Times* report on
Company [May 3, 1970] with the kind of adjectives producers only
dream about — "sizzlingly performed, inventively scored," "original," "uncompromising," "exemplary," "Sondheim has never
written a more sophisticated, more pertinent, or . . . more melodious score" — and then ended by declaring, "I didn't like the
show." Subjectivity can be confusing.

This is not an all-inclusive, totally comprehensive book on recorded musicals. That would require more than one volume and a
wheelbarrow to tote them around. This is a starter kit. It is user-friendly. This volume provides a select listing of the best and most
readily available shows (original casts, revival casts, studio casts,
film casts) in order to suggest a collection of representative musicals that span the genre's entire history. The book's scope, like
Mercutio's wound in *Romeo and Juliet*, is "not so deep as a well,
nor so wide as a church-door; but 'tis enough, 'twill serve."

Shows in this volume have been selected by using both objective
and subjective criteria. The objective criteria in Act One through
Act Four rely on annual awards ceremonies, namely the Antoinette
Perry [Tony] Awards, the New York Drama Critics Circle Award,
the Pulitzer Prize, and the recording industry's Grammy.

Rare, mint-condition, original cast albums affect devout musical
collectors the way antique Ming vases affect collectors of art, with
the inevitable consequence of extremely high prices. But for those
who just want to enjoy the music, reissues and revival or studio

casts will do just fine. Thus, the subjective criteria used for Act Five involve both budgetary considerations and that elusive element known as listening enjoyment. Subjective choices would include:

A. The show you force all your friends to listen to even if you have to tie them down.
B. The show you play so often that oxide begins to flake off the tape, or the record grooves have been worn through to the other side of the vinyl, or your CD player won't accept it any more because even *it* is tired of it.
C. The shows that make you want to sing and dance along even though you have no discernible talent for either (this is especially embarrassing when using a Walkman in a public place).
D. The shows that make you think, feel, laugh, cry, or write fan letters to the composers — even when they're dead.

As the critics cited above indicate, we are not all entertained by the same thing.

Some will prefer the romantic melodrama of, say, *Phantom of the Opera* [Act One, 1988] over the sharp personal realities of *A Chorus Line* [Act One, 1976] or the social commentary of *Don't Bother Me, I Can't Cope* [Act Four, 1972]. Those nostalgic for the 1960s might like *Grease* [Act Five] more than the 1940s big band sound of *Over Here!* [Act Five] or the swing dance music of *Sophisticated Ladies* [Act Five]. Lovers of country-western sounds might choose *The Best Little Whorehouse in Texas* [Act Five] in preference to the vintage blues of *Black and Blue* [Act Five] or the 1960s Rhythm and Blues stylings of *Dreamgirls* [Act Four, 1982]. The operatically inclined may gravitate more to *The Consul* [Act Two, 1949-1950] or *Porgy and Bess* [Act Five].

Similarly, there are listeners who prefer strong lyrics, no matter what the style, and shows that are *about* something, songs that have relevance, substance, an opinion — even an attitude — about life. They want their brains engaged along with their emotions. Clever words, witty words, words with bite, well-crafted, meaningful, and even dirty words grab their attention more forcefully than a rank of violins pursuing a lush melodic phrase. Others savor the violins, the romance of a "Shall We Dance?" "I Could Have Danced All Night," or "The Music of the Night." Some gifted composers provide both, bless them, and there are fans who enjoy just such a wide spectrum of styles. Fortunately, Broadway has something for every taste, narrow or eclectic.

To further help librarians and fans compile a well-balanced collection, the effort in Act Five — the subjective section — is to provide as diverse a selection of musical styles as possible, always keeping in mind the historical and artistic importance of individual shows, scores, or performances.

The musical stage has long provided listeners with a rich tapestry of savory sounds and evocative words, all set in an ever-evolving, make-believe world brimming with beauty and poetry, love and hate, joy and despair, and all movingly expressed in song and dance. This book is your passport to that world.

Acknowledgments

Books are written in that scariest of risky environments: alone. But just as an athlete can find an extra burst of adrenaline when the crowd roars its approval, so too does a writer find both sustenance and motivation, drive and inspiration from the encouragement of those cheering him on.

The first person to share the vision of this book and, more, to actively assist in its publication, was Peter Gellatly of The Haworth Press and editor of *Collection Management* journal (in which a condensed version first appeared).

Special thanks for Grammy research are due to Viki Goto of the National Academy of Recording Arts and Sciences' publications department.

The cheering was augmented by my own long-suffering booster club of the usual suspects who offered comments, listened to tunes, helped locate some old shows and obscure facts, provided unconditional encouragement and support, and put up with me in my normal antisocial writing mode: B. J. and Don Albert, Doug Bowe, Lydia DeHaro, Chuck and Sandy Gipe, Hatsuyo Hawkins, Susan Hicks, Carolyn Kahl, Harry Mallo, Dan Miller, Esperanza Moreno, Bud and Pilar Newman, Fletcher Newman, Ramon and Irma Ramirez, Estela Reyes, Juan A. Sandoval, Scott and Joy Segall, Ossie Spruell, Dolores Sweezey, Elka Tenner, Bill and Katie Young. Plus Max O. Preeo of *Show Music* magazine. And, of course, the indispensable Justine and Juliette.

Also, for giving me hope, Drs. Mario Palafox and Mark Reeves.

Excerpts from *Sondheim & Co.*, 2nd ed. by Craig Zaden. Copyright 1974, 1986 by Craig Zaden. Reprinted by permission of HarperCollins Publishers.

Excerpts from *Twenty Years on Broadway* by George M. Cohan. Copyright 1924, 1925 by George M. Cohan, renewed 1953 by

Agnes W. Cohan. Reprinted by permission of HarperCollins Publishers.

Thanks also to the following publishers for permission to quote from books cited in the text: Putnam, Signet, Viking, Southern Illinois University Press, and Diana Fleishman for permission to quote from John Houseman's *Run-Through*.

Overture:
America's Musical Heritage

Musical Comedy (Musicals). Type of musical entertainment, 20th cent., development of operetta, which relies for its popular success on a succession of catchy and easily memorable tunes, either as songs, duets, or choruses.

— Michael Kennedy,
Oxford Dictionary of Music[1]

Long ago and far away—to borrow a song title from Jerome Kern—there was a magical land called Tin Pan Alley. It was situated on the exotic isle of Manhattan, on 28th Street between Broadway and Fifth Avenue. From the turn of the century and for the next three decades, this small parcel of real estate was the main home of American popular music, originating songs that were sung on vaudeville stages, picked up by bands and orchestras, and, through the sale of sheet music, eventually danced to and hummed by ordinary people throughout the country.

It did not look magical. Or even prosperous. Just a block of grimy office buildings. But lettered in gold on most of the windows were the enchanted words, "Music Publishers," and coming through the windows onto the busy street below was a happy cacophony of tinny, rinky-tink noise as dozens of sorcerer song pluggers plunked away at upright pianos, demonstrating their musical magic for clients.

Those clients were the producers of variety shows in search of new material, and the stars of vaudeville shows wanting something that would spotlight their talents and bring in their fans. (Al Jolson was a master at it, entertaining the audience for hours with impromptu concerts while his cast stood around in a frozen tableau waiting to go on with the show.)

Not that songs relevant to the show's plot were unknown. The

American stage was swamped with European-styled operettas, even the best and most homespun of which steadfastly retained a foreign sound and look: Red-coated Mounties singing of stout-hearted men and Indian maidens; Prussian military types with pointed helmets warbling through their mustaches to women in hoop skirts barely concealing Wagnerian dimensions.

A brash young actor from a show business family changed all that: George M. Cohan Americanized the operetta into the musical comedy.

LOWBROW HIJINKS

Crash right through this show to-night. Speed! Speed! and lots of it; that's my idea of the thing. Perpetual motion. Laugh your heads off; have a good time; keep happy. Remember now, happy, happy, happy. . . . And don't forget the secret to it all. Speed! a whole lot of speed!

—George M. Cohan's advice to the cast of *The Governor's Son,* 1901[2]

Under Cohan's guidance, the often lugubrious and sonorous tempos of the operetta took on the cocky ebullience of Cohan himself, a song-and-dance man with the instincts of a master showman. His shows were a celebration of the American identity often with a flag-draped Cohan dancing—or, rather, prancing and strutting—boisterously across the stage. The shows that sprang from Cohan's prolific mind staked out this new form of entertainment as American territory. Cohan published over five hundred songs to help legitimize that claim; a statue of him in Times Square is a lasting tribute.

The next innovative step in this musical evolution came from a one-time Tin Pan Alley song plugger and composer named Jerome Kern. Kern succeeded in bringing graceful and imaginative melodies to the musical comedy while retaining its underlying American flavor. His small-scale musicals at the 300-seat Princess Theater used songs (with lyrics by Guy Bolton and P. G. Wodehouse) not just as star turns but to further the story.

Kern kept this up for three years (1915-1918) and, in turn, inspired others to take adventurous risks in Broadway composing, opening the door for all who came after. But it was Kern himself who set the standard against which all musicals were measured for decades to come: *Show Boat* [Act Five]. With Oscar Hammerstein II, a veteran of operettas and musical comedies ("Stout Hearted Men" was his and Sigmund Romberg's), Kern set out to revolutionize the genre and succeeded. The songs in *Show Boat* grew from the characters, the situation, the era. The various plot lines of miscegenation, heartbreak, sacrifice, and success upon the wicked stage had genuine emotional depth. It may have flirted with melodrama at times (a form mocked in one of the showboat's stage offerings), but the music held it to an even keel.

Serious musicals for the serious-minded have rarely dominated Broadway, however. The standard boy-meets-girl romantic comedy continued to hold sway. But thanks to Kern, the composers of these frivolities were now better able to turn the froth into something more solid.

During the 1930s, the chief architects of this new-found maturity were Richard Rodgers and Lorenz Hart, and a pair of brothers named George and Ira Gershwin. George was once a song plugger in the Alley. The work of these two preeminent teams was indicative of their youth and their times, characterized by contemporary music idioms and sharp, facile, lightly mocking lyrics.

Both teams were popular in the 1920s, Rodgers and Hart with *The Garrick Gaieties* revues, *Peggy-Ann*, *A Connecticut Yankee*, and *Present Arms*; the brothers Gershwin with *Lady Be Good!* (which introduced jazz to Broadway), *Tip-Toes*, *Oh, Kay* [Act Five], and *Funny Face* [see *My One and Only*, Act Five]. George took time out to compose a masterful jazz concert piece, "Rhapsody In Blue."

Rodgers and Hart kept pace in the 1930s with *Simple Simon* (which included their melancholy hit, "Ten Cents a Dance"), *Jumbo*, *On Your Toes* — featuring the ballet, "Slaughter on Tenth Avenue" [Act Five], and *Babes in Arms* [Act Five]. The Gershwins countered with the Pulitzer Prize-winning *Of Thee I Sing* [Act Three, 1932], *Let 'em Eat Cake* [Act Five], and the "folk opera" *Porgy and Bess* [Act Five]. George added a concerto and the concert work, *An American in Paris*. For lovers of musicals, the decade of the 1930s was a dizzying time.

George Gershwin died tragically and unexpectedly of a brain tumor in 1937 at the age of 38. By then his driving jazz rhythms had come to symbolize American music to the rest of the world. After George's death and a period of retirement, Ira again wrote the lyrics for some musicals — notably *Lady in the Dark* with Kurt Weill (in which Danny Kaye sang "Tchaikovsky," spewing out the tongue-twisting names of some 53 Russian composers in thirty seconds), and the Judy Garland film *A Star Is Born* — before permanently retiring in 1954.

By the 1940s, Jerome Kern was more involved with movies than theater (he and Dorothy Fields won an Oscar for "The Way You Look Tonight" in 1936 and Hollywood hung onto him). Larry Hart, after penning the lyrics for *Pal Joey* [Act Two, 1951-1952] and *By Jupiter*, was beset by personal problems and split with Rodgers in 1942; he died the following year at the age of 48.

As one prolific and creative era ended, another began with the torch being passed to men such as Cole Porter and Irving Berlin, and carried on by Rodgers and Hammerstein.

Irving Berlin was the eldest and most successful of the Broadway giants as the 1940s arrived. He could not read or write music and used a secretary for both (George Gershwin had applied for the job, but Berlin wisely advised him to stick with his own music). He could barely plunk out a simple melody on a made-to-order piano. But what a gift Berlin had for popular tunes and honest sentiment! "All by Myself," "Always," "I Love a Piano," "All Alone," "Say It With Music," "Mandy," "What'll I Do?" and "Blue Skies" were all Tin Pan Alley hits prior to Kern and Hammerstein writing *Show Boat*.

The Russian-born Berlin (born Israel Baline) was, in turn, a singing waiter, a composer of hit ragtime tunes ("Alexander's Ragtime Band" in 1911 was the cornerstone of his career); chief song contributor for *The Music Box Revues* and *Ziegfeld Follies* ("A Pretty Girl Is Like a Melody"); composer of Broadway scores such as *Face the Music* and *As Thousands Cheer* in the 1930s, *This Is the Army* ("Oh, How I Hate to Get Up in the Morning") and *Annie Get Your Gun* [Act Five] in the 1940s, and *Call Me Madam* in 1950; prolific composer of film scores for Fred Astaire and Ginger Rogers (*Top Hat, Carefree, Follow the Fleet*); and beloved composer of patriotic standards and holiday favorites, from "God Bless America" (1939) to "This Is a Great Country" (1962) and "Easter Parade" (1933) to "White Christmas" (1942) — the latter being a film song that won an Oscar. Berlin's lyrics were simple and straightforward, his melodies memorable.

There was nothing simple about a good Cole Porter song; it could get under your skin in the still of the night, haunt you and taunt you night and day, day and night. And just when you thought it was time for a waltz, he could begin a beguine. The antithesis of a Berlin ballad, a Porter song could bristle with satiric wit, fly to the moon on gossamer wings, puncture pomposity, shock with sophisticated ideas and double entendres, and play with words the way children play with jacks, scattering them around and then, with melodies both lovely and exotic, deftly snatch them up again.

Born into wealth, Porter became a celebrated international party favorite long before he had a hit show. He went from writing fight songs for Yale's football team to the Foreign Legion (a youthful escapade, marching — so goes the legend — with a small piano on his back), to the salons of Paris and the glitter of Broadway as if it were all preordained. The 1930s saw him composing his artful ditties for *The New Yorkers, Gay Divorce, You Never Know, Anything Goes* [Act Five], *Leave It to Me,* and *DuBarry Was a Lady.*

A horseback-riding accident in 1937 crushed both of Porter's legs, leaving him a pain-wracked cripple for the next 27 years, yet even *that* did not dim his wit for long and the 1940s saw him composing his unique brand of breezy banter in *Panama Hattie, Let's Face It, Mexican Hayride, Kiss Me, Kate* [Act One, 1949], *Out of This World,* and *Silk Stockings* [Act Five].

When asked for an opinion of a new Rodgers and Hammerstein show, that one-man song-writing team of Cole and Porter said the usual polite things but wondered aloud why it took two people to write a song.[3] Genius must have its due. But the teaming of Rodgers with Hammerstein in 1942 took the musical into another stage of development, just as *Show Boat* had. The first effort by Rodgers and Hammerstein combined ballet, humor, drama, and corn as high as an elephant's eye: *Oklahoma!* [Act Five]. The opening night reviews were sensational.

John Anderson, writing in the New York *Journal-American,*

called it "a beautiful and delightful show, fresh and imaginative," and was among the first to notice that "none of it has either the routine sight or sound of the usual showshop patchwork."

Howard Barnes of the New York *Herald Tribune* declared, "Songs, dances and a story have been triumphantly blended."

Lewis Nichols told readers of *The New York Times* that "Mr. Rodgers's scores never lack grace, but seldom have they been so well integrated." (Nichols also suggested that the title tune was one which the state of Oklahoma "would do well to seize as an anthem forthwith"; it did.)

Oklahoma! was a smash hit and so was the new team. Before the decade ended, Rodgers and Hammerstein had contributed *Carousel* [Act Two, 1945-1946] and *South Pacific* [Act One, 1950] to Broadway, picking up a Pulitzer Prize for the latter; they won an Oscar in 1945 for "It Might As Well Be Spring" (from the film *State Fair*). The 1950s brought forth *The King and I* [Act One, 1952], and *Flower Drum Song* [Act Five], and they moved into the 1960s with *The Sound of Music* [Act One, 1961].

> The music is not décor. It is core.
>
> — lyricist Tom Jones[4]

Rodgers and Hammerstein's chief competition in the 1950s was another team with many of the same virtues — Alan Jay Lerner and Frederick Loewe.

Both Rodgers and Loewe were adept at lush and evocative melodies that conjured up exotic climes and times, whether it was mysterious Bali Ha'i or the Scottish highlands, Oklahoma cornfields or California's goldfields, Siam or Covent Garden, San Francisco's Chinatown or Parisian high society, the Austrian alps or the towers of Camelot. All of their shows played well instrumentally.

Where Hammerstein, the graduate of operettas, was always good at individual songs of strong emotion that could stand on their own outside of a plot, Alan Jay Lerner's great gift of wit and words enabled him to adroitly walk that thin line between a character song and a song everyone could relate to. He was the one librettist who dared tackle George Bernard Shaw. And no one could top him at big centerpiece songs that not only advanced the plot but were a crucial part of the narrative, such as *Camelot*'s brilliant "Guenevere" in which the chorus sings of the discovery of Lancelot's love for the queen, his escape, her trial, and her rescue from the stake [Act Five].

Teamwork was also the order of the day for writers and lyricists Betty Comden and Adolph Green, who often were up on stage performing their own numbers. From the late 1940s through the 1950s and on into the 1960s, a bright new Comden and Green show was something to look forward to. First came *On the Town* in 1944 [Act Five] and *Wonderful Town* nine years later [Act One, 1953], both with music by Leonard Bernstein. They teamed with composer Jule Styne for *Bells Are Ringing* [Act Five], *Do Re Mi*, *Subways Are for Sleeping*, *Hallelujah, Baby* [Act One, 1968], and others.

Jule Styne spread his immense musical talent around, also working with Sammy Cahn on *High Button Shoes*, Leo Robin on *Gentlemen Prefer Blondes*, Carolyn Leigh and others on *Peter Pan* [Act Five], Stephen Sondheim on *Gypsy* [Act Four, 1959], and Bob Merrill on *Funny Girl* [Act Four, 1964].

A composer who wrote his own words and music in the Porter and Berlin tradition was Frank Loesser. After a few song hits in the 1930s, he made a quick name for himself with the nation's first World War II fight song, "Praise the Lord and Pass the Ammunition," the title coming from a widely quoted comment heard during the bombing of Pearl Harbor. More hit singles followed, notably "Spring Will Be a Little Late This Year," "Jingle Jangle Jingle" (for Tex Ritter), and "On a Slow Boat to China." Loesser won an Oscar in 1949 for "Baby, It's Cold Outside" (from the film *Neptune's Daughter*). After a Broadway hit starring Ray Bolger called *Where's Charley?* (which included the hit "Once in Love With Amy"), Loesser reached the heights in 1950 with *Guys and Dolls* [Act One, 1951]. In 1956 he experimented with sung dialogue in *The Most Happy Fella* [Act Two, 1956-1957], and won a Pulitzer Prize in 1961 with *How to Succeed in Business Without Really Trying* [Act One, 1962].

By then, Ira Gershwin was in retirement. Hammerstein died in 1960, Porter in 1964. Frank Loesser died in 1969. Berlin effectively retired in 1962 after *Mr. President*, though he lived on until 1989, dying at the age of 101. Richard Rodgers tried other partners after Hammerstein's death, including Stephen Sondheim (*Do I Hear a Waltz?*), wrote his own lyrics for one show [*No Strings*, Act Four, 1962], and died in 1979.

ON THROUGH THE SEASONS . . .

The 1960s were for the new breed, the youngsters, taking off from the great legacy left by Broadway's pioneers.

For Broadway's composers, the 1960s began like a marathon race, a great many entrants bunched together at the starting line, with the mass slowly stretching out as leaders began to break away from the pack, the lead changing a number of times as great individual shows opened and closed, until at the end there was one clear winner moving into the 1970s, tailed closely by a small number of remaining finishers, all talented, all having left their marks on musical history.

For reasons perhaps best attributed to the generation gap (in both composers and ticket-buying audiences), the growing popularity of rock and roll was very slow to work its way onto Broadway, and has yet to gain a firm foothold. With Elvis gyrating across America in the late 1950s and early 1960s, the most Broadway's best could offer was Cole Porter's "The Ritz Roll and Rock" in the film version of *Silk Stockings*, and Irving Berlin's politicians in *Mr. President* doing the "The Washington Twist" in the Oval Office (a score that also included a more heartfelt number called "Let's Go Back to the Waltz").

The closest thing to a rock musical was a 1960 satire about an Elvis clone being drafted. It was called *Bye Bye Birdie* [Act One, 1961]. The score was by newcomers Charles Strouse and Lee Adams. Likewise, the ever-escalating Vietnam War did not figure into the consciousness of the American musical until briefly in 1967 [*Hair*, Act Four, 1968; *Now Is the Time for All Good Men*, Act Five], and did not inspire a masterpiece until *Miss Saigon* [Act Five] — and that was first a hit in London.

In the first half of the 1960s, Broadway was in stasis, and in danger of becoming complacent.

In 1963 a beachhead was established on Broadway by the British (leading to a full-scale invasion by the 1980s). Lionel Bart imported

Oliver! [Act One, 1963], and with him came the Anthony Newley and Leslie Bricusse show, *Stop the World, I Want to Get Off* [Act Five]; they followed that with *The Roar of the Greasepaint, the Smell of the Crowd* [Act Five]. It was becoming clear that America no longer had an exclusive right to its own musical heritage.

Most of the 1960s witnessed little true innovation in the musical, though very talented people produced some excellent shows within the established musical-comedy structure.

Strouse and Adams collaborated on *Golden Boy* [Act Five], *It's a Bird It's a Plane It's Superman*, and ended the decade with *Applause* [Act One, 1970]. The team of Sheldon Harnick and Jerry Bock scored big with the Pulitzer-winning *Fiorello!* [Act One, 1960] and the blockbuster *Fiddler on the Roof* [Act One, 1965]. Jerry Herman, the 1960s' answer to Irving Berlin, produced the catchy melodies of *Hello, Dolly* [Act One, 1964] and *Mame* [Act Four, 1966]. Dorothy Fields, whose songs had graced the stage and screen since the 1940s, did the lyrics for *Redhead* [Act One, 1959] and *Sweet Charity* [Act Five]. In 1964 Barbra Streisand became a household name in *Funny Girl* [Act Four, 1964], with songs by Jule Styne and Bob Merrill. Composers Joe Darion and Mitch Leigh, like Lionel Bart, proved that a classic of literature could become a successful musical as they metamorphosed *Don Quixote* into *Man of La Mancha* [Act One, 1966].

A youngster (and one-time scriptwriter for the *Topper* TV series) named Stephen Sondheim teamed up with Leonard Bernstein in 1957 for *West Side Story* [Act Five], with Jule Styne in 1959 for *Gypsy* [Act Four, 1959], then went out on his own Cole Porterish-way to write *A Funny Thing Happened on the Way to the Forum* [Act One, 1963] and *Anyone Can Whistle* [Act Five] in 1964. His talent was the light at the end of the 1960s' tunnel, becoming brighter with each passing year.

With all this emerging talent, something had to come along to shake up the conventions the way *Show Boat* and *Oklahoma!* had, and it appeared in 1966 with Kander and Ebb's *Cabaret*. It was only their second musical.

John Kander and Fred Ebb began in 1965 with *Flora, the Red Menace* [Act Five], a musical about Red-baiting during the 1930s starring Liza Minnelli in her Broadway debut. They next chose to place songs in the context of an even more powerful drama: the rise of Nazism in Berlin during the 1920s, as seen through the eyes of a naive would-be writer and a jaded cabaret singer. *Cabaret* [Act One, 1967] was unconventional, compelling, and uncompromising, and it proved there was an audience for unflinching reality in a musical format. Subsequent Kander and Ebb works such as *Chicago* [Act Five], *The Act* [Act Five], *The Rink* [Act Five] and others, while entertaining and tuneful, did not match that emotional punch. (A 1991 revue of their work, *And the World Goes 'Round*, is available from RCA.)

Eleven years after Elvis first sang "Hound Dog," rock finally made it to a Broadway success in 1967 with *Hair*. It featured anti-war chanting, four-letter words, nudity, drug songs, hippies, and counterculture flower children. It was an outrageous hit. But, in terms of musical stylings, rock still did not become the dominant Broadway sound, not even after the success of the "rock opera" *Jesus Christ, Superstar* [Act Five], or the rock version of *Two Gentlemen of Verona* [Act One, 1972]. Rock's influence can be heard on Broadway, but not always in the forefront.

THE MODERN MUSICAL'S WORLD

It is no longer assumed that a musical is or should be an escapist entertainment. . . . The Broadway musical, instead, has opened itself more and more to the real world: the fearful, divided, confused real world we live in every day . . . [musicals] have gained something in variety, imaginative freedom, and truth to life.

—Julius Novick[5]

What emerged from the largely complacent 1960s—thanks to *Cabaret* and a few other groundbreakers—was the reality musical. One show and one composer epitomized that in the 1970s. The show was *A Chorus Line* [Act One, 1976], its score composed by Marvin Hamlisch and Edward Kleban. The leading composer of the 1970s was Stephen Sondheim who, in quick succession, wrote the scores for *Company* [Act One, 1971], *Follies* [Act One, 1972], *A Little Night Music* [Act One, 1973], *Pacific Overtures* [Act Two,

1975-1976], and *Sweeney Todd* [Act One, 1979] in the astonishing space of nine years.

Other good shows appeared in the 1970s, of course: *Annie* [Act One, 1977], *Grease* [Act Five], *I Love My Wife* [Act Five], *The Wiz* [Act One, 1975], and others, but no one show, and no one composer, ever dominated a decade quite like *A Chorus Line* and Sondheim.

Seemingly gone forever were the days when a producer, without a script, could hire a composer and say, "I'm not sure what the plot will be. Just give me three love songs, two comedy numbers, and, hmmm, how about a tap dance? Oh, my star is that guy who whistles in three octaves, so give me something for that. Setting? Well, make it . . . Brazil. My wife likes Latin rhythms. I'll be back to get the songs next week. Gotta go find a writer."

In terms of popular success, the 1980s belonged to a Britisher named Andrew Lloyd Webber. Sondheim gave him a run for his money, wonderfully fusing song with dialogue and action in *Into the Woods* [Act One, 1988], *Sunday in the Park With George* [Act Two, 1983-1984], and *Merrily We Roll Along.* Another imported musical based on a dramatic and epic novel, *Les Misérables* [Act One, 1987], had a spectacular run not just on Broadway but around the world. Richard Maltby, Jr. and David Shire emerged from Off-Broadway in the 1980s with *Baby* [Act Five], nominated for nine Tony Awards.

But when the smoke had cleared, and the critical brickbats were forgotten (Stephen Holden in *The New York Times* called him the master of "Bustling quasi-symphonic music [and] bravura pop spectacle"[6]), it was Andrew Lloyd Webber who kept rolling on. By the end of the decade, working with a variety of lyricists, he had composed *Jesus Christ, Superstar* [Act Five], *Evita* [Act One, 1980], *Cats* [Act One, 1983], *Phantom of the Opera* [Act One, 1988], and *Aspects of Love* — along with lesser works such as *Song and Dance* and *Starlight Express.* Still, the New York critics avidly took up what has come to be called "Webber-bashing," as when Howard Kissel reviewed *Song and Dance* in *Women's Wear Daily* (9/19/85), conjuring up the image of the Mozart play *Amadeus* to brand Lloyd Webber as "probably the Saliari of our time. His music is Mediocrity Incarnate but terribly commercial."

Yet this British composer with the prolific and profitable output clearly struck a resounding chord in many ears on both sides of the Atlantic, making him — if not the best or most inventive — surely the richest composer in Broadway's history. *People* magazine reported Lloyd Webber's estimated *daily* income for 1990 at $175,500.[7]

Alan Jay Lerner died in 1986; Frederick Loewe in 1988. Sondheim ended the decade teaching the art of the musical at Oxford and dashing off some tunes for Madonna to sing in the film *Dick Tracy* (winning an Oscar for "Sooner or Later"), then began the 1990s with a brilliant Off-Broadway offering called *Assassins* (RCA 60737-4-RC). Lloyd Webber entered the 1990s with a musical version of the Gloria Swanson film *Sunset Boulevard*. Ironically, toward the end of 1990 Sondheim found himself challenging Andrew Lloyd Webber on his home turf through London productions of several of his Broadway shows, a situation headlined by *The New York Times* this way: "West End Story: Sondheim Mania Hits London."[8]

As the 1990-1991 season got underway, enough revivals and revues were on display to prompt *Time*'s William A. Henry III to see them as an attempt to "reclaim the giddy simplicity of the past."[9] And yet the season closed with a moving Vietnam romantic tragedy, *Miss Saigon* [Act Five]; a cherished tale of childhood awakening in *The Secret Garden* [Act Five]; a calypso-flavored fantasy called *Once on This Island* [Act Five]; and a glitzy, nostalgic extravaganza, *The Will Rogers Follies* [Act One, 1991], with music by Cy Coleman and lyrics by Betty Comden and Adolph Green — still writing musicals 46 years after *On the Town*.

Whether American composers can regain the creative and adventurous high ground in the 1990s, or whether the heart of the musical will have permanently shifted to London's West End, Paris, Sydney, or elsewhere, becoming internationalized, remains to be seen. The battle is bound to be tunefully exciting.

SOUND IDEAS

One of the gifts bestowed by our technological era is that of sound reproduction. Without it only a relative handful of people would ever hear and enjoy the great musicals through original cast recordings.

Thomas Edison patented his "phonograph or speaking machine" on February 19, 1878, the sound being recorded on a hand-cranked cylinder wrapped in tin foil. Improvements and refinements have continued to this day, evolving from Edison's cylinders to Emile Berliner's very breakable shellac platters of 1887 with a single song on each side and revolving at 78 revolutions per minute (four minutes to a side), to long-playing, vinyl, 33 1/3 rpm albums in 1948, to magnetic tape and, most recently, to compact discs (CDs) with the sound preserved digitally through a binary code scanned with a laser beam rather than tracked with a stylus. ("Compact" because what once used to take up several feet of shelf space can, on CD, fit into a shoebox.) Audiophiles who drooled over hi-fi, stereo, eight-track, and quadraphonic sound proved to be just as enthralled with the arrival of CDs.

The quality of the sound has thus gone from flat and scratchy to concert hall quality in little more than a century, with most of the improvements coming in the space of about forty years. Or, to put it another way, all roughly within the lifetime of Irving Berlin.

Songs from musicals were often recorded from the earliest days of the record industry—the first such number by an original cast being attributed to "Old Folks at Home" from the show *When Johnny Comes Marching Home*, released by the Victor Talking Machine Company in 1904.[10] But it wasn't until 1943 and *Oklahoma!* that what we know as an original cast recording of a whole show was produced (by Decca on a series of 10-inch disks). (This is a point that can lead to heated debates among musical devotees. It all depends on definition. One camp insists that the honor of being the first original cast recording goes to *The Cradle Will Rock* [Act Five], a recording by the cast released on seven 12-inch discs by Musicraft Records in 1938. Most histories, however, still credit *Oklahoma!* because it includes the original musicians as well as the cast, making it a more complete representation of an original show.)

Columbia's 33 1/3 format became the new standard in 1948, and the business of recording musicals boomed (beginning with Cole Porter's *Kiss Me, Kate*). At times, an album could make a bigger profit than the show itself, while mint condition originals from the early days of recording can sell for hundreds and even thousands of dollars today.

Show tunes once dominated the airwaves and every show's composer was under heavy pressure to produce at least one song that could be recorded by a pop singer and become a hit outside the context of the plot. These were usually love songs; ballads suitable for dancing and romancing. This practice not only made money for the composer and artist but helped promote the show and thus sell more tickets. (It was said that *My Fair Lady* generated so many hit songs covered by so many singers that audiences could be heard humming the score on their way *into* the theater. Similarly, when producer David Merrick imported *The Roar of the Greasepaint, the Smell of the Crowd* from London in 1965, he kept a road show company on tour long enough for the songs to become part of the public consciousness before opening on Broadway, turning a London flop into a New York hit.)

The pressure on a Broadway composer to write a hit song is not as great as it once was. Rock music's Top 40 and Top 20 formats for the youth market now dominate radio to such a degree that finding a show tune on the radio or a jukebox today is virtually impossible. The show tunes of old are now mostly relegated to Vegas lounge acts, or automated soft music radio stations whose syrupy instrumental arrangements can be heard wafting through supermarkets, department stores, and all the better elevators.

This often prompts reports that the musical is dying or dead. The irony is that over the past twenty years, freed from the commercial pressure to produce hit singles for jukeboxes and radio, the musical has once more felt a surge of creative innovation in the direction of a total theatrical experience in which the traditional concept of songs is only a part. The form is again growing, maturing virtually unheard by the mass audience, tackling tough issues with dramatic musical forms, giving multilayered characters equally deep lyrics, and constantly exploring in new stylistic directions. It may once again be ahead of its time.

> The musical, you must remember, is America's most distinctive contribution to the theater. . . . Its potential is largely unexplored.
>
> —playwright Arthur Laurents[11]

Tin Pan Alley is physically gone and Broadway show tunes are no longer the songs the whole world sings. The individual publishing firms and their rinky-tink pianos have been swallowed up by conglomerate America, but its entrepreneurial, pioneering spirit lives on, and that spirit continues to evolve, adding new dimensions each year to the stunning heritage of the American musical experience.

The Recordings

The dates given in the first four Acts of this book correspond to the dates of the various awards organizations. The typical Broadway season does not follow a calendar year. To be eligible for a Tony, for example, a show has to open (in a theater seating 500 or more people) prior to a preannounced cutoff date, presently in May. This means that a show that opened in the latter half of 1990 *and* a show that opened in April of 1991 would both be eligible for the 1991 Tony Award. (This has caused some embarrassment when nominated shows might already have closed by the time of the awards.)

As the typical Broadway season runs through New Year's Day, the New York Drama Critics Circle Award's date more accurately straddles two years, as in "1958-1959."

Eligibility for a 1980 Grammy, however, required an album to have been released between October 1, 1979 and September 30, 1980, with the award presented in February of 1981.

Regarding record labels and inventory numbers, it should be kept in mind that companies often sell part or all of their stocks and even go out of business. Decca and Geffen, for example, were purchased by MCA, and MCA sold out to Matsushita late in 1990 for over $6 billion; Sony purchased Columbia in 1989 for over $2 billion. The inventory numbers may change as well, depending on whether the format is a vinyl album, cassette tape, or CD, and if the product is the original release or a reissue. Only the newer shows are available on CD, though some of the older ones are slowly being reissued in that format, often with additional songs that did not fit the time requirements of the old vinyl albums.

CDs are more expensive, of course, but are not as vulnerable to abuse as are tapes (stretchable, erasable) and records (warpable, scratchable). With the rapid phasing out of albums, the older shows are becoming increasingly difficult to find except at premium prices in catalogs catering to hard-core collectors. Some search tips are noted in Appendix A.

Unless otherwise noted, review quotes in the text are of opening night performances that appeared in the following morning's papers. It should be kept in mind that theater critics are judging the effect of an entire production, not just the songs. Often, a score can rise above sets, costumes, libretto and stage pacing.

Whenever possible, buyers are urged to stay with the original cast recording (film versions often drop some or most of a stage score and substitute new numbers, usually with the hope of reaping an Oscar for Best Original Song). However, films, stage revival versions (which sometimes contain new songs), and studio casts are noted when these are worth having or are the only ones readily available. There is a growing trend for contemporary studio cast recordings of old shows to be far more complete than the originals, and these are happily noted.

ADVISORY: SUSPECT WORDS AND IDEAS AT WORK

Warning for librarians: In this age of consternation over the lyric content of rock and rap music, and warning labels being "voluntarily" slapped on tapes, CDs, and albums (usually after threats of economic boycotts or possible government interference), keep in mind that the musical has grown up, matured. There are songs on award-winning scores that a radio station could not broadcast without endangering its license. Songs such as "Dance Ten, Looks Three" in *A Chorus Line* and "Sodomy" in *Hair,* or the opening bordello number in *Miss Saigon* and "By Threes" in *I Love My Wife*, to name just four, will always run afoul of the bluenoses, just as Cole Porter's "Love for Sale" in 1934 could only be played on the air instrumentally. In a modern musical, a love ballad such as "Some Enchanted Evening" might easily be a duet between two men or two women — not to shock, but to reflect changing attitudes.

On the subject of label advisories, the American Library Association stands opposed, feeling that "injustice and ignorance rather than justice and enlightenment result from such practices. . . . For the library to adopt or enforce any of these private systems . . . would violate the *Library Bill of Rights.*" However, arbitrarily removing such directives that have been affixed with the permission of the copyright holder would also be "unacceptable."[12] While Broadway musicals have not yet felt the censorious pressure aimed at youth-oriented recordings, the time may come, and restricted access might be advised.

Warning to all collectors: the shows listed here are the best, the top of the heap. Once hooked on them, collecting musicals can become addictive.

REFERENCE NOTES

1. Michael Kennedy, *Oxford Dictionary of Music* (New York: Oxford University Press, 1985), p. 489.

2. George M. Cohan, *Twenty Years on Broadway* (Westport, Connecticut: Greenwood Press, 1924), p. 185.

3. George Eells, *The Life That Late He Led* (New York: Putnam's, 1967) p. 255.

4. Tom Jones, "For People Who Hate Musicals," *The New York Times*, May 30, 1965.

5. Julius Novick, "In Search of a New Consensus," *Saturday Review*, April 3, 1976, pp. 39-42.

6. *The New York Times*, June 8, 1988.

7. *People*, July 23, 1990, p. 55.

8. *The New York Times*, September 30, 1990.

9. *Time*, November 12, 1990.

10. Joseph Nathan Kane, *Kane Book of Famous First Facts and Records* (New York: Ace Books, 1975), p. 445.

11. Craig Zaden, *Sondheim and Company* (New York: Harper and Row, 2nd edition, 1989), pp. 62-63.

12. American Library Association's Intellectual Freedom Committee, *Newsletter on Intellectual Freedom*, September 1990, pp. 152-153.

The cited Library Bill of Rights reads: "[Library] Materials should not be excluded because of the origin, background, or views of those contributing to their creation. . . . Materials should not be proscribed or removed because of partisan or doctrinal disapproval. Libraries should challenge censorship in the fulfillment of their responsibility to provide information and enlightenment. Libraries should cooperate with all persons and groups concerned with resisting abridgment of free expression and free access to ideas.

Act One:
The Antoinette Perry Award

> The Antoinette Perry Awards will be different in that the recipients will be chosen by a board representative of the whole theatre world and that nothing will be labeled "the best." If the [Theatre] Wing directors decide a contribution in any department of the theatre is outstanding, that will be sufficient reason for recognition. . . . The schedule of categories will be kept elastic, so that it can be changed from year to year to keep up with trends.
>
> — Brock Pemberton, producer
> and Theatre Wing executive, 1947[1]

The Tony Award, as it has come to be known, is a registered trademark of excellence bestowed annually by the American Theatre Wing, an organization of professionals devoted to fostering theater arts in America through education and community service. The silver medallion is mounted on a lucite stand and depicts the traditional masks of drama and comedy. It is Broadway's Oscar, presented since the late 1940s and named for the Wing's second Chairman of the Board, actress Antoinette Perry (1888-1946), who was described by Brock Pemberton as "a joyous person who hated pomposity." As of 1991, votes were cast by 624 theater professionals and journalists.

Over the years, the official designations, undoubtedly for want of a more neutral term, have come to use the word "best," as in Best Play, Best Book of a Musical, Best Performance by a Leading Actress in a Musical, and so on. Four nominees are usually named in each category. Sometimes an award is shared by two or more shows or individuals.

Unlike Hollywood's Oscars or television's Emmys, however, a category may have fewer nominees or even be completely eliminated in any given year if the number of outstanding shows or performances is deemed insufficient. In 1956, for example, only two shows were nominated as Best Musical; three were nominated in 1959, five in 1960, three in 1989. In 1985 the categories of Best Actor and Best Actress in a musical were eliminated.[2]

The awards ceremony itself was abruptly canceled one year (1965) when Helen Menken resigned as the Theatre Wing's president to protest the closing of the organization's training school due to financial difficulties. Producer Harold Prince persuaded her to return and take over the chairmanship of the awards, the school was reopened, and the Tonys came off as planned on June 13th.[3]

The first award for Best Musical went to Cole Porter's *Kiss Me, Kate* in 1949. There has been a Best Musical winner every year since, though not all of them won for Best Original Score. What follows is a chronological listing of winners in the categories of Best Musical and, when they differ, Best Original Score, along with a basic discography.

AND THE WINNER IS . . .

1949

Kiss Me, Kate (Cole Porter). Opened December 30, 1948. Cast: Alfred Drake, Patricia Morrison, Lisa Kirk, Harold Lang, Lorenzo Fuller, Harry Clark, and Jack Diamond.

A play within a play, the story revolves around a contemporary acting company trying to stage Shakespeare's *The Taming of the Shrew* in Baltimore. Its stars are beset by romantic and financial woes, which often follow them onto the stage and blend with the Bard's work (most hilariously in the presence of two gangsters, played by Clark and Diamond, trying to collect a gambling debt; they not only end up in costume as bit players, but sing the pun-filled "Brush Up Your Shakespeare").

"A show that strains a reviewer's supply of adjectives," wrote William Hawkins in the New York *World-Telegram*. "Here is the sprightliest, handsomest and most tuneful musical imaginable," agreed John Chapman in the New York *Daily News*. Another first-nighter, the *Journal-American*'s Robert Garland, called it "literate without being highbrow, sophisticated without being smarty, seasoned without being soiled, and funny without being vulgar.''

Porter cleverly took lines from Shakespeare and turned them into songs, most notably: "I've Come to Wive It Wealthily In Padua," "Were Thine That Special Face," and the ribald "Where Is the Life That Late I Led?" (Brooks Atkinson of *The New York Times* could not help commenting that Porter "has always enjoyed the luxury of rowdy tunes. . . . All his lyrics are literate, and as usual some of them would shock the editorial staff of *The Police Gazette*.")

Other key songs: "Wunderbar," "So in Love," "Too Darn Hot," "I Hate Men," "Always True to You in My Fashion," and the spritely "Tom, Dick, or Harry." John Lardner of the New York *Star* said of the songs, "You get the impression Mr. Porter had a lot of fun writing them."

The show also won Tonys for Best Score, Best Costumes, and Best Authors — Bella and Samuel Spawack. The show was such a hit that a race horse was named after it; on May 23, 1951, Kiss Me Kate paid $17.94 at Belmont.

The 1953 MGM film version, originally photographed in 3-D, is quite good and keeps most of the score but not the cast. The movie stars Howard Keel, Kathryn Grayson, Ann Miller, Bobby Van, and, as the singing thugs, Keenan Wynn and James Whitmore. The film contains an extra song, "From This Moment On," which was lifted from Porter's later show *Out of This World*. Future award-winning choreographer and director Bob Fosse has a dancing role as one of Ann Miller's three suitors.

One odd thing about the film is the opening scene where Keel and Grayson, as Fred Graham and Lilli Vanessi, audition a song for composer Cole Porter, played by Ron Randell. It is odd because the real Porter had been a cripple for eleven years before *Kiss Me, Kate* was written, a well-known fact at the time, yet MGM chose to have Randell walk around on two good legs.

Original cast: Columbia S 32609. Film: MGM 3077.

The only full-length recording is a 1990 studio cast starring Josephine Barstow, Thomas Hampson, Kim Criswell, George Dvorsky, Damon Evans, and David Garrison from EMI. It comes on two cassettes or CDs and is the first complete recording of the score, including the dance music, some previously neglected lyrics, and seven songs never before recorded (six were dropped during out-of-town tryouts): "I Sing of Love," "It Was Great Fun the First Time," "A Woman's Career," "We Shall Never Be Younger," "I'm Afraid, Sweetheart, I Love You," "If Ever Married I'm," and "What Does Your Servant Dream About?" This recording also features the best renditions of "Too Darn Hot" (by Evans) and "Always True to You in My Fashion" (by Criswell). EMI/Angel, 4D2S-54033.

1950

South Pacific (Richard Rodgers, Oscar Hammerstein). Opened April 7, 1949. Cast: Mary Martin, Ezio Pinza, Juanita Hall, Myron McCormick, and William Tabbert.

This was the second musical to win a Pulitzer Prize in Drama [see Act Three, 1932, for the first, *Of Thee I Sing*], and it was based on an earlier Pulitzer-winning book, James A. Michener's *Tales of the South Pacific*. Two tales — "Our Heroine" and "Fo' Dolla" — formed the basis of Hammerstein's script.

Mary Martin, conjuring up images of Kansas corn and Fourth of July flag waving, is all-American nurse Nellie Forbush, fresh from a secluded (and segregated) upbringing in Little Rock, Arkansas, and now stationed in the South Pacific during World War II. She falls in love with widower Emile De Becque, a French planter played by Ezio Pinza. His former marriage and children from his native wife give her pause, but by the end Martin overcomes her inbred prejudices. Tabbert, as Navy lieutenant Joe Cable, is not so flexible. His love for a native girl is torn apart by an upbringing that judges people by the color of their skin. In one of Hammerstein's strongest lyrics, Tabbert anguishes that you have to be "Carefully Taught" to hate.

Hit songs include: "Some Enchanted Evening," "Wonderful Guy," "Younger Than Springtime," "Happy Talk," "I'm Gonna Wash That Man Right Out of My Hair," "Bali Ha'i," "Cockeyed Optimist," and "Nothin' Like a Dame."

New York Post critic Richard Watts, Jr. was awestruck: "I do not think it is first-night excess which causes me to hail it as one of the finest musical plays in the history of the American theatre." Brooks Atkinson termed it "magnificent," and ventured the opinion that "Some Enchanted Evening" had a chance "to become reasonably immortal." The accolades were virtually unanimous.

The show swept the four musical acting categories, with Tonys going to Martin, Pinza, Hall, and McCormack. Joshua Logan won for directing and cowriting the script with Hammerstein.

The Logan-directed 1958 film starred Mitzi Gaynor, Ray Walston, John Kerr, Juanita Hall, France Nuyen, and, doing the singing for Rossano Brazzi, Giorgio Tozzi. The film's biggest flaw was the use of stage lighting effects in what was supposed to be a realistic setting.

Original cast: Columbia OL-4180. Film: RCA LOC-1032.

A 1987 revival by the New York City Opera garnered opposite reviews. *USA Today*'s David Patrick Stearns called the story "a bit wobbly 38 years after the show's premiere," and Peter Goodman of *Newsday* thought it "soft-headed, to go with its soft heart." Douglas Watt of the *Daily News* called the plot "creaky and obvious today," though the songs held up well. Clive Barnes, virtually alone among the major critics, thought the revival proved that the story was "still younger than springtime."

1951

Guys and Dolls (Frank Loesser). Opened November 24, 1950. Cast: Robert Alda, Vivian Blaine, Sam Levene, Isabel Bigley, Pat Rooney, Sr., Stubby Kaye.

The Broadway stage had never seen anything quite like it, the shady con artists, horseplayers, strippers, and bookies of Damon Runyon's marvelous short stories singing and dancing their way into audiences' hearts, hilariously fractured syntax intact. One high-roller is Sky Masterson (Alda, whose son Alan was 15 at the time), who falls for a Salvation Army missionary (Bigley); another is Nathan Detroit (Levene), trying to coax more mileage out of a fourteen-year engagement to dancer Adelaide (Blaine).

"Love for the new musical spread faster last night than fire through dry grass in a high wind," reported William Hawkins in the *World-Telegram*.

Most of the show's songs became big hits with the public: "A Bushel and a Peck," "Luck Be a Lady," "Sit Down, You're Rockin' the Boat" (a show-stopper by Kaye), "I'll Know," "If I Were a Bell," and "I've Never Been in Love Before" were all standouts, along with "The Oldest Established (Permanent Floating Crap Game)," "Marry the Man Today," and "Take Back Your Mink."

Alda and Bigley won Tonys, as did director George S. Kaufman, writers Jo Swerling and Abe Burrows (Runyon had been dead for four years), choreographer Michael Kidd, and composer Frank Loesser.

The 1955 film retained Blaine and Kaye but gave the leads to Marlon Brando (Sky), Frank Sinatra (Nathan), and Jean Simmons (Sarah Brown, the prohibitionist missionary). Added to the film score: "A Woman in Love," "Pet Me, Poppa," and "Adelaide."

A 1976 stage revival with an all black cast is a wonder to listen to — upbeat, sassy, and altogether splendid, it features James Randolph (Sky), Robert Guillaume (Nathan), Ernestine Jackson (Sarah), Norma Donaldson (Adelaide), and Ken Page in Stubby Kaye's role as Nicely-Nicely Johnson. (While questioning the propriety of an all black cast as being little more than "a stunt," the *New Yorker*'s Brendan Gill had no complaint about the 26-year-old score. In the issue of August 2, 1976, he wrote: "What one senses in every note and syllable of Loesser's handiwork is a formidably high intelligence, akin to Porter's and Sondheim's in the acuteness with which it applies itself to the seeming mere playfulness of popular song.")

Original cast: Decca 8036. Film: Decca ED-2332. 1976 revival: Motown M6-876 S1. (See Appendix D also.)

1952

The King and I (Rodgers and Hammerstein). Opened March 29, 1951. Cast: Yul Brynner, Gertrude Lawrence, Doretta Morrow.

First came Margaret Langdon's novel, *Anna and the King of Siam*, based on her life as an English governess in Thailand, working for a king with some 9000 wives (most of them largely ceremonial, one would hope). That became a 1946 movie with Rex Harrison and Irene Dunne. Finally, and even more memorable, came the lavish and exotic musical with its heartfelt songs that flowed gracefully from the characters and setting.

Lawrence arrives in Siam to teach the young prince the ways of the world (not least of all that tiny Siam is not at the center of the world), and ends up teaching (and emancipating) the king's many wives and legions of children. In time, Brynner, the all-powerful and all-stubborn king, also learns there is a world beyond himself.

The score is one of the most popular and tuneful of the era: "I Whistle a Happy Tune," "Hello Young Lovers," "A Puzzlement," "Getting to Know You," "Shall We Dance?" and "The March of the Siamese Children" are all theater classics. Both stars won Tonys for their performances; it was Gertrude Lawrence's last play.

Even this classic show drew some lukewarm notices. John McClain, in the New York *Journal-American*, said it was "not a great score according to Richard Rodgers's standards," and called it "a near miss" in which "there were no musical moments which made you almost jump out of the seat." He admitted, though, that "I shall probably be dinned to death by selections from this show for the next six months." The next six decades would have been a closer prediction.

Brynner last played the king in 1985, at which time John Beaufort of *The Christian Science Monitor* (1/11/85) wrote, "The score overflows with lush Rodgers melodies and lilting Hammerstein lyrics." Frank Rich of the *Times* (1/8/85) said of the star, "Man and role have long since merged into a fixed image that is as much a part of our collective consciousness as the Statue of Liberty."

The 1956 film starred Brynner and Deborah Kerr, whose singing was dubbed by Marni Nixon. Brynner won an Oscar.

There are at least eighteen versions of this score on record, and, because the composers kept adding to it over the years, none of them contains every bit of music.

Original cast: Decca, 9008. Film: Capitol, SW-740.

A 1964 revival at New York's Lincoln Center starred prima donna Risë Stevens and Darren McGavin and the recording includes most of the narrated ballet, "The Small House of Uncle

Thomas'' (not available on the original cast album or film score): RCA LSO-1092.

A 1977 revival recording with Brynner and Constance Towers added "Arrival at Bangkok," "Children Sing, Priests Chant," "The Royal Bangkok Academy," "So Big a World" (a solo for Brynner), "Western People Funny," and, instrumentally, "The Dance of Anna and Sir Edward" (it does not contain "The Small House of Uncle Thomas"): RCA ABL1-2610.

(There was also a non-musical television series based on the show, starring Yul Brynner, Samantha Eggar, and Keye Luke. Titled *Anna and the King*, the series played on CBS as a Sunday evening lead-in to *MASH* from late September of 1972 until the end of the year.)

1953

Wonderful Town (Leonard Bernstein, Betty Comden, Adolph Green). Opened February 25, 1953. Cast: Rosalind Russell, Edith Adams, George Gaynes, Henry Lascoe.

As with *The King and I*, *Wonderful Town* went through several incarnations before becoming a hit musical. They began with a series of *New Yorker* articles by Ruth McKenny which became the nonmusical play and 1946 film *My Sister Eileen*, written by Joseph Fields and Jerome Chodorov. The film starred Rosalind Russell who reprised her role as Ruth, a struggling New York writer, in the musical.

In addition to collecting rejection slips, Ruth must also endure her sister Eileen (a would-be actress played by Adams) effortlessly attracting every available man in sight, though this proves helpful in charming their way out of various awkward situations.

Bernstein's musical stylings were vibrant, lovely and funny, blending into an electrifying overture. John Chapman wrote in the *Daily News* that "there hasn't been anybody around like him since George Gershwin for jauntiness, tricky and intriguing modulations and graceful swoops into simple and pleasant melody."

Individually the tunes were a perfect match for the Comden and Green lyrics to "One Hundred Easy Ways (to Lose a Man)" (Russell does not list them all), "Christopher Street" (a lively tour of

Greenwich Village and its various eccentric inhabitants), "Conversation Piece," "Conga!" "My Darlin' Eileen," "Pass That Football" (in which an illiterate college student explains how an athlete can thrive in school), and "Wrong Note Rag." "What a Waste" shows how talented people must sometimes dilute their art for money.

"No one," observed Walter Kerr in the *Herald Tribune*, "is going to pretend that Miss Russell's singing voice is much more than an amiable croak," but he loved the way her "sheer animal spirits . . . set a whole stage to rocking around her." Adams had the better singing voice and showed it in "A Little Bit in Love" and "It's Love" (a duet with Gaynes). Russell won a Tony, as did Leonard Bernstein, authors Fields and Chodorov, and choreographer Donald Saddler.

Original cast: Decca 9010. 1990 reissue: MCA Broadway Gold Classics MCAC-10050.

1954

Kismet (Robert Wright, George Forrest, and the classical music of Alexander Borodin). Opened December 3, 1953. Cast: Alfred Drake, Doretta Morrow, Joan Diener, Henry Calvin, Richard Kiley.

"Lavish, tuneful and terrific," reported John McClain in the *Journal-American*, "a big and bountiful extravaganza in the old time tradition." Plus "scores of scrumptious-looking maidens expensively under-clad."

Once again Broadway looked to the past and found that it was good — it just needed music to jazz it up. *Kismet*, Turkish for fate or destiny, was an Arabian Nights fable featuring a poet/beggar named Hajj who becomes Emir of Baghdad, an evil Wazir, harems, caliphs, and magic. It was first presented as a nonmusical by Edward Knoblock in 1911 (with Otis Skinner as Hajj), on film in 1930 (Sidney Blackmer, Loretta Young), and again on the silver screen in 1942 (Ronald Colman, Marlene Dietrich).

For the musical, Wright and Forrest chose the sinuous melodies of Borodin, who did not object, having died 66 years before. Thus one of the Russian's *Polovetsian Dances* became the smash hit,

"Stranger in Paradise"; "Fate" came from Borodin's Symphony No. 2 in B Minor; and "Baubles, Bangles and Beads" was adapted from the scherzo of the String Quartet in D Major.

Other notable numbers: "Not Since Nineveh," "Was I Wazir?" (sung by Henry Calvin, later known as Sergeant Garcia in the *Zorro* TV series), "Rahadlakum," "The Olive Tree," "Sands of Time," and "Zubbediya, Samaris' Dance."

Accolades were not unanimous. Most critics praised the look of the show, but found the substance wanting. At the *Herald Tribune*, Walter Kerr noted, "It's the sort of show that would sell its soul for a joke, and the jokes should be better at the price." Brooks Atkinson at the *Times* was a tougher sell, saying "the lyrics comprise some of the most fearful poetry of our time."

On the plus side, William Hawkins of the *World-Telegram and Sun* declared *Kismet* to be "noisy, spectacular, and vigorous. The biggest and brightest of magical carpets, it may not be subtle or original, but nobody intended it to be. It is melodic and gay."

For his unwitting contribution, Borodin was awarded a posthumous Tony as Best Composer. Awards also went to Drake (as Hajj), and writers Charles Lederer and Luther Davis.

The 1955 film starred Howard Keel, Ann Blyth, Dolores Gray, Vic Damone, and Monty Woolley.

Original cast: Columbia OL-4850. Film: MGM 3281. A complete recording (2 CDs) by a studio cast of opera stars Donald Maxwell, Valerie Masterson, and David Rendall: That's Entertainment Records of London, 1170. (This 1990 issue also contains four songs from the failed 1978 all-black version that was set in Africa and titled *Timbuktu*; Douglas Watt of the *Daily News* dubbed the 1978 production "a gaudy bore with a pearl named Melba [Moore] bobbing about in it.")

Wright and Forrest made a career out of using classical music. They borrowed tunes from Edvard Grieg in 1944 for *Song of Norway*, and Heitor Villa-Lobos for *Magdalena* in 1948 — a show which Brooks Atkinson called "one of the most overpoweringly dull musical dramas of all time," which could explain why the "premiere" recording of it did not appear until 1989 on CBS Records, SMT-44945. The duo also revised Rachmaninoff for *Anya* in 1965.

1955

The Pajama Game (Richard Adler, Jerry Ross). Opened May 13, 1954. Cast: John Raitt, Janis Paige, Eddie Foy, Jr., Carol Haney.

7 1/2 Cents was the name of the original Book-of-the-Month Club novel, the title taken from the hourly wage hike demanded by workers at the Sleep-Tite Pajama Factory (and which also supplied the title for one of the songs). As the new superintendent, Raitt has to figure out how to meet the demand while increasing sales in order to keep the company from closing. Naturally, a love interest develops with Janis Paige, leader of the union's grievance committee.

The *Herald Tribune*'s Walter Kerr called it a "bright, brassy and jubilantly sassy show [that] takes a whole barrelful of gleaming new talents, and a handful of stimulating ideas as well, and sends them tumbling in happy profusion over the footlights." At the *New York Post*, Richard Watts, Jr., had a warning for capitalists saying, "the book, for all its hint of practical business background, isn't very interesting as either realism or satire." He also felt that the lyrics "are neither beautiful nor witty."

Standout songs included "Hey, There" (a big hit for Rosemary Clooney in 1954, maintaining the #1 spot on the Billboard charts for six straight weeks), "Steam Heat," and "Hernando's Hideaway." The score also boasted the rousing love song "There Once Was a Man," "I'm Not at All in Love," "Small Talk," and "A New Town Is a Blue Town." Haney won a Tony, as did the composers, Bob Fosse as choreographer, and authors George Abbott and Richard Bissell. (When Carol Haney broke her ankle, a stand-in from the chorus named Shirley MacLaine stepped in and became a star.)

The 1957 film with Raitt, Foy, Haney, and Doris Day is one of those rarities: a stage musical successfully transferred to film.

Original cast: Columbia OL-4840. Film: Columbia OL-5210.

1956

Damn Yankees (Richard Adler, Jerry Ross). Opened May 5, 1955. Cast: **Gwen Verdon**, Stephen Douglass, Ray Walston, Jean Stapleton, Jimmie Komack, Russ Brown.

Based on Douglass Wallop's novel, *The Year the Yankees Lost the Pennant* (though it sounds like a subtitle for *Gone With the Wind*), this fantasy tells the remarkable story of middle-aged Joe Boyd, who makes a deal with the Devil, giving up his soul for the chance to help the Washington Senators beat the unbeatable (and hated) New York Yankees. He is diabolically changed into a young phenom known as Joe Hardy, "Shoeless Joe From Hannibal, Mo."

Douglass is the ballplayer, Walston the Devil, and Verdon is Lola, the sexy temptress from Hades. (Of her super-heated performance, the *Herald Tribune*'s Walter Kerr wrote, "Miss Verdon is, I believe, some sort of a mobile designed by a man without a conscience . . . she is simply and insanely inspired.")   For their second Tony-winning musical in a row, Adler and Ross concocted "Whatever Lola Wants," "Two Lost Souls," and "(You Gotta Have) Heart," along with "A Little Brains," "The Game," "Those Were the Good Old Days," and "A Man Doesn't Know." (It was to be their last show. Ross died of tuberculosis at age 29 before *Damn Yankees* closed, and before he and Adler won Tonys for their songs.)

Tonys also went to Walston, Verdon, Brown, authors George Abbott and Douglass Wallop, and choreographer Bob Fosse.

Verdon and Walston repeated their roles in the 1958 film, while Tab Hunter played Joe Hardy.

Original cast: RCA LOC-1021. Film: RCA LOC-1047.

1957

My Fair Lady (Alan Jay Lerner, Frederick Loewe). Opened March 15, 1956. Cast: Rex Harrison, Julie Andrews, Stanley Holloway, Robert Coote.

It was an audacious undertaking, turning *Pygmalion* by George Bernard Shaw, one of the world's greatest playwrights, into an American musical. Surely the acerbic wit, the social commentary, the charming misogyny, would be hurt, or even lost! And in other hands, perhaps they would have been. But Alan Jay Lerner was as gifted a wordsmith with lyrics as Shaw was with dialogue, and the result of this inspired collaboration was one of the musical theater's greatest and most enduring triumphs.

Harrison is Henry Higgins, expert dialectician and staunch bachelor ("I'm an Ordinary Man," "A Hymn to Him"), who accepts the challenge of passing off a ragamuffin flower girl named Eliza Doolittle (Andrews) as a well-spoken member of the upper class. Eliza has simple desires ("Wouldn't It Be Loverly?") who wants to better herself, but not at the expense of her dignity ("Just You Wait," "Without You"). They strike sparks off one another until realizing their mutual needs and love at the end.

It has the kind of romantic ending American audiences doted on but which Shaw disdained. In the original, Higgins ends up as alone and as surly as he was at the start. Lerner changed that, with apologies to the ghost of Shaw, and created a classic.

"As fine a piece of work, of its kind, as our stage can be asked to give us," said John Chapman of the *Daily News*, "splendid and splendorous." "A felicitous blend of intellect, wit, rhythm and high spirits. A masterpiece of musical comedy legerdemain. A new landmark in the genre," according to Robert Coleman of the *Daily Mirror*. Such praise was practically universal.

Included in the unforgettable score: "With a Little Bit of Luck," "Get Me to the Church on Time," "Why Can't the English?" "The Rain in Spain," "I Could Have Danced All Night," "I've Grown Accustomed to Her Face," and "On the Street Where You Live."

Harrison and director Moss Hart were awarded Tonys, along with Lerner and Loewe. (Judy Holliday copped the Best Actress Tony — see Act Five, *Bells Are Ringing*.) Harrison added an Oscar for the 1964 film, while Audrey Hepburn as Eliza had her singing done by Marni Nixon.

Original cast: Columbia BT 5090. Film: Columbia KOS-2600. London cast: Columbia OS 2015 (same cast as on Broadway, but with a somewhat different approach from Harrison, who sings more than he speaks his lines).

For smooth listening enjoyment, there is *Nat King Cole Sings Selections From My Fair Lady*, 1965, his final album: Capitol SM2117.

1958

The Music Man (Meredith Willson). December 19, 1957. Cast: Robert Preston, Barbara Cook, David Burns, Pert Kelton, Iggie Wolfington, The Buffalo Bills, Eddie Hodges.

Meredith Willson's unpretentious musical salute to his home state of Iowa and its rock solid (and stolid) citizens seemed to come out of nowhere and take New York's sophisticates by storm. "Fresh, genial and warm-hearted corn," said Richard Watts in the *New York Post*, but he admitted it was also, "in some paradoxical manner, boldly original." Robert Coleman found it "delightfully nostalgic for those who have lived in whistle stops, and," he reminded his *Daily Mirror* readers, "first-rate fun for city slickers."

It was Willson's first Broadway musical, though the former piccolo player and flutist with the New York Philharmonic had some modest hits as a songwriter, including Tallulah Bankhead's radio theme, "May the Good Lord Bless and Keep You."

There was nothing in Willson's background to suggest that a musical about a con man selling nonexistent boys' bands to gullible lovers of barbershop quartets while falling in love with Marian the librarian could possibly succeed in cynical Manhattan. But it did, beating even *West Side Story* [Act Five] for the 1958 Best Musical Tony.

Perhaps the Gothamites liked the numbers that showed up their country cousins — "Iowa Stubborn" and "Ya Got Trouble," the latter warning of the insidious evils lurking in pool halls and dime novels. Or maybe it was the simple but honest love songs, from the wistful "Goodnight My Someone" and "Being in Love," to the declarative "Till There Was You." Surely the straw hats and barbershop quartets of "Sincere" and "Lida Rose," and the Sousa-like thundering of "Seventy-Six Trombones" would not have swayed the jaded city folk? Naw. All those tickets were probably purchased by tourists from Iowa.

Preston, Cook, Burns, and Willson all received Tonys.

Robert Preston repeated his role in the 1962 movie version and received an Oscar nomination; his costars were Shirley Jones, Buddy Hackett, Hermione Gingold, and Paul Ford.

Original cast: Capitol SWAO-990. Film: Warner Brothers 1459.

1991 studio cast with Timothy Nobel and Kathleen Brett: Telarc, CS-30276.

1959

Redhead (Albert Hague, Dorothy Fields). Opened February 5, 1959. Cast: Gwen Verdon, Richard Kiley, Leonard Stone, Doris Rich.

In the album's liner notes, lyricist Dorothy Fields offers the "unprejudiced" opinion that this show is "absolutely great!" Opinions have been known to differ; the reviewer for *Time* (2/16/59) praised the star ("Verdon gives a theatergoer the rare sensation that his ticket has been underpriced") but called the score "lackluster" and said the story "should be returned to the moths from which it was borrowed."

Redhead is, without a doubt, the only "romantic murder-mystery musical" set in 1907 London. It featured *Damn Yankees* star Verdon as Essie Whimple, a spinster and molder of statues for a waxworks museum of grisly villains. She falls in love with an American strongman (Kiley), hides out as a chorus girl in his theatrical troupe, and both end up searching for a killer who is terrorizing London—who turns out to be Kiley's best friend and fellow actor, George Poppett (Stone).

Verdon affects a British accent while singing "The Right Finger of My Left Hand," "Just for Once," "I Feel Merely Marvelous," "Look Who's in Love," and "I'll Try" (the last two being duets with Kiley). Kiley solos on "She's Not Enough Woman for Me" and "I'm Back in Circulation," earning his first Tony. Verdon, Stone (a tie with Russell Nype in *Goldilocks*), Fields, and choreographer Bob Fosse (Verdon's husband) were also honored.

Original cast: RCA LSO-1104.

1960

Fiorello! and *The Sound of Music*, the only tie to date for Best Musical.

Fiorello (Sheldon Harnick, Jerry Bock). Opened November 23, 1959. Cast: Tom Bosley, Patricia Wilson, Pat Stanley, Mark Dawson.

Bosley, who later gained TV fame playing Howard Cunningham for ten years in *Happy Days*, here portrays real-life politician Fiorello La Guardia as he battles the corrupt leadership of Tammany Hall and the Jimmy Walker administration, moving up from being a peoples' lawyer to mayor of New York City. The first scenes have him, a Republican, defending strikers at the Nifty Shirt-Waist Corporation in 1914. His secretary (Wilson) is in love with him, but he marries someone else and only as a widower does he begin to see that Wilson's devotion is not merely that of a good employee.

This political song and dance drew its satiric power from songs such as "Politics and Poker," "The Name's La Guardia" (the only number featuring Bosley as singer, backed by the entire cast), "The Bum Won," "On the Side of the Angels," and "Little Tin Box" (the fictional horn-of-plenty source of Tammany wealth). "When Did I Fall in Love?" "I Love a Cop" (a striker falls for the man who arrested her), and "Til Tomorrow" were the principal ballads. Eileen Rodgers belted out a tribute to Jimmy Walker called "Gentleman Jimmy."

"It is a hardboiled tale," said Frank Aston in the *World-Telegram*, "raucous, honest, blisteringly funny." John Chapman cast his ballot in the *Daily News*: "If we can't vote for LaGuardia any more, let's vote for Tom Bosley."

The show earned Tonys for Bosley, director George Abbott, composer Bock, and writers Abbott and Jerome Weidman. *Fiorello!* also became the third musical to win a Pulitzer Prize.

Original cast: Capitol SWAO-1321. It was not filmed.

(Two other New York City mayors also became the subjects of stage musicals. *Jimmy*, a 1969 musical by Bill and Patti Jacobs, featured impressionist Frank Gorshin as Jimmy Walker, Anita Gillette as his mistress, and Julie Wilson as his wife—who feelingly sang about the wayward Walker in "The Charmin' Son-of-a-Bitch." The show was a flop, but the score is engaging, especially when Gillette is singing: RCA LSO-1162. *Mayor, the Musical* was a 1985 Off-Broadway musical by Charles Strouse based on the memoirs of Ed Koch, with Lenny Wolpe as the embattled but ebullient ("How'm I Doin'?") Koch. The show focused on the difficulties of running a major metropolitan city. Song highlights include

"You Can Be a New Yorker Too," and "March of the Yuppies":
New York Music Company, Inc., NYMT 21.)

The Sound of Music (Rodgers and Hammerstein). Opened November 16, 1959. Cast: Mary Martin, Theodore Bikel, Patricia Neway, Lauri Peters, Brian Davies.

It is Austria, 1938, and religious postulant Maria is not singing with the other nuns but is, instead, somewhere atop an alp singing that the hills are alive with the sound of music. Life in a cloister does not seem to suit her. Packed off as governess to the uptight, overdisciplined children of Captain von Trapp, she soon loosens them up by singing "My Favorite Things," "Do-Re-Me," and "The Lonely Goatherd." Love with the Captain blossoms ("An Ordinary Couple") as the Nazis begin to overrun the country ("No Way to Stop It"). The nuns help engineer an escape from Austria and the Trapp Family Singers become famous the world over (though their ultimate success is not part of the script).

Other well-known songs: "Sixteen Going On Seventeen," "How Can Love Survive?" "So Long, Farewell," "Climb Ev'ry Mountain," and "Edelweiss."

Robert Coleman told his *Daily Mirror* readers that Mary Martin was "magnificent" and the show "a titanic hit," though qualifying that by calling it "a work that depends essentially upon its lyrics and music to make it the stunner it is." Brooks Atkinson at *The Times* thought even less of the script, calling it "hackneyed," and gave a kind of backhanded salute to the composer's "endless fund of cheerful melodies." Richard Watts, Jr. at the *Post* found the score "particularly rich in freshness and imagination."

Tonys went to Mary Martin and Patricia Neway (as Mother Superior). Howard Lindsay and Russel Crouse shared the writing Tony with Weidman and Abbott, and Richard Rodgers shared the composing honors with Jerry Bock (for *Fiorello!*).

The 1965 film starred Julie Andrews and Christopher Plummer (whose singing was dubbed by Bill Lee). It won an Oscar as Best Picture, the second year in a row the award went to a musical (*My Fair Lady* having won in 1964). The film was a huge international success, an indicator of which would be Mrs. Myra Franklin of Cardiff, Wales, who, by the year 1980, had seen it 940 times.[4] (The film also marked the only celluloid appearance of Marni Nixon, the behind-the-scenes singing voice for many Hollywood stars, as Sister Sophia.)

Original cast: Columbia KOS-202. Film: RCA LSOD-2005.

(Among the competitors that year was Richard Rodgers' daughter, Mary Rodgers, composer of *Once Upon a Mattress*, starring newcomer Carol Burnett.)

1961

Bye Bye Birdie (Charles Strouse, Lee Adams). Opened April 8, 1954. Cast: Dick Van Dyke, Chita Rivera, Paul Lynde, Susan Watson, Dick Gautier.

In this first rock musical, Conrad Birdie (Gautier) is a cross between Elvis Presley and Conway Twitty, a pompadoured, self-centered, hip-swinging rock star about to be drafted into the army. As a promotional stunt, he will say good-bye to all of America's lovestruck pubescent females by kissing their proxy, Kim MacAfee (Watson), on *The Ed Sullivan Show*. Albert Peterson (Van Dyke) is the struggling songwriter whose "One Last Kiss" will accompany the nationwide pucker and make him rich enough to marry his secretary Rose (Rivera), who only wants him to be an English teacher.

Brooks Atkinson at the *Times* thought the show "uneven" but realized he was in the minority: "Last evening, the audience was beside itself with pleasure. This department was able to control itself."

Most other critics were instantly won over. John Chapman of the *Daily News* called it "the funniest, most captivating and most expert musical comedy one could hope to see in several seasons of showgoing." The *Herald Tribune*'s Walter Kerr came to the conclusion that "the teen-agers of America may be attractive, after all," and called costar Susan Watson "a fetching little innocent." At the *Journal-American*, John McClain was ecstatic: "Hallelujah! We've finally got a bright, new, funny, fast, crazy musical going for us."

The lively and tuneful score features "A Lot of Livin' to Do," "Put on a Happy Face," "Rosie," and "(What's the Matter With) Kids." It also has a number of excellent songs dropped from the movie version, including: "Normal American Boy" (with Van Dyke and Rivera fielding embarrassing questions for Birdie at a news conference), "Spanish Rose," "Baby, Talk to Me," "An English Teacher," and "What Did I Ever See in Him?"

Van Dyke, writer Michael Stewart, and director Gower Champion took home Tonys (Champion also won as choreographer). Rivera was nominated but lost to Tammy Grimes [see Act Five, *The Unsinkable Molly Brown*].

The 1963 film starred Van Dyke, Janet Leigh, Ann-Margret, Jessie Pearson (as Birdie), and Bobby Rydell as Kim's boyfriend Hugo (originally a nonsinging role played on the stage by Michael J. Pollard). A title song was added to the film, and pop singing star Rydell was included in "One Boy" and "A Lot of Livin' to Do." A highlight of the film is watching Ann-Margret shedding her clothes from beneath a heavy sweater to the tune of "How Lovely to Be a Woman."

Original cast: Columbia KOS-2025. Film: RCA LSO-1081. Reissue of the film score: RCA 1081-2-R.

For details on the little-known sequel, *Bring Back Birdie*, see the alphabetical listing in Act Five.

1962

How to Succeed in Business Without Really Trying (Frank Loesser). Opened October 14, 1961. Cast: Robert Morse, Rudy Vallee, Bonnie Scott, Charles Nelson Reilly.

When executive Shepherd Mead wrote his original book of the same title, it was nothing more (or less) than a tongue-in-cheek, step-by-step plan for climbing the corporate ladder (step one was to find a way out of the mailroom). Making the book itself part of the musical's plot was a stroke of genius, as J. Pierpont Finch (Morse) religiously follows its precepts as his battle plan for reaching the top.

Reilly shines as a boot-licking toady in "(I Play It) The Company Way," and "Coffee Break," while Morse moves ever upward with "Grand Old Ivy" and his personal motto, "I Believe in You" (sung to his own image in a mirror, then, as love blooms, to his girlfriend Rosemary).

Other standout songs: "A Secretary Is Not a Toy," "Been a Long Day," "Paris Original," "Cinderella, Darling," and "Brotherhood of Man."

"It is slick, fast on its feet, and convulsively, cerebrally funny," said *Newsweek* (10/23/61). *Time* hailed it as "a light, bright spoof of corporate wheels and wiles," and declared Robert Morse "a superlative, tousle-haired, triple-jointed comic wonder who could coax laughs out of Mt. Rushmore." Calling Morse "the most ingratiating eager beaver who ever gnawed through someone else's rung on the ladder of success," *Time* described his approach this way: "Totally animated, Robert Morse never merely speaks lines. He dives after an ordinary joke with a twisting one-and-a-half gainer and makes it look like a pearl."

This style had a near opposite effect on John McCarten of *The New Yorker* (10/21/61): "[Morse] is given to all sorts of writhings, grimaces, and contortions, which tended to unnerve me, but he's a boy who grows on you . . . he becomes likable in a fresh, deceitful, unreliable, absolutely egomaniacal way."

Howard Taubman at the *Times* (10/16/61) said, "It belongs to the blue chips among modern musicals," while the songs "sharpen the ridicule" thanks to "lyrics with an edge and tunes with a grin."

Morse and Reilly earned Tonys, as did director Abe Burrows and cowriters Jack Weinstock and Willie Gilbert. The musical went on to win a Pulitzer Prize. Rudy Vallee set a Broadway performance record by staying with the production for over three years. Michele Lee joined Morse and Vallee in the 1967 film, which dropped some songs but retained the theatrical feeling of the production numbers and, best of all, preserved Morse's great performance.

Original cast: RCA LSO-1066. Film: United Artists 5151.

(After a few more shows such as *So Long, 174th Street* [Act Five], and some films, most notably *The Loved One* – in which his affected British accent kept slipping – and *A Guide for the Married Man*, Morse was virtually unseen again until a triumphant nonmusical return to Broadway in *Tru*, for which he won a 1990 Tony playing Truman Capote.)

1963

A Funny Thing Happened on the Way to the Forum (Stephen Sondheim). Opened May 8, 1962. Cast: Zero Mostel, Jack Gilford, David Burns, Brian Davies, John Carradine, Preshy Marker, Ronald Holgate.

"No one gets to the forum; no one even starts for it. And nothing really happens that isn't older than the forum, more ancient than the agora in Athens. But somehow you keep laughing," wrote Howard Taubman in *The New York Times*, probably while still guffawing and holding his sides. He called the show an "uninhibited romp," and that's exactly what it is. The songs were more than rest breaks, often being funny in their own right.

This fast-moving, convoluted comedy involves a Roman slave (Mostel) trying to win his freedom by procuring a girl (Marker) from a house of ill repute for his young master, Hero (Davies, fresh from a supporting role in *The Sound of Music*) before an egotistical centurion (Holgate) can come and claim her.

The vaudeville-like pace and complications are set with the opening number, "Comedy Tonight," which is followed by "Lovely," "Pretty Little Picture," the delightfully sexist "Everybody Ought to Have a Maid," "I'm Calm," "Bring Me My Bride," and "That Dirty Old Man."

Mostel and Burns won Tonys, as did director George Abbott and producer Harold Prince. The writing Tony went to *Forum*'s Burt Shevelove and Larry Gelbart (later a guiding force behind TV's *MASH* and Broadway's *City of Angels* — below, 1990).

The 1966 film starred Mostel, Gilford, Phil Silvers, Buster Keaton, and, in place of Davies, young Michael Crawford (who would win a Tony fifteen years later for *Phantom of the Opera*; see 1988 below for details). Director Richard Lester kept up a frantic pace in a realistic setting but dropped eight songs.

Original cast: Capitol SWAO 1717. Film: United Artists 5144.

Best Score

Oliver! (Lionel Bart). Opened in London June 30, 1960; in New York January 6, 1963. New York cast: Clive Revill, Georgia Brown, Bruce Prochnik, Alice Playton.

This was the first year (but not the last) when the Best Musical did not also win the Tony for Best Original Score. This singing and dancing version of *Oliver Twist* featured Revill as Fagin, the larcenous leader of a pack of thieving street urchins, and Prochnik as new recruit Oliver.

The score includes: "It's a Fine Life," "Where Is Love?"

"You've Got to Pick a Pocket or Two," "As Long as He Needs Me" (sung by Georgia Brown), "Who Will Buy?" "I'd Do Anything," "Oom-Pah-Pah," "My Name (Is Bill Sikes)," and "Consider Yourself (Part of the Family)."

John McClain of the *Journal-American* thought it "simply scrumptious." At the *World-Telegram*, Norman Nadel agreed: "On its own audacious, exuberant terms, *Oliver* is a work of art." Richard Watts at the *Post* found it "an exciting and stunningly beautiful musical play" with a score that had "a wonderfully fresh tunefulness and gusto about it." Not so easily charmed was Howard Taubman of the *Times*, who noted the show contained "more cuteness than one associates even with Dickens," and complained that it settled too often for "facile show-business razzmatazz."

All the critics agreed with the apparently conscious decision of Lionel Bart to tone down the ethnicity of Fagin, often held up with Shakespeare's Shylock—rightly or wrongly—as an example of antiSemitism. In the musical, Fagin is merely a conniving, almost charming, Cockney rascal and opportunist.

The 1968 Oscar-winning film directed by Sir Carol Reed starred Ron Moody (from the original London cast), Oliver Reed—the director's nephew—as the villainous Bill Sikes (the character's menacing solo song was dropped), Mark Lester as Oliver, and the delightful Shani Wallis in place of Georgia Brown as good-hearted Nancy.

Original cast: RCA LSOD-2004. Film: Colgems COSd-5501.

1964

Hello, Dolly! (Jerry Herman). Opened January 16, 1964. Cast: Carol Channing, David Burns, Eileen Brennan, Charles Nelson Reilly.

"The fact that it seems to me short on charm, warmth and the intangible quality of distinction," wrote Richard Watts, Jr., in the *New York Post* following opening night, "in no way alters my conviction that it will be an enormous popular success." He was correct. And he was also not alone in finding the musical to be shrewdly put together by masters of showmanship, likely to bring mixed reactions among the critics but raves from ticket buyers.

"A musical shot through with enchantment," said Howard Taubman in the *Times*, who added, "Were it not for lapses of taste, it could have been one of the notable ones." Gerald Bordman writes in *American Musical Theatre*, "The show was in no way innovative and made not the slightest pretense to artistic merit."[5] But it became a monster hit anyway, thanks to the overwhelming personality of star Carol Channing and the bright, catchy tunes of Jerry Herman.

Based on Thornton Wilder's nonmusical play, *The Matchmaker*, *Hello, Dolly!* follows the devious courtship of matchmaker Dolly Gallagher Levi as she tries to land the rich and onery Horace Vandergelder by pretending to look for a different match for him. A subplot involves the amorous adventures of two shop clerks out on the town pretending to be rich.

More than anything, the show belonged to Channing. John McClain of the *Journal-American* noted: ". . . there was that rare and undeniable electricity which jolts an audience on opening night, the sense of rapport that goes back and forth across the footlights." Walter Kerr agreed, telling his readers in the *Herald Tribune* that Channing filled the stage "with hair like orange seafoam, a contralto like a horse's neigh, and a confident swagger that promises to baby-sit for the entire house." She reminded Kerr of "all the blowsy glamor of the girls on the sheet music of 1916."

The score includes: "It Only Takes a Moment," "Before the Parade Passes By," "Ribbons Down My Back," "Dancing," "It Takes a Woman," "So Long Dearie," and, of course, the title song, made even more famous by a Louis Armstrong recording that hit #1 on the Billboard charts in May of 1964. Both major political parties wanted the melody for their 1964 campaign songs, with the Democrats ultimately using it for "Hello, Lyndon."

(Jerry Herman's trademark has been memorable music, so it was somewhat ironic when the very catchy melody of "Hello, Dolly" became the subject of a lawsuit filed by Hollywood composer Mack David, who charged that it was based on his 1948 song "Sunflower," as recorded by Frank Sinatra, Russ Morgan, and virtually every glee club in Kansas where "Sunflower" had been adopted as the state song. Apparently the catchy tune had caught in Herman's mind and, some fifteen years later, he inadvertently gave it new life in his hit show. Accidents will happen. Herman settled out of court for a reported half million dollars while retaining sole rights to the music that was now so identified with *Dolly*.)[6]

Dolly won 10 of its 11 Tony nominations, a record still standing in 1991, including awards to Channing, writer Michael Stewart, long-time Hollywood dancer Gower Champion as director, composer Jerry Herman, and David Merrick as producer.

The show was such a blockbuster that it became a vehicle for many stars over the years: Channing was superseded by Ginger Rogers in 1965, who was followed by Martha Raye in 1967. Betty Grable toured the states with it; Dorothy Lamour played Dolly for a week in 1967. Mary Martin took the show to Vietnam, Korea, and London. Pearl Bailey headed a 1967 all black cast.

The 1969 film, made at a staggering cost of $24 million, starred Barbra Streisand, Walter Matthau, and Michael Crawford. It was such a colossal flop that Harry and Michael Medved included it in their book, *The Hollywood Hall of Shame*, saying, "When the dust and glitter cleared after a massive publicity campaign, Fox found itself some $15 million in the hole."[7]

Original cast: RCA LSO-1087. Revival cast of Pearl Bailey and Cab Calloway: RCA LSO-1147. Film: 20th Century Fox 5103.

1965

Fiddler on the Roof (Jerry Bock, Sheldon Harnick). Opened September 22, 1964. Cast: Zero Mostel, Maria Karnilova, Beatrice Arthur, Bert Convy, Austin Pendleton, Joanna Merlin, Julia Migenes, Tanya Everett.

Zero Mostel is Tevye, the dairyman of the village of Anatevka, burdened by poverty, distressed by modern attitudes, and befuddled by the romantic yearnings of his five daughters, especially the three eldest ones, Tzeitel, Hodel, and Chava. (Bea Arthur is Yente the matchmaker, whose practical choices are always overridden by the girls' more romantic ones.) Every so often Tevye looks up and delivers a complaint and plea to God, but even that does not help. A pogrom by the tsar forces the villagers to leave at the end and seek new lives elsewhere, far from the home they love.

"To Life," "Tradition," "Sabbath Prayer," "Sunrise, Sunset,"

"Matchmaker, Matchmaker," "Miracle of Miracles," "Tevye's Dream," "Do You Love Me?" "Now I Have Everything," and "If I Were a Rich Man" all conjure up the moods and people of Sholom Aleichem's stories (adapted by Joseph Stein) and help capture its universal human spirit of survival, even when survival is as uncertain as that of a fiddler balancing on a pitched roof.

"The humor—and such a wealth of it—speaks to everyone," wrote Norman Nadel in the *World-Telegram*. "You don't have to be Jewish to love Tevye, or to appreciate his conversations with God." Jerry Bock, Nadel said, "has not superimposed tunes on a story; he has fashioned them so as to tell it most persuasively."

On the other hand, the *Herald Tribune*'s Walter Kerr thought the "easy quips" soiled the characterizations, and declared that *Fiddler* "might be an altogether charming musical if only the people of Anatevka did not pause every now and again to give their regards to Broadway, with remembrances to Herald Square."

Mostel and Karnilova (as his wife Golde) won acting Tonys. Joseph Stein won for writing, Harold Prince for producing, Jerome Robbins for directing and choreographing, Bock and Harnick for composing.

The 1971 film starred Israeli actor Topol, who also had the part in the 1967 London production. Shorn of Mostel's exuberant antics, Topol played the part of Tevye in a dignified, somber, and emotionally effective fashion. But the film dropped the song, "Now I Have Everything." Topol reprised the role on Broadway in 1990, earning a Tony nomination.

The reviews of the revival centered largely on the enduring appeal of the show. Mel Gussow, in *The New York Times* (11/19/90), said the 26-year-old show had become "a universally cherished folk musical" and "part of our musical heritage." Howard Kissel of the *Daily News* said the original had "touched a nerve that has had reverberations all around the world."

Original cast: RCA LSO-1093. Film: United Artists 10900. RCA's reissue of the original cast on CD (RCD1 7060) contains a previously unreleased song, "Rumor," featuring Bea Arthur and Leonard Frey.

Also recommended is a book by Richard Altman and Mervyn

Kaufman titled *The Making of a Musical: Fiddler on the Roof* (Crown, 1971).

(The difficulties inherent in making a hit out of ethnic material was made clear three years later when the same producer, Hal Prince, attempted to stage a musical version of the Nikos Kazantzakis book and Anthony Quinn movie, *Zorba the Greek*. On stage, *Zorba* was a flop, its faults as glaring as *Fiddler*'s virtues, and was labeled "synthetic" by *Time* (11/29/68): "the bouzouki music sounds as if it was piped in by Muzak [and] the dances have the look of old folk dances — any old folk.")

1966

Man of La Mancha (Joe Darion, Mitch Leigh). Opened November 22, 1965. Cast: Richard Kiley, Joan Diener, Irving Jacobson, Ray Middleton, Robert Rounseville.

In *Don Quixote*, completed in 1615, Miguel de Cervantes wrote: "He that publishes a book runs a very great hazard, since nothing can be more impossible than to compose one that may secure the approbation of every reader." Though he died in poverty a year later, Cervantes had indeed written a book for the ages to acclaim forevermore. But could such a long study of honor, chivalry, and madness be adapted to the musical comedy stage? Few thought so.

In a preface to the published script, author Dale Wasserman relates how potential backers were at first put off by it, seeing the show as "too radical, too 'special' and, most crushing of all, too intellectual. *Man of La Mancha* floundered rather than marched toward production, sustained only by the tenacity of those among us who shared the Quixotic dream."[8]

That it worked, became a smash hit, and won a Tony is as much a tribute to its creators as to Cervantes' story. And it is as much his story as Don Quixote's, for it begins with the author in prison, charged by his fellow inmates with being an idealist, to which he pleads guilty. He then beguiles them with the story of Don Quixote de La Mancha, a man so overcome by the woes of the world that he lost his wits and mistook windmills for giants and a whorish kitchen scullion for a great and virtuous lady. (A very Freudian approach by Cervantes, over 300 years before Freud.)

The most famous song to come out of the show was "The Impossible Dream," but just as moving are: "I, Don Quixote," "Dulcinea," "What Do You Want of Me?" "To Each His Dulcinea," and "Aldonza."

Norman Nadel was as enthused with Don Quixote as he had been with Tevye the year before, saying the show "mates theater and music with excitement and invention," while Walter Kerr again took the opposite stance, finding the aspirations in "The Impossible Dream" to be somewhat "vulgar," and carping that "Cervantes' rough landscape has been planted with pretty ordinary posies."

Kiley earned a Tony, as did composers Darion and Leigh and director Albert Marre (he also directed *Kismet*, in which Kiley and Diener had supporting roles; see 1954 above).

The 1972 film with Peter O'Toole and Sophia Loren was wretched, so much so that critic Leonard Maltin moaned: "Beautiful source material has been raped, murdered, and buried."[9]

Original cast: Kapp KS-5505. London cast with Diener and Keith Michell: Decca DXSA-7203. The London album is a double set with a lot of dialogue, including the windmill scene and Don Quixote's battle with the muleteers.

1967

Cabaret (John Kander, Fred Ebb). Opened November 20, 1966. Cast: Jill Haworth, Bert Convy, Joel Grey, Jack Gilford, Lotte Lenya.

Life doesn't have to be serious. Life can be a cabaret where, if you concentrate on the music, the dancing, the distracting entertainment, you won't be able to notice life's more distressing elements, let alone be forced to do something about them. Turn your face away from reality; eat, drink, and be merry, and just ignore those guys in the brown shirts and swastika armbands. They're part of a different show.

Walter Kerr in *The New York Times* called it, "A stunning musical. Brilliantly conceived." *Cabaret* was that and much more. Richard Watts, Jr., in the *New York Post*, said, "It is the glory of *Cabaret* that it can upset you while it gives theatrical satisfaction."

Fifteen years earlier, John van Druten had adapted the stories of

Christopher Isherwood into a play (and film) called *I Am a Camera*, showing the decadence of prewar Berlin. As a play it won the 1951-1952 New York Drama Critics Circle Award.

From that evolved *Cabaret*, the story of an American novelist (ex-ballplayer Convy, graduating from a supporting role in *Fiddler on the Roof*) looking for atmosphere and inspiration in the Berlin of 1929. He finds more than he can handle in the jaded cabaret performer Sally Bowles (Haworth). She's the star of the Kit Kat Klub, the show presided over by the manipulative and androgynous Master of Ceremonies (Grey). Gradually the subplot of growing Nazi menace comes into play through the romance of Herr Schultz, a Jew (Gilford) and his landlady Fraulein Schneider (Lenya) — who gives him up in favor of keeping her business license.

The musical's underlying themes are in intentionally disturbing contrast to the atmosphere of the ever-happy cabaret. The score includes: "Willkommen," "Don't Tell Mama," "Perfectly Marvelous," "Tomorrow Belongs to Me," "Why Should I Wake Up?" "The Money Song," "Married," "Meeskite," "If You Could See Her," and the hit title song.

Joel Grey and Peg Murray won Tonys, as did director Harold Prince, composers Kander and Ebb, and choreographer Ronald Field. Grey also appeared in a 1987 stage revival of the show.

The 1972 film starring Liza Minnelli and Joel Grey dropped many of the songs, adding "Mein Herr" and "Maybe This Time." Director Bob Fosse took a more realistic approach to the musical material, keeping it largely within the confines of the cabaret itself and thereby making the character and dialogue songs expendable. Also, the Gilford-Lenya love story was given to a younger couple and was successfully concluded with a marriage. Minnelli, Grey, and Fosse won Oscars.

Original cast: Columbia KOS-3040. Film: ABC 752.

1968

Hallelujah, Baby! (Jule Styne, Betty Comden, Adolph Green). Opened April 26, 1967. Cast: Leslie Uggams, Robert Hooks, Lillian Hayman, Allen Case.

In an attempt to depict sixty years of the Civil Rights movement, author Arthur Laurents followed the same three people through six decades of struggle against racial prejudice without letting them age a single day. Thus audiences were able to see how being born into different eras would have affected these characters' lives and ambitions. Most critics decided the show was about ten years too late but heaped praise on star Leslie Uggams.

Uggams (in her stage debut) is Georgina, daughter of a maid at the turn of the century, who's in love with Pullman porter Clem (Hooks). A white theatrical producer named Harvey (Case) hires Georgina — to play a maid.

In the 1920s the producer is the owner of a segregated nightclub (white patrons, black entertainers), Georgina is in the chorus, and Clem is a waiter.

In the 1930s Georgina is a singing witch in a WPA production of a jazzy *Macbeth*; Clem and Harvey are both on the breadline.

The 1940s find the two men in the army (Harvey is an officer, Clem is a sergeant) and Georgina is singing with the USO.

Georgina is a singing star in the 1950s, Clem is a civil rights activist, while Harvey owns an integrated nightclub and asks Georgina to marry him.

As the play enters the 1960s there is renewed hope that freedom and equality will be coming soon.

Song highlights include Uggams' solos: "Being Good," "Little Room," and the gospel-flavored title song. Hooks sings "Watch My Dust," Case solos on "Not Mine," and the cast gets together on "Smile, Smile," and "Talking to Yourself." Hayman, who won a Tony as Georgina's mother, sings of her daughter's talent, "I Don't Know Where She Got It." Most of the show's social commentary was in the libretto rather than the lyrics. Little of the time-tripping plot twists can be discerned just from listening to the songs.

Uggams shared a Tony with Patricia Routledge (for *Darling of the Day*, a flop by Jule Styne and E. Y. Harburg that played just 31 performances). Comden, Green, and Styne won for their score. The show had closed by then, playing only 293 performances.

Original cast: Columbia KOS-3090.

1969

1776 (Sherman Edwards). Opened March 16, 1969. Cast: William Daniels, Paul Hecht, Clifford David, Roy Poole, Rex Everhart, Ken Howard, Virginia Vestoff, Ronald Holgate, Betty Buckley.

The Founding Fathers are gathered in stifling Philadelphia to decide whether or not to break away from England. The power struggles over politics, land, slavery, and loyalty trigger heated and acrimonious debates, usually provoked by the disliked and obstinate John Adams (Daniels) against his more conservative foes. He and Ben Franklin (Everhart) prevail upon a reluctant Thomas Jefferson (Howard) to support their arguments with a Declaration of Independence. (Jefferson is reluctant because he is newly married and desires to be with his wife, played by Betty Buckley.) With more debate and some crucial compromises—particularly over slavery—the Declaration is signed and the American Revolution officially begins.

It was a gutsy choice to have such revered figures singing and dancing in their period costumes, but the gamble paid off with songs such as: "Sit Down, John," "Piddle, Twiddle and Resolve," "But, Mr. Adams," "Till Then," "The Lees of Old Virginia," "Momma, Look Sharp," "Is Anybody There?" "Cool, Cool, Considerate Men" (dropped from the film), and the powerful hypocrisy song, "Molasses to Rum," sung by South Carolina's Edward Rutledge (Clifford David).

Clive Barnes of the *Times* was beside himself: "It makes even an Englishman's heart beat a little bit faster. This is a musical with style, humanity, wit and passion." Richard P. Cooke in *The Wall Street Journal* (3/18/69) said this "semi-documentary" was "absorbing and exciting and the events of those remarkable months in Philadelphia come through admirably."

Holgate, as Richard Henry Lee, won the only acting Tony (Vestoff, as Abigail Adams, was the only other nominee from the show; William Daniels asked that his name be withdrawn due to a billing and category dispute). Peter Hunt won for his direction.

Daniels, Vestoff, and Howard reprised their roles in the 1972 film, with Ben Franklin played by Howard Da Silva.

Original cast: Columbia BOS-3310. Film: Columbia S-3174.

1970

Applause (Charles Strouse, Lee Adams). Opened March 30, 1970. Cast: Lauren Bacall, Len Cariou, Bonnie Franklin, Lee Roy Reams, Penny Fuller.

The book by Betty Comden and Adolph Green was based on the Bette Davis film *All About Eve*. The story revolves around stage star Margo Channing (Bacall) who finds her career slowly taken over by the sweetly treacherous ingénue Eve Harrington (Fuller), who manipulates her way into the spotlight and stardom without regard for who gets stepped on.

After a rousing overture, the show sparkles with: "Think How It's Gonna Be," "But Alive," "Who's That Girl?" (Margo's reaction to seeing herself on TV in an old movie, which can also be seen as Bacall spoofing her own career), "Fasten Your Seat Belts" (from a Bette Davis line in the original film), "Welcome to the Theatre" (Margo's bitterly ironic look at the "asylum" where ego games and backstabbing are all part of the magic and fun), "She's No Longer a Gypsy," "One of a Kind," "One Hallowe'en" (in which Eve discloses the root cause of her ruthless ambition was a cold and distant father), "Something Greater," and the title number headed by Bonnie Franklin (later of TV's *One Day at a Time*) and a group of chorus people — gypsies of the theater. Why do they work and slave so hard? For the sound that means love — applause.

Every critic loved Lauren Bacall, with superlatives ranging from "splendid" to "overpowering." *The Wall Street Journal*'s John J. O'Connor was among the captivated: "[Bacall] dances up a mean storm, unleashes a seductive baritone voice, flings herself about the stage recklessly, gets tossed about by the dancers and, throughout, manages to remain incredibly attractive, sexy and vibrant. It's a smashing performance."

Opinions were divided about the music, however. Clive Barnes of the *Times*: "Miss Bacall is a honey, and the book is among the best in years — so who is going to care too much about the second-rate music? Not, I am sure, the public."

Walter Kerr took time to tell readers of the *Times* of the little-known chorus line gypsy Bonnie Franklin, who "really has nothing to do with the show but to stop it," thanks to "a smile like the one they sometimes paint on lollipops." Said Kerr, "she needs only to be turned loose to take over."

Bacall and director Ron Field won Tonys. There was no original score category for 1970.

Technically, it was Bacall's singing debut, though she did warble a few stanzas with Hoagy Carmichael in her 1944 film debut, *To Have and Have Not*. With this show, Bacall was following in the footsteps of Rosalind Russell, another film star with a narrow singing range but lots of moxie, who first hit the musical stage at age 45 in *Wonderful Town* [see above, 1953]. Bacall was also 45 when *Applause* opened.

Original cast: ABC SOC-11.

1971

Company (Stephen Sondheim). Opened April 26, 1970. Cast: Dean Jones, Elaine Stritch, Barbara Barrie, Charles Kimbrough, George Coe, Donna McKechnie, Susan Browning, Beth Howland, Pamela Myers.

The Sondheim era officially begins here, with this watershed musical of contemporary American life, friendship, love, marriage, and alienated attitudes.

In a story without much of a plot in the traditional sense, Robert (Dean Jones) is a bachelor-about-town constantly urged by his married friends to give up his single life and join them in marital bliss — though what lies beneath the surface is seldom blissful, as the much-married Joanne (Stritch) elaborates in "The Little Things You Do Together." Robert's many girlfriends try but cannot pin him down ("You Could Drive a Person Crazy"), and the husbands he knows are envious of his freedom ("Have I Got a Girl for You"). Robert is eventually worn down enough to understand that making commitments is a big part of "Being Alive."

Sondheim's gift for social satire gets a good airing in "Another Hundred People" and "The Ladies Who Lunch," the latter a haunting evocation of the emptiness of artificially full lives. Highlights include: "Side by Side by Side," "What Would We Do

Without You?'' and ''Getting Married Today,'' the latter done at a manic pace by Beth Howland (Vera on TV's *Alice*).

Sondheim explained the show's concept to biographer Craig Zadan this way: ''We wanted a show where the audience would sit for two hours screaming their heads off with laughter and then go home and not be able to sleep.''[10]

One who didn't get much sleep (and maybe didn't do all that much screaming with laughter) was critic Walter Kerr. His review in the *Times* the next day said the show ''gets right down to brass tacks and brass knuckles without a moment's hesitation, staring contemporary society straight in the eye before spitting in it.'' The overall effect was too cold, cynical, and distant for his taste, though Kerr admitted to admiring large parts of the show.

Company won 7 of its 15 nominations, but none for the splendid ensemble cast. Harold Prince picked up two Tonys as producer and director, and George Furth won for his book. Sondheim won for his brilliant score.

Original cast: Columbia OS-3550.

A 60-minute TV documentary on the recording of the cast album was made by director D. A. Pennebaker and aired on October 25, 1970. The 18-hour marathon recording session and the perfectionism of the composer, musicians, and performers was captured as never before. Elaine Stritch, for example, spent three hoarse hours trying to do a perfect take on ''The Ladies Who Lunch'' before giving up in tearful exhaustion; it was completed the next day to a prerecorded music track. RCA released the film on home video in 1992.

The documentary was sponsored by Chrysler-Plymouth after Eastern Airlines backed out, reportedly because one character, a stewardess, deliberately misses her next flight in order to stay with Robert.[11]

1972

Two Gentlemen of Verona (Galt MacDermot, John Guare). **Opened July 27, 1971.** Cast: Jonelle Allen, Clifton Davis, Raul Julia, Diana Davila.

The Bard of Avon meets the composers of *Hair*, resulting in a rousing, delightful rock musical that has very little regard for time or place (there are motor scooters, bicycles, and telephones in this adaptation).

The basic plot is Shakespeare's: Proteus and Valentine are two young nobles of Verona with diametrically opposed characters — one steadfast and loyal, the other deceitful and opportunistic. Both go to seek their fortune in Milan and fall for the same girl. There follows a series of escapades with disguises, misunderstandings, outlaws, misdelivered love letters, and assorted complications.

Musical highlights include the Duke of Milan's "Bring All the Boys Back Home" (a Vietnam-inspired political hypocrisy speech), "Thurio's Samba" (a song most governmental entities and parents' groups would declare unfit for a radio broadcast), "Night Letter," "Hot Lover," "What Does a Lover Pack?" "Love's Revenge," and "Calla Lily Lady."

The musical moved to Broadway after a smaller debut in Central Park as part of Joseph Papp's New York Shakespeare Festival. The expanded version met with general critical acclaim. "Crazy and wonderful," wrote Martin Gottfried in *Women's Wear Daily*. While characterizing the creators as "a dramatic demolition team" turned loose on the Bard of Avon, T. E. Kalem of *Time* (12/13/71) singled out Jonelle Allen as "a one-woman heat wave." At the *Daily News*, Douglas Watt termed Allen "a bundle of sensuous joy all by herself" and lauded the "cheerfully nutty lyrics."

The only other Tony the show won was for its book, by John Guare and Mel Shapiro.

Original cast: ABC BCSY-1001 (double album).

(Co-star Clifton Davis went on to play the Rev. Reuben Gregory on TV's *Amen*, while Raul Julia has become a star of stage and film — see 1982 below.)

Best Score

Follies (Stephen Sondheim). Opened April 4, 1971. Cast: Alexis Smith, Gene Nelson, John McMartin, Yvonne DeCarlo, Dorothy Collins, Mary McCarty, Ethel Shutta, Victoria Mallory, Fifi D'Orsay.

The Original Score Tony for 1972 went to Stephen Sondheim for *Follies*, a tour de force in which the middle-aged stars of a long ago Follies hold a reunion in a theater that is about to be torn down. The exploration of their post-Follies lives and loves and the choices they made ranges from the poignant to the emotionally shattering, with dramatic songs structured in the styles of old masters such as Cole Porter, the Gershwins, Berlin, Richard Rodgers, and Oscar Hammerstein.

Song highlights: "Waiting for the Girls Upstairs," "Broadway Baby," "The Road You Didn't Take" (John McMartin), "In Buddy's Eyes," "Who's That Woman?" "Too Many Mornings," "The Right Girl," "Could I Leave You" (Alexis Smith), "You're Gonna Love Tomorrow," "Losing My Mind" (Dorothy Collins), "Buddy's Blues" (Gene Nelson), and the greatest survival song ever composed, sung by Yvonne DeCarlo, "I'm Still Here."

(The historical references to politicians and fads in "I'm Still Here" might stump most younger listeners, and could serve as a trivia quiz for some adults. The song was used to fine comic effect by Shirley MacLaine in the 1990 film *Postcards From the Edge*.)

In his *Time* review of the show (4/12/71), T. E. Kalen wrote, "The frontier of the American musical theater is wherever Harold Prince and Stephen Sondheim are."

Alexis Smith and choreographer Michael Bennett won Tonys.

Original cast: Capitol SO-761. London cast: Geffen 24183-4. The London cast not only contains some new songs, but some that were left off the original cast album. It stars Diana Rigg, Julia McKenzie, Daniel Massey, and David Healy (whose solo on "The Right Girl" was ever-so-slightly expurgated for British record buyers). Broadway veteran Dolores Gray belts out "I'm Still Here." New highlights include: "Ah, But Underneath" (a saucy, Cole Porter-like number done splendidly by Diana Rigg of TV's *The Avengers*), "Country House," "Social Dancing," and "Make the Most of Your Music."

See Act Four, 1986, for the Grammy-winning *Follies in Concert*.

1973

A Little Night Music (Stephen Sondheim). Opened February 25, 1973. Cast: Glynis Johns, Len Cariou, Hermione Gingold, Patricia Elliot, Victoria Mallory.

Based on the 1956 Ingmar Bergman film, *Smiles of a Summer Night*, the musical is set in turn-of-the-century Sweden and the songs are invariably in Viennese waltz tempos. This startling departure for Sondheim was more proof of his unwillingness to be typecast and his desire to work with challenging ideas and forms. *A Little Night Music* is a romp, with various couples — not necessarily married to each other — playing a sophisticated game of musical beds until finally getting themselves sorted out.

The biggest hit from the show — propelled to prominence by a 1975 Judy Collins recording — was "Send in the Clowns," a song composed for Glynis Johns during out-of-town tryouts (the song won the 1975 Grammy as Song of the Year). Other numbers: "The Glamorous Life," "Remember," "You Must Meet My Wife," "Liaisons" (Gingold's lament about the decline of scandalous affairs), "Every Day a Little Death" (a wife's feelings about her husband's extramarital affair), "A Weekend in the Country," and "The Miller's Son," a rambunctious tune about sowing wild oats sung by Petra the maid (D. Jamin-Bartlett).

Critics basically found the show tuneful and eye-filling, but — a favorite term for a Sondheim show — distant. "The atmosphere is sterile," wrote Douglas Watt of the *Daily News*. "Though much of the talk and activity are given over to sex, there seems to be little of it around [and] stunning as it is to gaze upon and as clever as its score is, [the show] remains too literary and precious a work to stir the emotions."

At *The Wall Street Journal*, Edwin Wilson termed Sondheim "the cleverest lyricist working today" and found the show "lovely to look at and a pleasure to hear." Echoing those sentiments, T. E. Kalem wrote in *Time* (3/12/73), "This is a jewelled music box of a show: lovely to look at, delightful to listen to, and perhaps too exquisite, fragile and muted ever to be quite humanly affecting."

On the plus side, Jack Kroll of *Newsweek* saw the show as "an emerald in a box of gooseberries," while Richard Watts at the *Post* found the "delightful" score "fresh and charming." Martin Gottfried at *Women's Wear Daily* had two conflicting views; while commending the score as "enchanting, without question his finest yet," Gottfried panned the production as a whole, reporting that "the show has little life, little musical theatricality and little reason for its own existence.''

Johns and Elliot won Tonys, as did Hugh Wheeler for writing the book. And Sondheim won his third composing Tony in a row.

The 1978 film with Elizabeth Taylor, Diana Rigg, Gingold, and Cariou, directed by Harold Prince, was a disaster. Not only was it slow and boring, but Taylor's voice was not up to the task. ''The Miller's Son'' was dropped.

Original cast: Columbia KS-32265. London cast (with Jean Simmons, Hermione Gingold, and Joss Ackland): RCA 5090-4-RG.

1974

Raisin (Judd Woldin, Robert Brittan). Opened October 18, 1973. Cast: Joe Morton, Ernestine Jackson, Virginia Capers, Deborah Allen, Ralph Carter.

''Pure magic!'' raved Clive Barnes in *The New York Times*. ''A tremendous blaze of new black talent!'' lauded Clarence B. Jones in the New York *Amsterdam News*. ''It restores your faith in the theatre, moves you to tears, makes you stand up and cheer!'' cheered Maurice Peterson in *Essence*. Richard L. Coe at *The Washington Post* declared, ''At last! Something worth shouting about!'' Such understatement did not begin to express the spiritual lift *Raisin* could give an audience.

This musical rendering of Lorraine Hansberry's timeless story of a black family's middle-class aspirations in moving to an all white neighborhood, *A Raisin in the Sun*, was both faithful to the original and a joyful event on its own merits.

Joe Morton's pent-up ambitions and rage as Walter Lee Younger fairly burst from the recording in ''Man Say,'' ''Runnin' to Meet the Man,'' and ''It's a Deal.'' From the ironically comic ''Not Anymore'' to the gospel-flavored ''He Come Down This Morning,'' *Raisin* is a moving, foot-tapping delight. Virginia Capers won a Tony as Mama Younger; Morton was beaten by Christopher Plummer as a singing *Cyrano*, which played only 49 performances.

Original cast: Columbia KS-32754.

(Joe Morton went on to star in the film *Brother From Another Planet*, *Terminator 2: Judgment Day*, and TV's *Equal Justice*.)

Best Score

Gigi (Alan Jay Lerner, Frederick Loewe). Opened November 13, 1973. Cast: Alfred Drake, Agnes Moorehead, Daniel Massey, Karin Wolfe, Maria Karnilova, George Gaines.

Despite Woldin and Brittan's superb adaptation of *Raisin* (many of the songs incorporated some of Hansberry's original lines of dialogue), and the fact that *Raisin* ran for 744 *more* performances, the Tony Award for original musical score went to Broadway veterans Lerner and Loewe for *Gigi*.

Gigi, of course, was an original and brilliant 1958 MGM film with Maurice Chevalier, Leslie Caron, Louis Jourdan, Isabel Jeans, and Hermione Gingold. It told the story of a young girl in Paris at the turn of the century whose aunt tries to raise her to be a courtesan, and of the rich, jaded Gaston, who falls for her before the transition is complete. The story was from a novel by Colette. The film, director, score, and title song won Oscars. Chevalier was presented with an honorary Oscar. So what was it doing winning a Broadway Tony sixteen years later?

Four new songs, for starters: "The Earth and Other Minor Things," "Paris Is Paris Again," "In This Wide, Wide World," and, the best of the lot, "The Contract," in which Gigi's Aunt Alicia haggles over the girl's prenuptial details like a hard nosed robber-baron.

Film songs dropped from the play were "The Parisians" and "Say a Prayer for Me Tonight" (first composed for, but dropped from, *My Fair Lady*), but preserved intact (and with some added lyrics here and there) were: "Thank Heaven for Little Girls," "It's a Bore," "The Night They Invented Champagne," "I Remember It Well," "I'm Glad I'm Not Young Anymore," the delightful title song, and Gaston's sung soliloquy as he suddenly realizes that Gigi the little girl is now Gigi the alarmingly alluring young lady.

Chevalier was replaced on stage by Alfred Drake, who poured his smooth voice over the music like syrup on hotcakes. He wisely did not affect a French accent.

Broadway cast: RCA ABK1-0404. Film: MGM SE-3641 ST.

The film score was reissued in 1990 on CBS Special Products, AT 45395, and, unlike the MGM album, contains quite a bit of dialogue as lead-in for the songs, as well as the montage where Jeans gives Caron a cram course in how to attract a man.

1975

The Wiz (Charlie Smalls). Opened January 5, 1975. Cast: Stephanie Mills, Tiger Haynes, Ted Ross, Hinton Battle, Andre DeShields.

This all black musical rendering of L. Frank Baum's *The Wonderful Wizard of Oz* was the brainchild of producer Ken Harper and it turned out to be a terrific and successful concept, without a lot of help from the critics.

"The songs are mostly dull, the lyrics commonplace and the music uninspired," carped Douglas Watt in the *Daily News*, while admitting the show was "so enormously good-natured, spectacular looking and slickly done that it is hard to resist." Clive Barnes, noting in the *Times*, however superfluously, that "Criticism is not objective," reported, "I found myself unmoved for too much of the evening, but I was respectfully unmoved, not insultingly unmoved." He disliked the "blaring, relentless rhythms" of the music as well.

Martin Gottfried, writing for the *New York Post*, questioned the propriety of the casting decision, saying, "an all-black anything never had any business anywhere," feeling the concept to be too patronizing. He liked the first act but was "left with deep disappointment that the second act fell apart." (Gottfried also noted the lack of drug references by the black cast, and wrote that Baum himself "was no stranger to hallucinogens, which should be obvious from the trippy story. If further clues were needed, one need only remember the poppy fields outside Emerald City.")

At *Women's Wear Daily*, Howard Kissel thought the songs "sometimes sound more like a potential collection of hit singles than a dramatic score." Edwin Wilson told *Wall Street Journal* readers, "The book for the new musical is undistinguished in every respect except its audacity." Still, he conceded "the show is alive: a triumph of spirit and performance over material."

The contemporary Motown soul sound was a long way from the Harold Arlen and E. Y. Harburg score for the Judy Garland film classic, and yet it remained Baum's story of Dorothy following the yellow brick road to Oz with the Scarecrow, Cowardly Lion, and Tin Woodsman. Only this time, instead of "We're Off to See the Wizard," they're singing: "Ease on Down the Road," "I Was Born on the Day Before Yesterday," "Slide Some Oil to Me," "Be a Lion," "What Would I Do if I Could Feel," "Y'All Got It!" "Everybody Rejoice," and "Don't Nobody Bring Me No Bad News."

Ted Ross won a Tony as the Cowardly Lion, and so did Dee Dee Bridgewater as the good witch Glinda. Geoffrey Holder was presented with a directing Tony, and Charlie Smalls won for his score.

The 1978 film starred Diana Ross, Michael Jackson, Nipsey Russell, Ted Ross, and Richard Pryor as the Wizard, with arrangements by Quincy Jones. Diana Ross, being too old for schoolgirl Dorothy, was turned into a schoolteacher for the film. The movie reportedly lost $11 million.

Original cast: Atlantic SD-18137. Film: MCA 2-14000.

1976

A Chorus Line (Marvin Hamlisch, Edward Kleban). Opened April 15, 1975. Cast: Carole Bishop, Pamela Blair, Wayne Cilento, Kay Cole, Priscilla Lopez, Donna McKechnie, Sammy Williams.

If greatness is to be measured in longevity, *A Chorus Line* is Broadway's greatest musical, having entertained and moved audiences for a record-breaking fifteen years (6,137 shows).

The title song of *Applause* [above, 1970] celebrated the usually nameless, faceless toilers of the chorus, the theater's gypsies; *A Chorus Line* gives them an entire show. It takes more than that, of course, to produce such a stunning hit, and the show's universality lies in its honesty. It is more than the laid-bare emotions of a group of dancers auditioning for a few roles. In their personal revelations, hopes, dreams, and desires, they become every one of us, auditioning for a place in the world.

The score is filled with great numbers: "I Hope I Get It," "At the Ballet," "Hello Twelve, Hello Thirteen, Hello Love," "Nothing," "The Music and the Mirror," "Dance: Ten; Looks: Three," and the theme of all our aspirations, "What I Did for Love."

"A dazzling show: driving, compassionate and finally thrilling," said Martin Gottfried in the *New York Post*, "It is a major event in the development of the American musical theater." Douglas Watt of the *Daily News* hailed it as a "daringly simple, brilliantly staged entertainment . . . the most exciting Broadway musical in several seasons." No less enthused was Clive Barnes at the *Times* who not only found it "devastatingly effective," but said "it is a show that must dance, jog and whirl its way into the history of the musical theater." And so it did.

McKechnie, Williams, and Bishop received Tonys, as did director Michael Bennett, writers James Kirkwood and Nicholas Dante, and composers Hamlisch and Kleban.

Lovers of the musical waited nine years for a film version, only to be rewarded for their patience with one of the worst translations to film ever perpetrated. The great "Hello Twelve" ensemble number was thrown out, and "What I Did for Love" was turned into a mere love song, no longer having any special significance to the story or the subtext. No one from the original cast was in it. The film serves as a reminder that with fewer musicals being made into movies, the originals need to be preserved even if they have to be taped live on stage.

Original cast: Columbia PS-33581.

Two books about the show are also recommended: Denny Martin Flinn's *What They Did for Love* (Bantam Books, 1989), and *On the Line*, compiled by Robert Viagas, Tommie Walsh, Baayork Lee and the original cast (Morrow, 1990). A third book also serves as a biography of the director: *A Chorus Line and the Musicals of Michael Bennett*, by Ken Mandelbaum (St. Martin's Press, 1989).

1977

Annie (Charles Strouse, Martin Charnin). Opened April 21, 1977. Cast: Andrea McArdle, Reid Shelton, Dorothy Loudon, Sandy Faison, Robert Fitch, Danielle Brisebois (later of TV's *Archie's Place*).

Cartoonist Harold Gray's Little Orphan Annie brings uplifting songs to her Depression-era search for her parents, along with an eternal optimism, her mutt Sandy, rich Daddy Warbucks, and a score that, in the wrong hands, could have sunk spunkiness to the level of the truly offensive.

Indeed, cynics were wont to scoff. On the TV series *Barney Miller*, Hal Linden once commiserated with a tourist, the victim of a terrifying armed robbery and a day spent in the police station, who shrugged and replied, "Well, it was better than seeing *Annie*."[12]

Time (5/2/77) groused that "The music of Charles Strouse would scarcely inspire an organ-grinder's monkey to rattle his cup, and Martin Charnin's lyrics are for beginning lip readers."

An opposing opinion was expressed in *Newsweek*'s review (5/2/77), which noted "it's not easy to write corny but catchy tunes," and called the show "an incredible achievement . . . a deliberate rejection of the musical theater's recent hard-won sophistication." Annie herself was hailed as "the mascot of the new age of hope, optimism and simplicity that's coming in with President Carter." (Theater reviewers are not to be confused with political pundits.)

However cynical one's hindsight may be, the score is a delight, with 13-year-old McArdle's wonderfully rich voice making the most of "Maybe," "Tomorrow," "I Don't Need Anything But You," and "The Hard-Knock Life." If anything, the little girl with the big voice doesn't have enough to sing. Loudon, playing the greedy superintendent of a Dickensian orphanage, has a field day with "Little Girls" and "Easy Street." A poignant lament in a "Hooverville" camp of the homeless, "We'd Like to Thank You (Herbert Hoover)," more than makes up for the unabashedly sunny "Tomorrow" (which Annie belts out while standing on Franklin Roosevelt's desk).

Tonys went to Loudon, Thomas Meehan for the book, and Strouse and Charnin (who also directed) for Best Score. McArdle was nominated in the same category as Loudon; she was no novice but a performer since the age of three, mostly in TV commercials. As a teen her big voice was so true and strong that McArdle sang the national anthem in Seattle at the 50th major league All-Star game in 1979.

The real trouper of the show, however, proved to be Sandy. This part airedale terrier and Irish setter was found in a Connecticut dog pound, purchased for $8.00, and cast in the nonsinging role on the day he was scheduled to be put to sleep. Sandy showed his gratitude for this new leash on life by becoming a star and staying with the production for six years and 2,377 performances. Sandy chowed down at Sardi's, shook hands with Jimmy Carter and Muhammad Ali, and lived anything but a dog's life. He even had a 94-page book published in 1978: *Sandy: The Autobiography of a Star* (Simon and Schuster, "as told to" William Berloni, who rescued Sandy from the pound, and Allison Thomas). Sandy died of arthritis in August, 1990, at the age of 80 (16 in dog years).[13]

John Huston directed the regrettable 1982 movie version starring Albert Finney (a world-class actor but not much of a singer), Carol Burnett, Bernadette Peters, and young Aileen Quinn as Annie. It cost $42 million to make, causing the Medved brothers to dub it one of the decade's "prize porkers."[14] The socially significant "We Want to Thank You" was dropped, along with most of the show's guts, while enough sunny, meaningless new songs were added to drastically tip the show's balance toward the relentlessly cute and maudlin, a mood not helped by the obvious (and futile) attempt to have Quinn come off as a new Shirley Temple when the role called for an older, Dead End-type kid.

Original cast: Columbia PS-34712.

1978

Ain't Misbehavin' (Thomas "Fats" Waller, Richard Maltby, Jr., and various lyricists). Opened May 9, 1978. Cast: Ken Page, Nell Carter, Andre DeShields, Amelia McQueen, Charlaine Woodard.

Fats Waller was the clown prince of jazz, a brilliant virtuoso of the stride style at the piano or organ, a composer of hit songs, a showman who'd prop a bottle of gin on the nearest piano and commence to jam, jive, and jump at the least provocation. The spoken asides on his recordings ("Well, alright now!") are legendary, for here was an entertainer whose outgoing personality could not be held in check, not even by the primitive studio technology of the 1930s and 1940s.

As conceived and directed by Richard Maltby, Jr. *Ain't Misbehavin'* is not just a biography of Waller through his music, but a recreation of the times in which he lived, seemingly playing his piano with three hands at a time.

The score contains Waller's finest hits as well as some lesser known and even forgotten works all deserving to be remembered: "Lookin' Good But Feelin' Bad," "'T Ain't Nobody's Bizness if I Do," "Honeysuckle Rose," "Squeeze Me," "Handful of Keys" (with lyrics by Maltby), "I've Got a Feeling I'm Falling," "The Joint Is Jumpin'," "Lounging at the Waldorf," "The Viper's Drag," "Mean to Me," "Keepin' Out of Mischief Now," "Black and Blue," "Two Sleepy People," "Ain't Misbehavin'," and more (the album is a double set).

Did the old music get through to the modern generation of critics? "Jump for joy!" wrote Douglas Watt in the *Daily News*. "Those five kindred souls up there on the stage could fill heaven with their youthful verve." He particularly singled out "chunky Nell Carter, a black Mae West with a voice that could sound reveille for an entire regiment or croon it to sleep."

Newsweek's Jack Kroll (5/22/78) said the show "celebrates the Falstaffian Waller, and it does so with irresistible joy, gladness and energy." And Richard Eder at the *Times* proclaimed the show to be "a whole cluster of marvels," especially the songs: "A whole series of the jazz worlds of the time, uptown and downtown, raffish and posh — the posh had an edge of mockery to it — funny and startlingly beautiful, came to life."

Nell Carter and director Richard Maltby, Jr., took home Tonys.

Original cast: RCA CBL2-2965. Many of Waller's recordings are available on compilation albums by a number of firms.

Both Carter and DeShields won Outstanding Individual Achievement Emmys in 1982 for an NBC production of *Ain't Misbehavin'*. (At the time, Nell Carter was in her second season as Nell Harper on NBC's long-running series *Gimme a Break*.)

Best Score

On the Twentieth Century (Cy Coleman, Betty Comden, Adolph Green). Opened February 19, 1978. Cast: Madeline Kahn, John Cullum, George Coe, Imogene Coca, and Kevin Kline (a future Oscar-winner for *A Fish Called Wanda*).

The 1978 Tony for original score went to Cy Coleman, Betty Comden, and Adolph Green for *On the Twentieth Century*, a show set on a famous old transcontinental train, the Twentieth Century Limited. It was based on a Ben Hecht and Charles MacArthur play of the same name (which was filmed in 1934 as *Twentieth Century*, a screwball comedy starring John Barrymore and Carole Lombard). The biggest hit of the musical version was the train itself, as *Variety* could not resist noting: "It's ominous when an audience leaves a musical whistling the scenery." It chugged its way through 460 performances.

The basic plot involves a producer (Cullum) trying to regain his fame by persuading a former star (Kahn) to make a comeback in his latest show, all the while being interrupted by a religious fanatic played by Imogene Coca. Some memorable numbers, composed largely in a comic operetta style (inexplicably so, as the show is set in the jazz age, but one gets used to it), were: "Repent," "She's a Nut," "I Rise Again," "I Have Written a Play," "Together," "Our Private World," and "Sextet."

Though he thought Cullum "wonderfully entertaining" and Kline "dazzlingly funny," Douglas Watt of the *Daily News* called the show "an uneasy comic operetta," and the music "a sweeping, extravagant, overly ambitious score that too often works against the brisk, farcical nature of the piece." At the *Post*, Clive Barnes disagreed, saying, "Coleman has found the perfect musical idiom for the show — something slightly North East of opera." Richard Eder of the *Times* found in the music "grandiloquent and amusing suggestions of everything from Tchaikovsky through Puccini and Friml and up through Kurt Weill."

Original cast: Columbia JS-35330.

1979

Sweeney Todd (Stephen Sondheim). Opened March 1, 1979. Cast: Len Cariou, Angela Lansbury, Victor Garber, Ken Jennings, Merle Louise, Edmund Lyndeck, Sarah Rice, Joaquin Romaguera, Jack Eric Williams.

Both the *New York Post* and the *Soho News* appropriately headlined their reviews with the phrase "bloody good" in describing this macabre and chilling musical about Todd, the Demon Barber of Fleet Street, who slashes throats with a merry abandon while his cohort Mrs. Lovett (Lansbury) bakes the victims into meat pies — and she's running a thriving business with them. There is no doubt Sweeney (Cariou) is quite bonkers, truth be told, having been unjustly jailed by a judge who wanted his wife and who now has designs on his daughter as well. Todd has been driven insane by thoughts of vengeance not only on the judge but on any who stand in his way, innocent or not. He sings love songs to his gleaming razors. This is not a well man.

A bizarre plot for a musical, with a score to match — for this is no ordinary collection of songs but a through-composed musical (a term adapted from the German word *dutchkomponiert*), referring to a show that is completely worked out in music, a style in which there is little or no spoken dialogue, and is as close to an opera as one can get without engaging a fat lady with a horned helmet to deliver a closing aria.

There are songs, of course, songs of an astonishing variety: "No Place Like London," "The Worst Pies in London," "The Ballad of Sweeney Todd," "Green Finch and Linnet Bird," "Johanna," "Pretty Women," "A Little Priest" (a creepily hilarious taste tour of Mrs. Lovett's special ingredients), and "Not While I'm Around" are among the best of Sondheim's ever-growing repertoire.

While it may not be to everyone's aesthetic (or gastronomic) taste, for those who like the occasional goosebumps and raised hair at the back of the neck, this show is quite a dazzling accomplishment.

Cariou, Lansbury, director Hal Prince, author Hugh Wheeler, scenic designer Eugene Lee, costumer Franne Lee, and composer Sondheim all received Tonys.

Original cast: RCA CBL2-2965 (double set).

(There was also a non-musical, 1936 British horror film called *Sweeney Todd*, starring the aptly named Tod Slaughter.)

1980

Evita (Andrew Lloyd Webber, Tim Rice). Opened in New York September 25, 1979. Cast: Patti LuPone, Mandy Patinkin, Bob Gunton.

The trend for through-composed musicals continued with *Evita*, the story of Eva Peron's rise from poverty to immense power in dictatorial Argentina, with a sung narrative commentary provided by Patinkin as Ché, a student activist based on revolutionary Ché Guevara.

Tim Rice's lyrics are powerful and compelling, sardonic and satiric. Patinkin is mesmerizing in "Oh What a Circus," "And the Money Kept Rolling In (and Out)," and "Waltz for Eva and Ché"; LuPone's amazing voice can belt out "Buenos Aires," turn wistful in "Don't Cry for Me Argentina," be snappish in "Rainbow High," and uncompromising in "The Actress Hasn't Learned the Lines (You'd Like to Hear)." Other standout numbers: "Another Suitcase in Another Hall," "On This Night of a Thousand Stars," "High Flying, Adored," and "Santa Evita."

Virtually all the critics panned the historical inaccuracy of Ché's presence, informing readers that Ché had, in fact, never met Eva Peron and was a high school student at the time. But in using the persona of an internationally known revolutionary as commentator and as a symbol of the undercurrent of growing disenchantment with the Peron regime, the decision is not only dramatically justified but comes across as a brilliant balancing act. Still, there was carping.

Walter Kerr so disliked the through-composed aspect — in that it *told* what was afoot as opposed to showing it ("We are condemned to hearing what we want to know") — that he felt it put the audience "into the kind of emotional limbo we inhabit when we're just back from the dentist but the novocaine hasn't worn off yet." As for the score, Kerr conjured up the images of two Hollywood veterans of the 1940s and told his *Times* readers it "sometimes sounds as though Max Steiner had arranged it for Carmen Miranda."

Douglas Watt of the *Daily News* termed the show "spectacularly vulgar . . . dispiriting and even pointless," and referred to LuPone as "colorless" and "a dud." T. E. Kalem of *Time* (10/8/79) called her "incendiary," while "Patinkin pours Brechtian acid into the role" of Ché.

Patinkin, LuPone, director Hal Prince, author Rice, and composer Andrew Lloyd Webber all won Tonys.

Original Broadway cast: MCA 2-11007 (double set).

LuPone went on to star in a revival of Cole Porter's *Anything*

Goes [Act Five] and on TV's *Life Goes On*; Patinkin divided his time and talent between stage (*Sunday in the Park With George*, Act Two, 1983-1984, *The Secret Garden*, Act Five), film (*Alien Nation*, *Yenta*, *The Princess Bride*, *Dick Tracy*), and the recording studio (*Mandy Patinkin*, CBS FMT 44943, *Dress Casual*, CBS FMT 45998).

1981

42nd Street (Harry Warren, Al Dubin). Opened August 25, 1980. Cast: Tammy Grimes, Jerry Orbach, Lee Roy Reams, Joseph Bova, Carole Cook.

There's this director, see, who's trying to make a comeback and, gee, wouldn't you know it, his leading lady just broke her ankle and now the cute but inexperienced understudy has to go on in her place, so go out there a nobody, honey, but ya gotta come back a star!

If that sounds familiar, if that sounds like the basic (some would say "classic") plot of every backstage musical ever churned out by Hollywood, there is a good reason: *42nd Street* is the stage version of a 1933 Ruby Keeler, Warner Baxter movie of the same name, using the same songs, plus some from *Dames*, *Gold Diggers of 1933*, and *Gold Diggers of 1935*, and recreating the sensational old Busby Berkeley dance routines.

The Warren-Dubin songs are certainly classics: "You're Getting to Be a Habit With Me" (using more drug analogies in a 1930s love song than even a rap group would try to get away with in the 1990s), "Shadow Waltz," "Dames," "We're in the Money," "Lullaby of Broadway," "Shuffle off to Buffalo," and "42nd Street" had long lives on the nation's hit parades, and still longer lives on the late, late show. They hold up very well. So well that when the show closed early in 1989 it had racked up 3,486 performances.

It did not begin on an auspicious note. *The New York Times* noted the day after opening night that the show "has been surrounded by a series of bizarre events" since coming to town, not least of which are the rumors of "bitter dissension" between director Gower

Champion and producer David Merrick, and Merrick's delays in opening the show in New York.

Then there were the writers, Michael Stewart and Mark Bramble. Their own battles with Merrick over writing credit were so frustrating that Stewart, on the day the show opened, said on National Public Radio that he was through with musical theater. "I don't love it anymore," said the veteran writer [*Hello, Dolly!* above, 1964] and lyricist [*I Love My Wife*, Act Five]. "I loved it for 20 years. I like it, I respect it, but my heart does not quicken when I hear an overture anymore."[15]

But the strangest twist came when director Gower Champion died of a rare blood cancer (waldenström's macroglobulinemia) just hours before the first curtain went up. Merrick decided to keep the director's death a secret until after the cast had taken its tenth curtain call of the night. Then, amid the tumultuous applause and good feelings, the producer went up on stage and dropped his bombshell, sending shock waves through the cast and audiei :e alike. The cast party became a wake.

Gower Champion was awarded a posthumous Tony for his choreography.

Original cast: RCA CBL1-3891.

Best Score

Woman of the Year (John Kander, Fred Ebb). Opened March 29, 1981. Cast: Lauren Bacall, Harry Guardino, Roderick Cook, Marilyn Cooper, Rex Everhart.

Although *42nd Street* copped the big prize, nearly all the rest, including Original Score, went to John Kander and Fred Ebb's *Woman of the Year*, which was based on a nonmusical 1942 movie with Katharine Hepburn and Spencer Tracy as a globe-trotting journalist and sportswriter who get on each other's nerves so much that they get married.

This incarnation starred Bacall as the over-serious political commentator, Tess Harding, and Guardino as Sam Craig, a cartoonist. It is easy to see they were meant for each other when, in the title song, Tess refers to him as arrogant, brutish, insensitive, and a chauvinist while Sam publicly ridicules her in his strip as a big-mouthed character he dubs Tessie Cat. In turn, she calls him a detestable little weasel, a beady-eyed runt, and vermin. No one ever said the road to love wasn't rocky, especially not in a musical where obstacles are a precondition for happiness.

Song highlights: "See You in the Funny Papers," "When You're Right, You're Right" (in which Tess admits to rarely being wrong about anything), "One of the Boys," "It Isn't Working," "I Told You So," "I Wrote the Book" (the book, sings Tess, on how to be tough and on how to lose a man), "Sometimes a Day Goes By," "The Poker Game," "Happy in the Morning" (an ode to not waking up alone), and the title number, Tess's hymn to herself.

As with her musical debut in *Applause* [above, 1970], Bacall was the critics' darling. In *Time* (4/13/81), T. E. Kalem gushed, "Bacall is a tigress of a performer. . . . From that growly, smoky voice, seemingly filtered through bourbon and cigarettes, to the lightning stride and the imperiously tossed head, she is a creature of animal grace and jungle danger. Bacallelujah!"

Frank Rich of the *Times*: "By making life and art look as easy and elegant as a perfect song, Miss Bacall embodies the very spirit of the carefree American musical." But he dubbed the show as merely "amiable." Clive Barnes at the *Post* saw it as "not faultless, but terrific."

Bacall and costar Marilyn Cooper received Tonys, as did author Peter Stone.

Original cast: Arista AL-8303.

1982

Nine (Maury Yeston). Opened May 9, 1982. Cast: Raul Julia, Karen Akers, Taina Elg, Liliane Montevecchi, Shelly Burch, Anita Morris, Kathi Moss.

Nine was a good age for Guido Contini (Julia), for that was when his mother (Elg) sang him a song ("Nine") and another, not so motherly woman (Moss), introduced him and his friends to the many varied pleasures of the flesh ("Be Italian"). But all that is learned through flashback.

When we first meet Guido he is an adult who never really grew up, a self-centered, womanizing movie director with writer's block who retreats to a spa to concentrate. But there from the dreamlike mist arise all the women in his life to taunt and frustrate him, from his mother to his wife (Akers) and his mistress (Morris), among others, many many others: *Time*'s review (5/24/82) noted that there were "21 — count 'em — 21 girls, many of them leggy thoroughbreds." The review also said the show's lyrics "would sound puerile coming from a sixth-grader," but found Yeston's music "refreshingly versatile and fetchingly melodic." (Yeston was a professor of music theory at Yale.)

Newsweek (5/24/82) described the parade of women as more like a "pride of lionesses," and called *Nine* "a brilliant show, but not an endearing or compelling one." It was based on Federico Fellini's 1963 film *8 1/2*.

Other high points: "Guido's Song" (Julia's hymn to himself; he is the only adult male in the cast), "My Husband Makes Movies," "Not Since Chaplin," "Folies Bérgères," "The Grand Canal," "Simple," "I Can't Make This Movie," and "The Waltz From *Nine*."

Montevecchi and director Tommy Tune won Tonys.

Original cast: Columbia CK-38325.

(Raul Julia has since established himself in dramatic films as well, giving standout performances in *Kiss of the Spider Woman*, *Compromising Positions*, *The Morning After*, *Moon Over Parador*, *Tequila Sunrise*, *Romero*, *Mack the Knife*, *Havana*, *Presumed Innocent*, and *The Addams Family*.)

1983

Cats (Andrew Lloyd Webber, T. S. Eliot). Opened on Broadway October 7, 1982. Cast: Betty Buckley, Harry Groener, Stephen Hanan, Ken Page.

T. S. Eliot once observed that what people desire today is to be "distracted from distraction by distraction." Had he lived to see it, Eliot might well have applied that comment on shallowness to this $4.5 million musical based on a slim book of his poems.

Eliot's cat verses (collected in 1939 in *Old Possum's Book of Practical Cats*) were started to amuse a very young godson, and children today delight in their whimsy, and in watching actors dressed and made-up as cats dancing around an oversized stage setting. Many critics, on the other hand, turned positively catty writing about it.

Frank Rich of *The New York Times* called *Cats* a "collection of anthropomorphic variety turns" in a show that "sometimes curls up and takes a catnap." As for the vague storyline of selecting one cat at the annual ball who will ascend to cat heaven (the "Heaviside Layer") and be reborn, Rich wrote: "If you blink, you'll miss the plot."

The New Yorker (8/20/90) called it, "A mighty spectacle about mighty little." Composer Gretchen Cryer said the show "enraged" her and likened it to spreading on millions of dollars of icing "when there's no cake there at all."[16]

Howard Kissel of *Women's Wear Daily* cynically observed that Webber's music "is remarkable largely for the shamelessness with which it seems to recycle other people's tunes," and that *Cats*, "in its potent blend of pretension and mindless spectacle . . . will doubtless be a Broadway fixture for years to come."

Cats could be said to have broken new ground in that it wasn't actually *about* anything. Arguably plotless, virtually formless, the songs are little more than character sketches of cats—rough, tough, battling cats like Growltiger; pesky cats who are into everything like Mungojerrie and Rumpelteazer; proud but mangy cats who prowl the waterfront like Grizabella; and contrary cats like Rum Tum Tugger, who always want what isn't offered. There are the mascot cats, Gus from the theater and Skimbleshanks from the railway yard. Did you ever hear a sound from out of nowhere, or see a broken vase without a culprit? It must be Macavity, the mystery cat. In Eliot's poems, feline and human personalities blend, then dance to Lloyd Webber's music.

There is a lot of music—the score comes on two cassettes. Songs include: "Jellicle Songs for Jellicle Cats," "The Naming of Cats," "The Rum Tum Tugger," "Grizabella, the Glamour Cat," "Bustopher Jones," "Mungojerrie and Rumpleteazer," "Old Deuteronomy," "The Jellicle Ball," "The Old Gumbie Cat," "Gus, the Theatre Cat," and "Memory" (the lyric by director Trevor Nunn based on some fragments of Eliot's noncat poems).

Clive Barnes called it "a potent theatrical cocktail," but termed the score "breathtakingly unoriginal yet superbly professional."

The best way to appreciate the score outside of the theater is with *Cats, the Book of the Musical* (Harvest/Harcourt Brace Jovanovich, 1983); it is crammed with color photos and lyrics.

Webber, Buckley, and Nunn received Tonys, as did T. S. Eliot for the book, though he died in 1965 and knew nothing about the musical. This fact prompted columnist Russell Baker to concoct an interview with the dead poet in *The New York Times* (5/25/83) in which Baker declared, "Dead people don't write Broadway musicals, despite the impression you get when you see one."

Original cast: Geffen 2G5G 2031.

1984

La Cage Aux Folles (Jerry Herman). Opened August 21, 1983. Cast: George Hearn, Gene Barry, Jay Garner.

Based on a nonmusical French farce, the Broadway version not only has songs but more heart.

The title refers to a nightclub in St. Tropez specializing in female impersonators (freely translated as The Bird Cage). Its owner Georges (Gene Barry, the suave star of TV's *Bat Masterson* and *Burke's Law*) has had a 20-year marriage with his star Albin, aka Zaza (George Hearn). Propriety and the feelings of his son (the product of a long ago one-night stand), force Georges to temporarily disown Albin so the son may safely marry the daughter of an antigay politician. By the final curtain, the son learns the error of his intolerance while Georges and Albin have found a deeper love and respect for each other.

The general consensus was positive, though the reviews made it sound like *Hello, Dolly!* in drag. Frank Rich of *The Times* saw it "as shamelessly calculating as a candidate for public office," filled with "almost unflagging tunefulness," and "as synthetic and padded as the transvestites' cleavage." To Rich, it was "the schmaltziest, most old-fashioned major musical Broadway has seen since *Annie,* and it's likely to be just as popular with children of all ages."

Yes, even with children, because despite the gay theme the show is aimed at the whole family: ". . . naughty but nice, bedizened but respectable," according to Douglas Watt in the *Daily News*, though he found Jerry Herman's songs "all pretty familiar and even pretty much alike. They're not in the least distinguished, either musically or lyrically, but they're entirely serviceable, like [Harvey] Fierstein's book."

Clive Barnes in the *New York Post* called it Herman's "best musical yet," featuring "breezy, swingy Broadway music that you thought had, at least briefly, disappeared from style."

There is little tendency in the songs to preach about tolerance, and the score shys away from anything confrontational or dramatic with the exception of "I Am What I Am" (a 1980s version of a hit show tune from the 1960s, "I've Gotta Be Me").

Highlights include: "We Are What We Are," "With You on My Arm," "Masculinity," "Song on the Sand," "Cocktail Counterpoint," "Look Over There," and "The Best of Times." A gimmick was to have several members of the transvestite chorus played by real women.

Tonys went to Hearn, director Arthur Laurents, author Harvey Fierstein, and composer Jerry Herman (his first Tony since *Hello, Dolly!* twenty years before). Herman heralded the win as a return to Broadway's roots of hummable, melodic songs.

Original cast: RCA HBE1-4824.

La Cage was undoubtedly a great popular success, with road show companies soon fanning out across the country. It not only topped the awards ceremony that year, but did so by beating both the blatantly heterosexual *Baby* [Act Five] and Stephen Sondheim's *Sunday in the Park With George* [Act Two, 1983-1984], which won both the Drama Critics Circle Award and Pulitzer Prize.

(George Hearn earned an Emmy the following year for a PBS presentation of *Sweeney Todd*.)

1985

Big River (Roger Miller). Opened April 25, 1985. Cast: Ron Richardson, Daniel H. Jenkins, Rene Auberjonois, John Goodman, Susan Browning, Bob Gunton.

The big river is the Mississippi and cast upon it poling a raft are none other than delinquent Huck Finn (Jenkins) and Jim the runaway slave (Richardson), sharing adventures and philosophy as they head for freedom.

Composer Roger Miller had never written a musical before, but was widely respected as a Country-Western singer/composer of exceptional if quirky talent, with award-winning hits such as "Dang Me" and "King of the Road" behind him (not to mention the classics "You Can't Rollerskate in a Buffalo Herd," "Chug-a-Lug," "Engine Engine No. 9," "One Dyin' and a-Buryin'," and "I Believe in Sunshine"). This was just the sort of down-home flavor Mark Twain's story required, and Miller delivered—earning a Tony to go along with his eleven Grammys.

Auberjonois was the Duke and Gunton the King. Highlights include: "Guv'ment" (sung by Huck's Pap, played by John Goodman of TV's *Roseanne*), "Hand for the Hog," "Muddy Water," "River in the Rain," "The Royal Nonsuch," "Worlds Apart," "Leavin's Not the Only Way to Go," and "Free at Last."

Time (5/20/85) called it "a sweet, small, no-stars musical" with songs "as full of unforced charm as Huck himself." *Newsweek* (5/6/85) hailed it, saying, "At last this sinister season has produced a musical replete with talent and intelligent ambition."

Richardson won a Tony as featured actor. Awards also went to director Des McAnuff and author William Hauptman.

Original cast: MCA-6147. (The out-of-print album is worth looking for; unlike the cassette, the album contains a two-page plot synopsis, photos, a complete cast/character listing, and all of the lyrics are printed on the inner sleeve.)

1986

The Mystery of Edwin Drood (Rupert Holmes). Opened August 21, 1985. Cast: George Rose, Cleo Laine, Betty Buckley.

When Charles Dickens died, he did so without the forethought of finishing his last novel, or even being considerate enough to leave a clue as to who killed his title character, Edwin Drood. The resolution of the mystery will always remain a matter of conjecture and that is just the point of the musical: After seeing Dickens' plot dramatized with songs, the audience gets to vote on who the culprit might be, the proceedings moved along by George Rose as the Chairman.

The *Times*'s Frank Rich found this climactic device "both delightful and ingenious," and lauded Rose for playing the part "with a tongue so far up his cheek that one half-expects it to emerge from his ear." Not everyone saw it that way. Patricia O'Haire of the *Daily News* said *Drood* was "campier than Boy Scout Jamboree and as suspenseful as waiting for the lottery numbers to be announced."

Rupert Holmes conveniently supplied "confession" lyrics for a number of suspects, so the guilty party could change from one night to the next. And the whole play was staged as if in a London music hall of 1873, with the actors mingling at times with the audience and the Chairman (owner/producer) cheerfully supplying narration and cues as they go along.

Songs include: "There You Are," "A Man Could Go Quite Mad," "The Wages of Sin," "Off to the Races," "Don't Quit While You're Ahead," and "The Garden Path to Hell." George Rose received a Tony; director Wilford Leach and writer/composer Holmes were also honored.

Original cast: Polydor 827 969-4 Y-1.

The audio cassette has only one guilty culprit on it—Cleo Laine as a perverted den mother (an opium den, that is). The CD version, though minus one song ("Ceylon"), contains all the possible endings. If the CD is not available, the alternative lyrics can be found in the published script (Nelson Doubleday, 1986).

1987

Les Misérables (Claude-Michel Schönberg, Jean-Marc Natel, Alain Boublil, Herbert Knetzmer). Opened March 12, 1987. Cast: Colm Wilkinson, Terrence Mann, Randy Graff, Judy Kuhn, Frances Ruffelle, Michael McGuire, David Bryant, Jennifer Butt, Leo Burmester.

"Insurrection is the truth's outburst of rage," wrote Victor Hugo in his sprawling masterpiece, "the paving stones that insurrection tears up throw off the spark of right." He saw the stones hurled by "that vast foam called the wrath of the people."

The biggest, most expensive musical up to that time, *Les Misérables* covers 17 years in the life of fugitive Jean Valjean and in the history of France, climaxing in the failed uprising of 1832 with fierce and inspiring battles on the barricaded streets.

Hugo's basic plot was freed from his literary embroidery and boiled down to its essentials. After 19 years in prison for stealing a loaf of bread, Jean Valjean (Wilkinson) is paroled but is soon hounded by the implacable Inspector Javert (Mann) for breaking that parole. Valjean, his prison number branded on his chest and forced back into crime by a system that exploits exconvicts, is befriended by a bishop and turns his life around. He changes his identity and we next see him eight years later; through hard work and devotion he has become the prosperous and respected mayor of Montreuil-sur-Mer.

In this capacity he inadvertently seals the penurious downfall of Fantine (Graff), a deserted mother who has turned to prostitution in order to support the small child she has left in the care of a despicable innkeeper. Feeling responsible for Fantine's last destitute hours of life, Valjean vows to care for young Cosette all his days. At the same time, his identity is discovered by Javert, who resumes his merciless hunt (the Inspector's whole philosophy of jurisprudence rests on his belief that people do not change: once a thief, always a thief).

Valjean liberates Cosette (Kuhn) from the clutches of the evil Thenardier and his wife (Burmester and Butt) and the two live in quiet solitude for nine years. Then Cosette meets and falls in love with Marius (Bryant), a young firebrand. (He, in turn, is loved by Thenardier's daughter, Eponine, who will sacrifice herself for this unrequited love.) Their love pulls Valjean into the political furies about to erupt in a student rebellion and once again brings him to Javert's unremitting notice.

During the battle with the National Guard, Valjean saves Javert from the rebels, then pulls the wounded Marius from a massacre on a barricaded street and into the underground sewers of Paris. Javert stops them, then lets them go. Torn by the realization that the thief he has been pursuing for 17 years may just be a better man than he, Javert kills himself. Cosette and Marius marry, and Jean Valjean dies, his vow to Fantine fulfilled. Her spirit, and the ghosts of Eponine and the rebels, appear to carry him to heaven.

Though it was a spectacular hit, critics were generally mixed about the show and its music. Clive Barnes, in the *New York Post*, called it "the stuff of theatrical legend," and "magnificent, red-blooded, two-fisted theater." (Though he did feel that the good tunes were "repeated *ad nauseam* during the long evening.")

Howard Kissel in the *Daily News* found the lyrics "unbelievably simple-minded" and the music "drivel—singsong, repetitious, emotionally dead." Jack Curry of *USA Today* must have seen a different show that same night, for he heard "soaring music" that "intensifies our emotional reaction to a sublime point."

Musical numbers include: "I Dreamed a Dream," "Lovely Ladies," "Master of the House," "Do You Hear the People Sing?" "Who Am I?" "One Day More," "Look Down," "In My Life," "Bring Him Home," "Dog Eats Dog."

Frances Ruffelle as Eponine and Michael Maguire as rebel leader Enjolras won Tonys for their performances. Trevor Nunn and John Caird shared directing honors for the show, while Boublil and Schönberg were honored for the book and, with translator Kretzmer, the score. (Both Wilkinson and Mann were nominated for their lead roles but lost to Robert Lindsay in the revival of *Me and My Gal*, a bit of British fluff from 1935.)

Original Broadway cast (highlights): Geffen MSG 24151. The complete, "symphonic" recording: Relativity/First Night Records, 88561-1027-2 [see Act Four, 1990, for details].

Also recommended is Edward Behr's *The Complete Book of Les Misérables* (Arcade, 1989).

1988

The Phantom of the Opera (Andrew Lloyd Webber, Charles Hart, Richard Stilgoe). Opened in London October 9, 1986; in New York January 26, 1988. Cast: Michael Crawford, Sarah Brightman, Steve Barton, Judy Kaye.

Take George Du Maurier's 1894 melodrama *Trilby*, about the evil Svengali who hypnotizes young Trilby and teaches her to sing, mix generously with an Edgar Allen Poe atmosphere, and what emerges will be a fair approximation of Gaston Leroux's 1911 novel, *The Phantom of the Opera* — a spooky soap opera.

In modern times, the tale has been a favorite largely with horror film buffs who remember Lon Chaney and Claude Rains in the role of the disfigured and disgruntled composer Eric who lives in the dank catacombs and gloomy lake beneath the Paris Opera.

The films focused on terror and hideous make-up. The musical had loftier aims and focused on the star-crossed romantic triangle of the masked and demented Phantom, his lovely protégé personally groomed to take the opera world by storm, and Raoul, the man she loves. (Murderer Eric seems to get away with his nefarious deeds at the final curtain when, as a mob closes in, he uses a conjuring trick to vanish from sight.)

Webber was soundly trounced by critics who found his music heavy-handed and repetitious (by overuse of the device of "contra-faction," the repeating of certain themes at different times, ostensibly to unify a work), as well as derivative from too many classics.

Michael Feingold in *The Village Voice* (2/2/88) wrote that "Webber's music isn't that painful to hear, if you don't mind its being so soiled from previous use." He called Lloyd Webber "a secondhand music peddler" with a "pathetic aural imagination" of his own, which "was outpaced years ago by his apparently exhaustive memory. I don't accuse him of plagiarism; he never quotes more than 3 1/2 bars of anyone else's work verbatim."

Feingold went on to identify snatches of melody apparently lifted from Kurt Weill, Leonard Bernstein, Stephen Sondheim, Puccini, and Humperdinck, and attributed the composer's success to the un-refined taste of "The semi-educated middle-class world [that] loves Andrew Lloyd Webber best of all theater composers."

Stephen Holden in *The New York Times* (6/5/88) said the show was filled with "derivativeness and pomposity" that "caters to an enduring public sweet tooth for blustery, high-flown romance." Doug Watt in the *Daily News* called it "a dark operetta whose 'operatic' passages consist mainly of pastiches in scenes imitating Verdi, Mozart, Richard Strauss, Offenbach and others," a style he termed "unabashed and cleverly derivative."

The New Yorker (8/20/90) called the show "negligible" but fun, though only "if you're not bothered by theatre that cares not a whit for words and contains not one ghost of an idea."

Frank Rich of the *Times* liked some of the songs, but disliked hearing them so often: "There are some lovely tunes, arguably [Lloyd Webber's] best yet, and, as always, they are recycled endlessly; if you don't leave the theater humming the songs, you've got a hearing disability."

Perhaps never before had a composer of such overwhelming popularity taken such heat for his efforts and ended up so financially rewarded at the same time. *Phantom*, the show the critics loved to hate, was an unqualified success; as late as 1991, road show productions were pulling in well over a million dollars a week. When star Michael Crawford donated a pair of tickets to charity for a Los Angeles performance, KABC-TV auctioned them off for $27,500.[17]

As with *Cats*, the spectacle of the total theatrical experience is needed to fully appreciate the score—the large curving staircase of the opera's masked ball, the boat ride across the underground lake, the dropped chandelier (Feingold complained that it came down too slowly), the necessary conjuring tricks, and the athleticism of Crawford as the murderous Phantom, were all stunning visual devices.

Crawford, who won a Tony, played the physically demanding role in over 1,300 performances in London, New York, and Los Angeles, his talent and singular endurance making him a matinee idol to thousands of fans. Those critics who loved the show cited Crawford as the principle reason.

David Patrick Sterns of *USA Today* felt the show was "basically a bodice-ripping love story" and "what keeps this wobbly blockbuster from collapsing under its own grandeur is Michael Crawford [who] galvanizes the show into great theater." Clive Barnes, calling the show "Phantastic," said Crawford gave "a performance that will rank in the annals of the musical for all time."

Memorable moments: "The Music of the Night," "Angel of Music," "All I Ask of You," "Wishing You Were Somehow Here," and "The Point of No Return."

London cast (complete score): Polydor 831 273-4. Highlights: Polydor POL 831563. The Broadway cast, being virtually the same as the London cast, was not recorded. A recording of the Toronto cast starring Colm Wilkinson and Rebecca Caine is on Polygram 847 689-2.

Recommended to go along with the score is George Perry's *The Complete Phantom of the Opera* book (Henry Holt & Co., 1987).

(The show could also have won a merchandising award, having spawned tie-in products as diverse as bath towels and pop-up books, key chains, dolls, masks, capes, and posters.)

Best Score

Into the Woods (Stephen Sondheim). Opened November 5, 1987. Cast: Joanna Gleason, Bernadette Peters, Ben Wright, Chip Zien, Tom Aldridge, Kim Crosby, Joy Franz, Danielle Fereland, Barbara Bryne, and Robert Westenberg.

Despite its immense popularity, *Phantom* did not get the Original Score Tony. That went to Broadway's own Stephen Sondheim for his Freud-fraught fairy tale, *Into the Woods*.

This strange story takes some well known characters such as Cinderella and her stepmother, Red Ridinghood, Jack (of beanstalk fame), Rapunzel, a couple of princes, a witch, a baker and his wife, and a giant, and puts them into the same dark mysterious woods where their stories become hopelessly entangled.

All goes well in the first act, but, in the second act the happily-ever-after counted on by the characters starts to come unraveled. Cindy's prince cheats on her. The evil stepmother cuts off the toes of her daughters to try and squeeze them into the glass slipper. Rapunzel is squished by the giant. Fingers of blame are pointed in all directions. And the moral of this cautionary tale is that people make mistakes, witches are not always evil, and endings are not always happy. The woods, like life, have many dark and unexplored paths that perhaps are better left that way.

Sondheim's concept of the score moved him to deliberately prune the lyrics until they appear, on the surface, to be little more than sung dialogue rather than traditional songs. That is deceptive, as **multiple listenings** (and a reading of the book) make clear.

Musical sequences include: "Hello, Little Girl" (sung to Red Ridinghood by the Wolf—who, given the lyrics, might just as well be a sleazy habitué of Times Square), "A Very Nice Prince," "Maybe They're Magic," "It Takes Two," "On the Steps of the Palace," "Agony," "Moments in the Woods," "Your Fault," "No One Is Alone."

Tonys. also went to Gleason (as the Baker's Wife) and author James Lapine.

Reviews were decidedly mixed. *Time*'s William A. Henry III called it "the best show yet from the most creative mind in the musical theater today," and "that joyous rarity, a work of sophisticated artistic ambition and deep political purpose that affords non-stop pleasure, [it is] an elixir of delight." But Douglas Watt of the New York *Daily News* (11/13/87) called the songs "surprisingly weak," and said Sondheim had "trouble trying to thread his way through the twists and turns of the dizzying plot."

Watt's colleague on the *Daily News*, Howard Kissel, thought the lyrics were "ingenious" and that the music "weaves in and out of the dialogue seamlessly" (11/6/87). *Newsday*'s review headline of November 6, 1987, was: "Witty and Beguiling *Into the Woods*," while just the opposite appeared in *The Wall Street Journal* on November 10: "Sondheim Loses His Way in a Fairy-Tale Forest."

Frank Rich of the *Times* found the story "convoluted," but added: "To hear 'No One Is Alone,' the cathartic and beautiful final song of *Into the Woods,* is to be overwhelmed once more by the continuity of one of the American theater's most extraordinary song-writing careers."

Original cast: RCA 6796-4-RC. London cast with Julia McKenzie and Clive Carter: RCA 60752-4-RC. The script was published in 1989 by Theatre Communications Group.

1989

Jerome Robbins' Broadway (music and lyrics from Irving Berlin, Leonard Bernstein, Jerry Bock, Sammy Cahn, Betty Comden, Adolph Green, Richard Rodgers, Oscar Hammerstein, Sheldon Harnick, Carolyn Leigh, Stephen Sondheim, Jule Styne, among others). Opened February 26, 1989. Cast: A 62-member ensemble cast of dancers and singers, with featured vocalists Jason Alexander, Faith Prince, Michael Lynch, Debbie Shapiro, Charlotte d'Amboise, Susann Fletcher, Scott Wise, and Robert LaFosse.

In what would be his last show, choreographer/director Jerome Robbins put together a musical montage of highlights from across the spectrum of his twenty years in the business. In this double-cassette package are newly staged numbers from *On the Town*, *Billion Dollar Baby*, *A Funny Thing Happened on the Way to the Forum*, *High Button Shoes*, *West Side Story*, *The King and I*, *Gypsy*, *Peter Pan*, *Miss Liberty*, *Call Me Madam*, and *Fiddler on the Roof*.

The effect of all these classic shows nearly overcame the critics. Howard Kissel of the *Daily News*: "At a time when what passes for musical theater is mainly about computerized scenic effects, this look backward is enormously exhilarating." Frank Rich of the *Times*: "[Robbins] pulls off the miracle of re-creating that ecstatic baptism, that first glimpse of Broadway lights, of every Broadway theatergoer's youth." He dubbed the show, "a one-evening tour of an entire era."

At the *Post*, Clive Barnes was overjoyed: "This is magnificent," he wrote, adding, "I promise you a hell of a good time."

It was a big show, even more expensive to mount than *Les Misérables*, requiring $340,000 a week. One set alone, seen for barely thirty seconds by the audience, contained 11,000 lights and cost $150,000 to create. After two years and 675 performances of near capacity audiences, it lost money.[18]

Jason Alexander, Scott Wise, Debbie Shapiro, and Jerome Robbins received Tonys.

Original cast: RCA 60150.

(There were no shows nominated in the Best Original Score category in 1989.)

1990

City of Angels (Cy Coleman, David Zippel). Opened December 11, 1989. Cast: James Naughton, Gregg Edelman, Randy Graff, Rene Auberjonois, Kay McClelland, Dee Hoty, Rachel York.

Neon reflecting off wet streets. A sultry sax blowing in the night. Large men of few words wearing shoulder holsters. Dolls and molls, gats and gams. Tough repartee. The scene is Hollywood, the 1940s, Raymond Chandler country.

Crime novelist and script writer Stine (Edelman) is the creator of a Philip Marlowe-like detective named Stone (Naughton), and he has difficulty keeping his real life and his fictional life separate — to the point where he sings duets with his made-up gumshoe.

While the pulp shamus has his share of troubles with murderers and lecherous women, writer Stine has his own problems with studio executives, a secretary, and a wife, all of whom end up with fictional counterparts in his script. It takes the writing and detecting skills of both the real writer and the imaginary detective to help each other out of a jam at the end.

Songs include: "Double Talk," "What You Don't Know About Women," "You Gotta Look Out for Yourself," "The Tennis Song," "Lost and Found," "You're Nothing Without Me," "L. A. Blues," "With Every Breath I Take," "You Can Always Count on Me" (the creed of every fictional secretary in love with her boss), and "All You Have to Do Is Wait," a show-stopping calypso-styled number from Shawn Elliott as Lt. Munoz in which he envisions various enjoyable means of execution for bothersome detective Stone.

The innovative staging invoked the black and white look of 1940s movie thrillers whenever Stone was on the job and Cy Coleman's music beautifully captured the sound of the era with everything from jazz, blues, and scat to big band swinging. (Though classically trained, Coleman is a gifted and innovative jazz pianist, as much at home jamming with his combo in a smokey nightspot as he is on Broadway.)

Clive Barnes in the *New York Post* saw it as "definitely, almost defiantly, both nostalgic and different. . . . It is also funny, ingenious and lots of other good things." Frank Rich agreed with the man who once held his place at the *Times*, saying, "Only the fear of missing the next gag quiets the audiences down. To make matters sweeter, the jokes sometimes subside just long enough to permit a show-stopping song or performance or two to make their own ruckus at center stage."

Naughton and Graff (as Stone and his secretary) were awarded Tonys, as was author Larry Gelbart, and composers Coleman and

Zippel. In accepting his Tony, Coleman generously paid tribute to the wonderful pit orchestra.

Original cast: Columbia CT 46067.

1991

The Will Rogers Follies: A Life in Revue (Cy Coleman, Betty Comden, Adolph Green). Opened: May 1, 1991. Cast: Keith Carradine, Dee Hoty, Cady Huffman, Paul Ukena, Jr., Dick Latessa, and a chorus of 16 leggy, highly coordinated women billed as The New Ziegfeld Girls.

"This, I suspect, is the musical audiences were really waiting for," wrote David Richards in *The New York Times* (5/12/91), "all the time the paid drumbeaters told them they were waiting for *Miss Saigon.*'"

Of course, it depends on whether one's theatrical menu includes meat or seven courses of lighter-than-air pastry. *Will Rogers* is a confectioner's delight.

The Will Rogers Follies was a show panned in most reviews for its lack of substance but praised lavishly for director Tommy Tune's eye for colorful spectacle. That, and sheer, joyous entertainment value, was enough to earn it the top prize. It's hard to vote against something that makes you smile so much.

The time is the present day and the whimsy (in the same year when the film *Ghost* was nominated for a Best Picture Oscar) is that Will Rogers (Carradine) has come back from the dead to recreate the Follies for a modern audience. He spins his lariat and homilies while firing off one-liners between costumed extravaganzas, a real trick roper (Vince Bruce), and even a dog act called Brackney's Madcap Mutts (other famous Ziegfeld stars such as Fanny Brice and W. C. Fields do not appear, perhaps being too happy in Entertainer Heaven to make the trip). The thin plot covers Rogers' romance with and marriage to Betty Blake (Hoty). The pretaped voice of the never seen Ziegfeld was provided by Gregory Peck (who appears on the recording, along with the dogs).

Frank Rich disagreed with colleague David Richards; his opening night review informed readers that the show was "disjointed," and "a drippingly pious testimonial [that] crashlands with a whopping thud a good half act or so before Rogers has his fatal airplane crash in Alaska.''

Edith Oliver at *The New Yorker* (5/13/91) found the music "pleasing," the lyrics "nimble," but, overall, it struck her as "a spectacle that is hollow at the core." At *The Village Voice* (5/21/91), Michael Feingold termed the score "second-rate Cy Coleman" and said, "If technical genius were all, it would be the greatest musical ever made; you've never seen such an unending flow of razzle followed by dazzle."

Unfortunately, the razzle and dazzle of the flashy costumes, tricky chorus routines, eye-filling sets, and inventive lighting effects during the many-limbed dance numbers will not translate well to an audio recording without a picture-filled booklet. Still, the Coleman/Comden/Green team knows its way around a show tune. Songs include: "Willamania," "Give a Man Enough Rope," "My Unknown Someone," "The Big Time," "It's a Boy," "Let's Go Flying," "Favorite Son," "Look Around," "My Big Mistake," "Never Met a Man I Didn't Like." The recording is greatly enhanced by the banjos of Larry Campbell and Scott Kuney, with Campbell also playing a fiery fiddle.

Nominated for 11 Tonys, it won six. Along with the Best Musical award, Tonys went to Willa Kim for costumes, Jules Fisher for lighting, Tommy Tune for direction and choreography, and to Comden, Green, and Coleman for the score — Coleman's second in a row. (The three composers sang their acceptance and thanks.)

Original cast: Columbia (Sony) CT 48606.

REFERENCE NOTES

1. *The New York Times*, March 23, 1947.

2. Isabelle Stevenson, *The Tony Award* (New York: Crown Publishers, Inc.), 1987, pp. 47, 59, 65, 189.

3. *The New York Times*, April 21, 1965.

4. Patrick Robertson, *Movie Facts and Feats: A Guinness Record Book* (New York: Sterling Publishing, 1980), p. 220.

5. Gerald Bordman, *American Musical Theatre: A Chronicle* (New York: Oxford University Press, 1978), p. 633.

6. David Ewen, *All the Years of American Popular Music* (Englewood Cliffs, New Jersey: Prentice-Hall, 1977), p. 454.

7. Harry Medved and Michael Medved, *The Hollywood Hall of Shame* (New York: Putnam Publishing Co., 1984), p. 212.

8. Dale Wasserman, Preface to *Man of La Mancha* (New York: Random House, 1966), p. viii.

9. Leonard Maltin, *Leonard Maltin's TV Movies and Video Guide* (New York: Signet/New American Library, 1989), p. 692.

10. Craig Zaden, *Sondheim and Company*, 2nd edition (New York: Harper and Row, 1989), p. 119.

11. *The New York Times*, October 25, 1970.

12. Jack Mingo and John Javna, *Prime Time Proverbs* (New York: Harmony Books, 1989), p. 159.

13. *Time*, September 10, 1990; *Newsweek*, September 10, 1990.

14. Harry Medved and Michael Medved, *The Hollywood Hall of Shame* (New York: Putnam Publishing Company, 1984), p. 203.

15. *The New York Times*, August 26, 1980.

16. Al Kasha and Joel Hirschhorn, (*Notes on Broadway*. New York: Simon and Schuster, 1987), p. 87.

17. *The Los Angeles Times*, April 26, 1990.

18. Rick Gore, "Broadway, Street of Dreams," *National Geographic*, September, 1990, 178 (Number 3), p. 75.

Act Two:
The New York Drama Critics
Circle Award

Once or twice a year, as regularly as the season itself comes along, Broadway rises to denounce the critics as negative scourges that give nothing at all constructive to the theatre.

—The New York Times, October 24, 1935

The New York Drama Critics Circle Award was first announced in October of 1935, its creation largely designed to offset the image of critics as "negative scourges" by providing something constructive in the way of encouragement. (George Bernard Shaw, a former critic who, as a playwright, came in for his share of negativity, once quipped that a drama critic was a person "who leaves no turn unstoned."[1])

Another powerful motivation was a general dislike for the choices made by the Pulitzer Prize committee over the previous two years. In 1934, the Pulitzer jury unanimously voted for Maxwell Anderson's *Mary of Scotland* as Best Drama, but that choice was overturned by the Pulitzer's advisory committee; the prize went instead to Sidney Kingsley's play about doctors, *Men in White*. The next Pulitzer went to Zöe Akins for adapting Edith Wharton's *The Old Maid*. Neither choice was critically acclaimed.

Attempts had been made in the past to form a critics organization—a group the *Times* called "the theatre's most harassed little band"—but none amounted to much. This time, the idea worked. Seventeen of New York's most influential and respected critics—among them such luminaries as George Jean Nathan, Brooks Atkinson, Walter Winchell, Percy Hammond, Joseph Wood Krutch, John Mason Brown, and Robert Benchley—met at the Algonquin

Hotel and formed the nucleus of the Drama Critics Circle, which continues to this day.

The Circle Award was first given for the best dramatic play of the 1935-1936 season, the winner being Maxwell Anderson's *Winterset*. It was nine years later that the first musical was honored; by 1950, musicals had become a regular, separate category.

While the Tonys are awarded largely by theater professionals to their peers, the Circle Award is bestowed by those who some in the business might consider their archenemies, the drama critics. As one might expect, the two groups do not always agree.

1945-1946

Carousel (Richard Rodgers, Oscar Hammerstein). Opened April 19, 1945. Cast: John Raitt, Jan Clayton, Jean Darling, Christine Johnson.

Based on Ferenc Molnar's *Liliom*, a stage hit for many years as a straight drama, *Carousel* is a tragic love story about two disparate people—the rough and tumble carny barker Billy Bigelow (Raitt), and the sweet and homespun Julie Jordan (Clayton).

Billy is not much of a husband until fatherhood looms. His desire to be a good provider gets him involved in a robbery where he is killed. The final scenes begin in the afterlife fifteen years later where, true to form, Billy is trying to gate-crash heaven through a rear door. To redeem himself, Billy is allowed to return to earth where he must perform a good deed inside of twenty-four hours and does so by helping his morose teenage daughter learn to enjoy life. (He sings "You'll Never Walk Alone" in her ear during her graduation ceremony.)

As corny as it sounds, the musical works. Rodgers and Hammerstein were masters of honest sentimentality and nowhere is it more abundant than in *Carousel*. The elegant songs range from "You're a Queer One, Julie Jordan" and "Mister Snow," to the haunting "If I Loved You," the happy "June Is Bustin' Out All Over," and, above all, Billy's "Soliloquy" on fatherhood, best known as "My Boy Bill."

"Yes, yes, a thousand times yes," wrote Robert Garland of New York's *Journal-American*. "Casting is perfection. Jan Clayton, making her Broadway debut as Julie, is lovely to look at, lovelier to listen to." Garland, referring to himself as "a professional fault-finder by trade," gladly reported: "I can't find anything to complain about."

Wilella Waldorf of the *New York Post* found fault with the songs, saying "there is no doubt that it is not the sort of score one goes out humming," and declared *Carousel* to be "no great vocal treat." Ward Morehouse at the *Times*, on the other hand, laid all doubts aside: "It's a hit, and of that there can be no doubt."

The 1956 movie starred Gordon MacRae, Shirley Jones, Barbara Ruick, Robert Rounseville and Cameron Mitchell.

Original cast: MCA-2033. Film: Capitol SW 694. 1987 studio cast of Babara Cook, Samuel Ramey, and Sarah Brightman: MCA Classics MCAC-6209.

1946-1947

Brigadoon (Alan Jay Lerner, Frederick Loewe). Opened March 13, 1947. Cast: David Brooks, Marion Bell, Pamela Britton, Lee Sullivan.

Once every hundred years, for just one day, a village in the high-lands of Scotland appears out of the mist and comes to life. That is Brigadoon. Two Americans, Tommy and Jeff, stumble into the vil-lage shortly after it appears and Tom promptly falls in love with a lass named Fiona MacLaren, and she with him. But should she or any inhabitant leave the village, the magical spell it is under will be broken and immortality lost. Tommy leaves but is drawn back to Scotland and, because in musicals love can conquer all, sees the village reappear long enough to accept him.

This first successful collaboration between Lerner and Loewe contains some of their most charming songs: "The Heather on the Hill," "Come to Me, Bend to Me," "Almost Like Being in Love," "There But for You Go I," "Down on MacConnachy Square," and "My Mother's Wedding Day."

Reviews were almost universally favorable. At the *Times*, Brooks Atkinson raved that "all the arts of the theatre have been woven into a singing pattern of enchantment." John Chapman at the *Daily News* ate it up, saying, "It is a brand new delight for hungry theatregoers."

The 1954 MGM film starred Gene Kelly, Van Johnson, and Cyd Charisse, and was directed by Vincente Minnelli (who used a sound stage with painted backdrops substituting for the hills of Scotland).

Original cast: RCA LSO-1001 (e). Film: MGM 3135 (Carol Richards sings for Cyd Charisse). Studio cast (1973) of Shirley Jones, Jack Cassidy, Susan Johnson, and Frank Porretta: Columbia Special Products COS 2540. This includes "The Love of My Life," a song not on the other two versions.

1947-1948

No award was presented in the musical category.

1948-1949

South Pacific (Rodgers and Hammerstein). Also a Tony winner. See Act One (1950) for details.

1949-1950

The Consul (Gian-Carlo Menotti). Opened March 15, 1950. Cast: Patricia Neway, Cornell MacNeil, Marie Powers, Gloria Lane, Maria Andreassi, Andrew McKinley, George Jongeyans (aka George Gaynes), Leon Lishner.

"I have an absolute loathing for musical comedy," Menotti told biographer John Gruen. "I hate musicals, especially those with operatic pretensions, such as *My Fair Lady*."[2] Perhaps it was this loathing, combined with his love for opera, that made Menotti perversely stage his operas in Broadway theaters.

Menotti wrote his first opera in his native Italy at the age of 11; at 16, his family moved to Philadelphia where the protégé continued to write serious music—the Metropolitan Opera performed his *Amelia Goes to the Ball* when he was 26. An opera on spiritualism called *The Medium* opened on Broadway in 1946 and had a long run.[3]

His next Broadway opera (billed as a "musical drama" so as not to scare away customers) was *The Consul*, a contemporary pot-boiler involving a woman's struggle to flee political persecution in an unnamed Iron Curtain country while being continually stifled by an indifferent bureaucracy. The Consul of the title is never seen. Everyone must deal with his secretary who reduces all comers to a number and case file, then dismisses them. Her child dies, her husband is imprisoned, and in despair heroine Magda Sorel (Neway) takes the traditional operatic way out by committing suicide. (She sticks her head in an oven as the curtain falls.)

It was as if George Orwell had joined forces with Franz Kafka to become the Gilbert and Sullivan of the Cold War. Backers were forewarned: "My opera," Menotti told them, "is vaaary gloomy." Menotti not only composed the music, and wrote his own lyrics, but also served as director, explaining to *Time*: "As stage director I am always faithful to the composer." For this work, Menotti also received a Pulitzer Prize in music and had his portrait painted for the cover of *Time*.[4]

The basic idea was inspired by the suicide of a refugee woman at Ellis Island who was forbidden entry to the United States. "I cannot abide little people who, given a little power, wield it inflexibly and cruelly," said Menotti in explaining the bureaucratic source of his inspiration.[5]

Original cast: Decca DX-101 (M).

(A decade later, Neway would win a Tony as Mother Superior in Rodgers and Hammerstein's *The Sound of Music* — see Act One, 1960, for details.)

1950-1951

Guys and Dolls (Frank Loesser). A Tony winner. See Act One (1951) for details.

1951-1952

Pal Joey (Richard Rodgers, Lorenz Hart, John O'Hara). Opened January 3, 1952. Cast: Vivienne Segal, Harold Lang, Helen Gallagher, Elaine Stritch.

This was a revival of the original 1940 musical with a new cast. The show, based on an epistolary novel by John O'Hara (in the form of letters signed "Pal Joey") that was itself formed from stories that appeared in *The New Yorker*, was a breakthrough in that it featured a cad as the central character. Joey is a self-centered crooner who uses women as stepping stones to the top of the heap, leaving a trail of broken hearts in his wake. Thanks to an equally rapacious woman who sets him up as a nightclub owner only to dump him before he can dump her, Joey's fall from the top is just as rapid as his rise. Helen Gallagher won a Tony in a supporting role.

In reviewing the original production, Sidney B. Whipple of the New York *World-Telegram* (12/26/40) found it to be "a bright, novel, gay and tuneful work," though he worried about "lyrics that sometimes skirt dangerously close to the risque and sometimes plunge right into it — but always wittily." Burns Mantle at the *Daily News* reported that "Rodgers and Hart have spattered the score with pleasant songs," adding, "neither is it cheaply or slyly smutty." Brooks Atkinson at the *Times* admired the result but, in referring to Joey, asked, "Although it is expertly done, can you draw sweet water from a foul well?"

The score contains that wonderful Rodgers and Hart standard, "Bewitched, Bothered, and Bewildered," as well as: "You Mustn't Kick It Around," "I Could Write a Book," "What Is a Man?" "Zip" (with a lyric that purports to show what goes through the mind of Gypsy Rose Lee as she's stripping), "That Terrific Rainbow," "Plant You Now, Dig You Later," "Pal Joey (What Do I Care for a Dame?)," "In Our Little Den (of Iniquity)," and "Take Him."

The 1957 film starred Frank Sinatra, Rita Hayworth (her singing done by Jo Ann Greer), and Kim Novak (her singing done by Trudi Erwin). The character of Joey was softened a little for the film, and some lyrics were laundered.

The original 1940 cast of Gene Kelly, June Havoc, Van Johnson, and Vivienne Segal was not recorded. The show made Kelly such a hot commodity that he moved to Hollywood for a long and glorious film career. He did not return to Broadway until 1958, and then as director of *Flower Drum Song* [Act 5].

Studio cast (1950) of Vivienne Segal and Harold Lang: Columbia Chart Busters JST 4364 (1988 reissue). Revival cast (Segal and Lang, though starring on stage, are replaced on the recording by Jane Froman and Dick Beavers): Capitol S-310. Film: Capitol W-912.

1952-1953

Wonderful Town (Bernstein, Comden, Green). A Tony winner. See Act One (1953) for details.

1953-1954

The Golden Apple (Jerome Moross, John Latouche). Opened March 11, 1954. Cast: Jonathan Lucas, Kaye Ballard, Stephen Douglass, Jack Whiting, Dean Michener, Nola Day, Priscilla Gillette, Bibi Osterwald, David Hooks, Barton Naumaw.

The Iliad and *The Odyssey* transplanted to a small Washington town named Angel's Roost, circa 1900. Far-fetched? It went something like this: Lucas plays a traveling notions salesman named Paris, while Ballard (who has a few notions of her own) is Helen, wife of Sheriff Menelaus (Michener). Helen has as much resistance to males as Ado Annie had in *Oklahoma!* and is swept off in a balloon by Paris to the town of Rhododendron (where the sly Mayor Hector is played by Whiting). Douglass is Ulysses Spelvin, just returned from the Spanish-American War, who leads the pursuit to bring back the runaway Helen.

During the ten-year quest, Ulysses finds his men slowly seduced by the allures of the big city, from a nympho named Calypso to the enticing and hula-dancing Sirens. Circe, a woman without mercy, attempts to deal with the intrepid Ulysses by offering him a golden apple, once a talisman of luck but now a symbol of greed and lust for power. Other characters included Ajax Finucane, Agamemnon Nimmin, Nestor Neider, Homer Pickins, Diomede Kunkel, Achilles Akins, and Patroclus Whiting.

There were no spoken lines. What wasn't sung was conveyed in dance and pantomime. Would such a departure from tradition set well with audiences? Robert Coleman of the *Daily Mirror* was convinced when the audience "rocked the rafters with robust applause." He declared, "It is art, without being arty, [an] evening of sheer delight." Richard Watts, Jr., also fell under its spell, calling the show "a thorough delight in its freshness, imagination, charm and brightness." The verses, wrote music critic Virgil Thomson in the *Herald Tribune*, "are vivacious, sparkling, ingenious and at many moments very, very funny. . . . And its orchestra makes far lovelier sounds than we are used to hearing in a musical."

More support came from John Chapman of the *Daily News*: "It is an off-beat, off-rhyme, off-harmony musical which lifts our Broadway song-and-dance theatre right off the comfortable seat of its pants and then gives it a kick in said pants." Over at the *Journal-American*, John McClain called it "some sort of milestone in the American musical theatre."

Among the numbers are: "By Goona-Goona Lagoon," "Helen Is Always Willing," "The Judgment of Paris," "Store-bought Suit," "Circe, Circe," "Calypso," "Doomed, Doomed, Doomed," and "Lazy Afternoon." Despite the raves. there were just 125 performances.

Original cast: RCA LOC-1014. Reissued on Elektra EKL-5000.

1954-1955

The Saint of Bleecker Street (Gian-Carlo Menotti). Opened December 27, 1954. Cast: Virginia Copeland, Gloria Lane, David Poleri, Gabrielle Ruggiero, Leon Lishner, Maria Di Gerlando, David Aiken.

Menotti's most ambitious opera had a cast of 30, a chorus of 30, and a 58-piece orchestra. Set in New York's Little Italy, *The Saint of Bleecker Street* is the story of religious-minded Annina (Copeland), her cynical and unbelieving brother Michele (Poleri) who is beaten trying to keep her from a religious parade, and Michele's mistress (Lane). Annina, who has visions and stigmata, wants to become a nun, a career choice strenuously objected to by Michele. When his mistress suggests there may be a subconscious incestuous motive in his stance, Michele murders her. Annina, wrote *Time* (1/10/55), then "becomes the bride of Christ in a chilling ritual." She dies during the ceremony.

Menotti was raised a Catholic but had said publicly his faith was lost and he was now a man of reason. This opera was his way of bringing his worlds of religion, opera, and reason together. To those who felt matters were unresolved by the end, the composer told *Time*, "I offer no solutions. I am satisfied if I shock, that is, if I create strong emotion."

William Hawkins (New York *World-Telegram*) said, "This is a major chapter in a major career. . . . [Menotti] again must be rated a genius." To John Chapman at the *Daily News*, "Menotti's score is a thing of thrills and surprises—somber, gentle, gay and explosive in turn." *Time* lauded the show's various musical forms and pointed out that the opera was attempting to show "all the kinds of human love . . . mother love, conjugal, fraternal, carnal, even incestuous love."

Audiences in the 1950s were not quite up to so much love all at one time. The opera hung on for just 92 performances, but long enough to impress the New York critics as well as the Pulitzer Prize committee which gave Menotti his second award in the serious music category.

Original cast: RCA CBM2-2714 (M) reissued double set.

1955-1956

My Fair Lady (Lerner and Loewe). A Tony winner. See Act One (1957) for details.

1956-1957

The Most Happy Fella (Frank Loesser). Opened May 3, 1956. Cast: Robert Weede, Art Lund, Jo Sullivan, Susan Johnson, Shorty Long.

"The riches are almost beyond counting," gushed Walter Kerr in the *Herald Tribune*, said riches ranging from "the freedom and the melodic fury of opera, or at least operetta" to "all those tumbling, rollicking, hell-kicking outbursts that belong to the very best vaudeville . . . the ambitious tunes swell mightily, and the torrid ones explode." He did have one reservation: "The overabundance [of riches] is damaging. It tends to choke the movement of the action."

Frank Loesser's near-operatic musical was based on Sidney Howard's 1925 Pulitzer Prize-winning stage hit, *They Knew What They Wanted* (which became a 1940 nonmusical film with Carole Lombard and Charles Laughton). Loesser labeled the 40-song score an "extended musical comedy," though the story of the love of an aging vintner for a young waitress who marries and then cheats on him with a hired hand is not the usual stuff of comedy.

That didn't bother John McClain at the *Journal-American*: "This brilliant and ambitious solo effort is, in my manual, merely a great, great musical by a guy who likes to write a lot of music and would rather have the people sing the story than talk it."

Some songs from the score found big commercial success, especially "Big D," "Happy to Make Your Acquaintance," "Joey, Joey, Joey," and, as recorded by The Four Lads, "Standing on the Corner (Watching All the Girls Go By)." One-time opera star Weede was nominated for a Tony but lost to Rex Harrison in *My Fair Lady*.

Cast: Columbia Special Products CO3L-240 M (3 records).

1957-1958

The Music Man (Meredith Willson). A Tony winner. See Act One (1958) for details.

1958-1959

La Plume de Ma Tante (Robert Dhery, Gerard Calvi). Opened November 11, 1958. Cast: Robert Dhery, Colette Brosset, Pierre Olaf, Jacques Legras, Roger Caccia, Jean LeFevre, Christian Duvaleix.

The title means "The Pen of My Aunt" and has nothing at all to do with the show. A French revue imported from England (it had already played in both countries for five years), it ran for 835 performances at New York's Royale Theater and featured a series of pantomime skits nearly devoid of dialogue. It was also largely lacking in lyrics. Many of the skits, however, were accompanied by music, thus qualifying it (barely) as a musical.

Newsweek (1/24/58) called it "inspired gaiety" and "a grabbagful of assorted bonbons," adding that the "musical pickings are slim but pleasing." One of the most talked about sight gags featured monks pulling seriously on bell ropes as the scene segued into a lively maypole dance. Another was a chorus line with one girl continually high-kicking the wrong leg.

Language was not a barrier. *Time* (1/24/58) noted that the show spoke "the international language of leers and leaps, pratfalls and double takes, cupboards and manholes," while Dhery delivered commentary in "a kind of compound-fractured English." Much of the "calisthenic comedy" action "moves to rhythmically gay and tinny music."

La Plume de Ma Tante was also nominated for a Tony but lost to *Redhead*. The entire cast, however, was awarded a special Tony for its contribution to the dramatic arts.

Obviously, this is one of those musicals that works best on stage and should be seen rather than heard. It does not translate well to audio recording, though there is one — of all the scores in this book, it is perhaps the most difficult to find.

Original cast: Vogue (F) LD-691-30.

1959-1960

Fiorello! (Bock, Harnick). A Tony winner. See Act One (1960) for details.

1960-1961

Carnival (Bob Merrill, Michael Stewart). Opened April 13, 1961. Cast: Jerry Orbach, James Mitchell, Anna Maria Alberghetti, Kaye Ballard, Pierre Olaf.

It began as a 1953 musical movie called *Lili* with Leslie Caron and Mel Ferrer that produced the hit song "Hi Lili, Hi Lo." A new score was written for the stage version, but the plot of a young girl falling in love with a bitter, crippled puppeteer remained.

Lili (Alberghetti) is a penniless young orphan taken in by a touring carnival. She mistakenly falls for Marco (Mitchell), a magician and heel who, it is said, would cheat his own mother. The puppeteer is Paul Berthalet (Orbach), whose outlook on life is so bleak that he sings "I've Got to Find a Reason (to Go on Living)," and sings to one of his puppets, "Everybody Likes You (And No One Likes Me)." Manic depression is his guiding philosophy of life, until he meets Lili. As the theme says, "Love Makes the World Go Round," and eventually Lili sees through Marco and comes to love Paul, which goes a long way toward lifting his gloom and improving his puppet show.

Gower Champion directed the musical, with a score that included: "Grand Imperial Cirque De Paris," "Sword, Rose and Cape" (Marco's attempt to impress and seduce Lili with macho posturing), "Humming" (Ballard's angry and funny diatribe against Marco's womanizing), "Yes, My Heart," "A Very Nice Man," "Mira" (in which Lili sings of her hometown), and "Yum Ticky (Ticky Tum Tum)," which showed off Alberghetti's clear, pure voice and impressive vocal range.

Calling Alberghetti "a wispy little sorceress," John Chapman of the *Daily News* declared the musical to be "enchantment from the moment the houselights go down." Howard Taubman of the *Times* said, "It bursts with the vitality of Broadway know-how, and yet is hardly ever vulgar." In the *Mirror*, Robert Coleman reported: "The first-nighters blistered their palms in affectionate welcome to the town's new song and dance triumph." Walter Kerr, writing for the *Herald Tribune*, found the show "distant," and complained that "Lili herself leaves our hearts untugged."

Alberghetti won a Tony, sharing the honor with Diahann Carroll in *No Strings* [Act Four, 1962].

Original cast: MGM E (M)/SE (S)-3946 OC. 1989 Reissue: Polygram 837 195-4.

1961-1962

How to Succeed in Business Without Really Trying (Frank Loesser). A Tony winner. See Act One (1962) for details.

1962-1963

No award was given in the musical category. Yet this was the season of *A Funny Thing Happened on the Way to the Forum* and *Oliver!* [Act One, 1963], as well as *Stop the World, I Want to Get Off* [Act Five] and *She Loves Me* [Act Four, 1963].

1963-1964

Hello, Dolly! (Herman). A Tony winner. See Act One (1964) for details.

1964-1965

Fiddler on the Roof (Bock, Harnick). A Tony winner. See Act One (1965) for details.

1965-1966

Man of La Mancha (Darion, Leigh). A Tony winner. See Act One (1966) for details.

1966-1967

Cabaret (Kander, Ebb). A Tony winner. See Act One (1967) for details.

1967-1968

Your Own Thing (Donald Driver, Hal Hester, Danny Apolinar). Opened Off-Broadway January 13, 1968. Cast: Danny Apolinar, Imogene Bliss, Marcia Rodd, Leland Palmer, Tom Ligon.

A rock musical treatment of Shakespeare's *Twelfth Night* wherein twin siblings, separated by a shipwreck, find each other again after a series of adventures involving disguises, misplaced love, and misunderstandings. The switch to a modern setting made Duke Orsino into a booking agent named Orson (Ligon), while Olivia (Rodd) owns a disco and Viola (Palmer) is a rock singer disguised as a man. (When Orson finds himself inexplicably falling for the disguised Viola, he handles it by readjusting his psyche through psychology books on latent homosexuality.)

James Davis, reviewing the show for the New York *Daily News*, offered the opinion that Shakespeare wrote the original play while drunk and called the story "a brutal bore." Jerry Tallmer at the *New York Post* found the rock songs "not only generally excellent but, oh, rarity, specifically pertinent."

Musical numbers included: "Baby! Baby! (Somethin's Happ'nin'),'' "No One's Perfect, Dear," "I'm on My Way to the Top," "The Apocalypse Fugue" (Viola's rock group is named The Apocalypse), "The Now Generation," and "(When You're)

Young and in Love." Two songs kept Shakespeare's words as lyrics: "Come Away, Death" and "She Never Told Her Love."

At *The New York Times* (1/15/68) Clive Barnes called the show "cheerful, joyful, and blissfully irreverent to Shakespeare and everything else," and even gave a hand to the rock score: "The music is always engaging and far from consistently strident." This was the first Off-Broadway musical to receive the Circle Award, beating out the Tony winner, *Hallelujah, Baby!* [Act One, 1968].

Original cast: RCA LOC (M)/LSO (S)-1148.

1968-1969

1776 (Sherman Edwards). A Tony winner. See Act One (1969) for details.

1969-1970

Company (Sondheim). A Tony winner. See Act One (1971) for details.

1970-1971

Follies (Sondheim). The score won a Tony. See Act One (1972) for details.

1971-1972

Two Gentlemen of Verona (MacDermot, Guare). A Tony winner. See Act One (1972) for details.

1972-1973

A Little Night Music (Sondheim). A Tony winner. See Act One (1973) for details.

1973-1974

Candide (Bernstein, Wheeler, Wilbur). Opened March 8, 1974. Cast: Lewis Stadlen, Jim Corti, Mark Baker, David Horwitz, Maureen Brennan, Sam Freed.

Leonard Bernstein, John Latouche, and Richard Wilbur first teamed with Lillian Hellman to do a musical of Voltaire's biting satire in 1956. At the time, Tom Donnelly of the *World-Telegram* applauded Bernstein's music as "lush, lovely, and electric. When it isn't voluptuous as velvet, it is as frostily pretty as a diamond bell [and] is one of the most attractive scores anyone has written for the theater."

The show flopped. One reason may have been underscored in Robert Coleman's review in the *Daily Mirror*: "It's for those who don't demand lacy icing on their entertainment cake, who can stand a lot of bitter with a little sweet. It's not for softies, but for the hardy who can tear the tinsel off reality and take it in stride." That, in a nutshell, did not describe America in 1956, a year when the top-selling songs on juke boxes were "The Great Pretender" by the Platters, "Hot Diggitty" by Perry Como, Elvis Presley's "Don't Be Cruel," Doris Day's "Que Sera, Sera," and Hugo Winterhalter's "Canadian Sunset."

Despite lasting only 73 performances, the music lived on in recordings and kept hope alive for a revival. That chance came in 1974 with a new book by Hugh Wheeler and some additional lyrics from Stephen Sondheim, with direction by Harold Prince. This time, it did indeed become the best of all possible musical worlds: Clive Barnes wrote, "I loved it and loved it. I think Voltaire would have loved it too. If he didn't — to hell with him."

Voltaire's ironic satire involves simple-hearted Candide's search for his beloved Cunegunde, kidnapped during a war. The two of them, along with the ever-optimistic philosopher Dr. Pangloss, see and suffer incredible miseries, from the extremes of the Inquisition to shipwrecks, slavery, pirates, tortures, rape, and more, before finding the perfect land — the non-existent El Dorado.

Songs in the revival include: "Life Is Happiness Indeed," "The Best of All Possible Worlds," "Oh Happy We," "Auto Da Fe (What a Day)," "I Am Easily Assimilated," "Sheep's Song," and "You Were Dead, You Know."

Revival cast: Columbia S2X 32923.

The original cast of Barbara Cook, Max Adrian, and Robert Rounseville has been reissued by CBS Masterworks on MT 38732. A 1991 studio cast of opera singers combines both scores under the direction of Leonard Bernstein: Deutsche Gramaphon 429 734-4.

1974-1975

A Chorus Line (Hamlisch, Kleban). A Tony winner. See Act One (1976) for details.

1975-1976

Pacific Overtures (Stephen Sondheim). Opened January 11, 1976. Cast: Mako, Yuki Shimoda, Soon-Teck Oh, Sab Shimono, Isao Sato.

East meets West as Commodore Matthew Perry's gunboat diplomacy forces Japan out of its isolation to open trade relations with the rest of the world, circa 1853. It was staged in traditional kabuki style with white make-up and men playing the female roles (until the final number, which was set in modern Japan). It was another stylistic gamble by Sondheim and an artistic, if not commercial, success.

Clive Barnes at the *Times* found it "beguiling and sometimes bewildering," and suggested that "Sondheim's music is in a style that might be called Japonaiserie (Leonard Bernstein quite often seems to be trysting with Madame Butterfly in the orchestra pit)," while the lyrics "are totally Western and — as is the custom with Mr. Sondheim — devilish, wittily and delightfully clever." Douglas Watt at the *Daily News* dismissed the show as "prevailingly dull" and "a mish-mash" that was "as thin and insubstantial as the painted screens used for scenery."

On the contrary, Martin Gottfried of the *Post* thought it an "exquisite, enchanting, touching, intelligent and altogether remarkable work of theater art." Howard Kissel of *Women's Wear Daily* saw it as "the production in which the team that sets Broadway's highest standards most fully meets the astonishing objectives they set themselves."

Musical highlights include: "Four Black Dragons," "Chrysanthemum Tea," "Welcome to Kanagawa," "Someone in a Tree," "The Advantages of Floating in the Middle of the Sea," "Please Hello," "A Bowler Hat," "Pretty Lady," and "Next."

Nominated for nine Tonys, it won for scenic design and costumes; it was the year of *A Chorus Line* [Act One, 1976].

Original cast: RCA ARL1-1367.

1976-1977

Annie (Strouse, Charnin). A Tony winner. See Act One (1977) for details.

1977-1978

Ain't Misbehavin' (Waller, Maltby et al.). A Tony winner. See Act one (1978) for details.

1978-1979

Sweeney Todd (Sondheim). A Tony winner. See Act One (1979) for details.

1979-1980

Evita (Webber, Rice). A Tony winner. See Act One (1980) for details.

1980-1981

No award was presented in the musical category. It was the season of *42nd Street* and *Woman of the Year* [Act One, 1981], and *Sophisticated Ladies* [Act Five].

1981-1982

No award was presented in the musical category. It was the year of *Nine* [Act One, 1982], *Dreamgirls* [Act Four, 1982], and *Pump Boys and Dinettes* [Act Five].

1982-1983

Little Shop of Horrors (Alan Menken, Howard Ashman). Opened July 22, 1982. Cast: Ellen Greene, Lee Wilkof, Hy Anzell, Jennifer Leigh Warren, Franc Luz, Sheila Kay Davis, and Leilani Jones, with Martin P. Robinson and Ron Taylor as Audrey II.

This odd musical began as a quickie exploitation, darkly comic horror movie by director Roger Corman in 1960 (with a then-unknown supporting player named Jack Nicholson). The story concerns a meek and mild man named Seymour who stumbles upon a monstrous, talking, meat-eating plant from outer space, and names it after his girlfriend, Audrey. To stay alive, it must be supplied with fresh, human blood. Only when he has to choose between the plant and Audrey (who's about to become its dinner) does he see the error of his botanical ways. By then it's too late. Audrey dies after being attacked by the plant. A distraught Seymour feeds her body to Audrey II and then climbs in after it with a machete, determined to kill the plant. After a struggle, the plant spits out the machete and heads for the audience as the lights go out.

Marilyn Stasio of the *New York Post* (5/24/82) called it a "delightfully warped project" with a "gleefully gruesome book," which had a score ranging from "rock-'n'-roll rousers to slippery Latin rip-offs and gooey ballads suitable for dancing belly-to-belly down the gym floor."

A 1960s-styled girl group provided singing commentary as a kind of Greek chorus. There was also a sadistic dentist who becomes plant food for Audrey II. Musical numbers include: "Skid Row (Downtown)," "Da-Doo," "Grow for Me," "Somewhere That's Green," "Dentist!" "Git It (Feed Me)," "Suddenly, Seymour," "Suppertime," "The Meek Shall Inherit."

The musical was filmed in 1986 with Ellen Greene, Rick Moranis, Steve Martin, and, as the voice of the plant, Levi Stubbs of the Four Tops. There was also an ambiguously happy ending for the film, with Seymour and Audrey destroying the plant (perhaps) and living happily ever after (maybe). A couple of songs were dropped from the film to make way for a new song that was nominated for an Oscar, "Mean Green Mother From Outer Space."

Ellen Greene, whom *Time* said had a voice "that buckles theater walls," seems reined in during her big film number, "Suddenly, Seymour," as if she were trying not to overpower Rick Moranis. On the original cast album, she belts and growls out the song in grand style.

Original cast: Geffen GHSP-2020. Film: Geffen GHS-24125.

Also recommended is *The Little Shop of Horrors Book* by John McCarty and Mark Thomas McGee (St. Martin's Press, 1988).

1983-1984

Sunday in the Park With George (Stephen Sondheim). Opened May 2, 1984. Cast: Mandy Patinkin, Bernadette Peters, Charles Kimbrough (of TV's *Murphy Brown*), Barbara Bryne, Dana Ivey.

Using George Seurat's pointillist painting *A Sunday Afternoon on the Island of La Grande Jatte* as the centerpiece, *Sunday in the Park With George* delves brilliantly into the creative mind and spirit of all artists (or writers) who put their work ahead of everything else. The show is a hymn to creativity and the importance of individual vision.

George is on stage painting throughout the first act, with the many figures in his work modeled by an assortment of actors and cardboard cutouts. Totally absorbed in his work, he has no time for romance and lives only through his art. While others are out enjoying life, his fate (and chosen dedication) is to observe and record (and sometimes reshape) what he sees, but not to interact. His finished masterpiece comes at the price of a lost love. (The real life Seurat died at 31 without ever selling a painting.)

In the second act, a modern George of a hundred years later is shown just as absorbed in his creation of darting laser lights and futuristic shapes called a Chromolume. And like his distant ancestor, the new George also has to battle against critical disapproval (there are more than a few jabs at shortsighted critics and lovers of the merely conventional) while constantly in need of funds. A visit to the site of the original painting helps tie the two artists together.

Hamlet instructed the players to "fit the action to the word, the word to the action"; in *Sunday in the Park With George* Sondheim goes the Bard one better and deftly fits the music to the action, and the action to the music, producing a seamless whole where underscoring is as important as the lyrics; traditional show tunes are pushed aside in favor of a totally integrated score of dialogue and music. To fully appreciate this masterful musical, the video of the PBS presentation is highly recommended (available from Karl/Lorimar Home Video).

Musical highlights include: "Color and Light," "Gossip," "Finishing the Hat," "Beautiful," "Children and Art," "Lesson #8," "Move On," "Sunday," and the brilliant "Putting It Together" (often referred to as "Art Isn't Easy").

Jack Kroll sang the show's praises in *Newsweek* (5/14/84), calling it an evening of "beauty, wit, nobility and ardor." Sondheim's score was termed "original even for him." Overall, "To say that this show breaks new ground is not enough; it also breaks new sky, new water, new flesh and new spirit."

It did not, however, break attendance records, possibly because it was written by creative people as an explanation of themselves and of the forces by which they are driven and thus had limited appeal to a general audience. Though the show also won a Pulitzer Prize in drama, it lost the Tony to Jerry Herman's *La Cage aux Folles* [Act One, 1984] and closed at a financial loss after 540 performances.

Original cast: RCA HBC1-5042. A double set.

1984-1985

No award was presented in the musical category. This was the season of *Big River* [Act One, 1985].

1985-1986

No award was presented in the musical category. This was the season of *The Mystery of Edwin Drood* [Act One, 1986].

1986-1987

Les Misérables (Schönberg, Doublil, Knetzmer). A Tony winner. See Act One (1987) for details.

1987-1988

Into the Woods (Sondheim). A Tony winner for its score. See Act One (1988) for details.

1988-1989

No award was presented in the musical category. This was the season of *Jerome Robbins' Broadway* [Act One, 1989], and *Black and Blue* [Act Five].

1989-1990

City of Angels (Coleman, Zippel). A Tony winner. See Act One (1990) for details.

1990-1991

The Will Rogers Follies: A Life in Revue (Coleman, Comden, Green). After years of berating Broadway's producers and creators for their safe, old-fashioned, and predictable fare, the critics in 1991 gave their Circle Award not to the dramatic import *Miss Saigon*, but to the most old-fashioned show imaginable, a glittering, nostalgic look back at the Ziegfeld Follies and one of its stars, folksy commentator Will Rogers.

A Tony winner. See Act One (1991) for details.

REFERENCE NOTES

1. C. R. S. Marsden, *The Dictionary of Outrageous Quotations* (Topsfield, Massachusetts: Salem House Publishers, 1988), p. 22.

2. John Gruen, *Menotti: A Biography* (New York: Macmillan, 1978), p. 99.

3. *Webster's American Biographies* (Springfield, Massachusetts: G. & C. Merriam Company, 1975), p. 714.

4. *Time*, May 1, 1950.

5. *Time*, March 27, 1950.

Act Three:
The Pulitzer Prize

> Annual, for the original American play performed in New York, which shall best represent the educational value and power of the stage in raising the standard of good morals, good taste and good manners, One thousand dollars ($1000).
>
> — Joseph Pulitzer's bequest[1]

Joseph Pulitzer was a Hungarian emigrant whose life in America included service in the union army during the Civil War, election to the Missouri legislature and the U.S. House of Representatives and, most notably, a long career in journalism as editor and publisher of the St. Louis *Post-Dispatch* and the New York *World*.[2]

Pulitzer died in 1911, leaving enough funds to endow the Journalism School at Columbia University (where students are taught *not* to emulate his penchant for aggressive yellow journalism popular during the Spanish-American War), and the annual awarding of cash Pulitzer Prizes for individual achievement in journalism, letters, and music.

Columbia's advisory board revised and shortened the above bequest in 1928 so the award could go to the play "which shall best represent the educational value and power of the stage," dropping all mention of morals and manners; added to that line in 1934 was this qualifier: "preferably one dealing with American life."

Even that did not appease everyone. When Robert Sherwood's *Idiot's Delight* was named Best Play in 1936, Clayton Hamilton, a critic and Pulitzer jury member for 16 years, told *The New York Times* the play violated the new condition not only because it was set in Italy, but, he complained, "the only American character is a song-and-dance artist accompanied by a moronic blonde."[3]

As described in the introduction to Act Two, the choices of the Pulitzer Prize committee have not always been met with general approval, the dissatisfaction leading to the creation of the New York Drama Critics Circle Award.

The music category is the province of "serious" music — symphonies, operas, and so on [see Menotti's contributions in Act Two, 1949-1959, and 1954-1955]. The more traditional Broadway musical falls into the drama category, established in 1918, which nearly always goes to a straight, nonmusical play. There have been a half-dozen exceptions to date.

1932

Of Thee I Sing (George and Ira Gershwin). Cast: William Gaxton, Victor Moore, Dudley Clements, Lois Moran, Grace Brinkley.

Such was the reputation of the writers and composers that advance ticket sales — with prices ranging from $1.00 to $5.00 — hit $5,300 the first day and $4,500 the second day.[4] It proved to be money well spent.

The libretto by George S. Kaufman and Morrie Ryskind is a delightfully barbed satire on American politics. In an effort to secure a strong but safe platform on which to run John P. Wintergreen (Gaxton) for president, his party settles on love. To drum up popular support they arrange a beauty contest in Atlantic City, the winner to become Mrs. Wintergreen and the marriage to be performed as the new president takes his oath of office. The party's campaign song becomes "Love Is Sweeping the Country" as the public takes the candidate (if not the issues) to its heart.

The devastating political jokes and one-liners fly fast and furious throughout the play, perfectly matched by George Gershwin's music and Ira Gershwin's snappy lyrics. (Only the authors and Ira, not George, were cited by the Pulitzer committee.)

The songs include: "Wintergreen for President," "Who Is the Lucky Girl to Be?" "Because, Because, Because," "Mine," "Some Girls Can Bake a Pie," "Of Thee I Sing (Baby)," "Illegitimate Daughter of an Illegitimate Son of an Illegitimate Nephew of Napoleon," "Jilted," and "I'm About to Be a Mother."

Time magazine (12/26/31) called it "the drollest, merriest musical nonsensity to come down the theatrical pike this season," reporting that Ira Gershwin "has packed the lyrics full of foolishness and funny rhymes."

Brooks Atkinson of *The New York Times* (12/28/31) hailed it as George Gershwin's "most brilliant score," adding: "Whether it is satire, wit, doggerel or fantasy, Mr. Gershwin pours music out in full measure, and in many voices. Although the book is lively, Mr. Gershwin is exuberant. He has not only ideas but enthusiasm."

Atkinson, though at times finding the unremitting satire "tiresome," applauded the overall effect: "The authors have transposed the charlatanry of national politics into a hurly-burly of riotous campaign slogans, political knavery, comic national dilemmas and general burlesque. They have fitted the dunce's cap to politics and government, and crowded an evening with laughter."

The original cast was not recorded.

A 1952 revival cast featuring Jack Carson, Paul Hartman, Lenore Lonergan, and Betty Oakes is on Capitol T-11651.

A 1972 television cast with Carroll O'Connor, Cloris Leachman, Michelle Lee, and Jack Gilford is on Columbia S31763.

A terrific 1987 studio cast production with Larry Kert, Jack Gilford, and Maureen McGovern is on CBS S2T 42522, usually sold together with the musical's sequel, *Let 'em Eat Cake* [Act Five].

1950

South Pacific (Rodgers and Hammerstein). A Tony winner. See Act One (1950) for details.

1960

Fiorello! (Bock, Harnick). A Tony winner. See Act One (1960) for details.

1962

How to Succeed in Business Without Really Trying (Frank Loesser). A Tony winner. See Act One (1962) for details.

1976

A Chorus Line (Hamlisch, Kleban). A Tony winner. See Act One (1976) for details.

1985

Sunday in the Park With George (Sondheim). A Drama Critics Circle Award winner. See Act Two (1983-1984) for details.

REFERENCE NOTES

1. Kathryn Coe and William H. Cardell, editors, *The Pulitzer Prize Plays* (New York: Random House, 1935), p. 1.

2. *The New York Times*, May 6, 1936.

3. *The New York Times*, May 5, 1936.

4. *The New York Times*, December 27, 1931.

Act Four:
The Grammy Award

gram-o-phone . . . n. a phonograph. [1887; orig. a trademark; appar. inversion of *phonogram* now obs. name for a phonographic cylinder].

—The Random House Dictionary
of the English Language

Named for the early gramophone machines, the Grammy has been awarded annually by the National Academy of Recording Arts & Sciences in a variety of categories since 1958. Over the years the announcement of winners has moved from obscurity to one which involves a high profile annual television event. Some 6,000 professionals in the recording industry make the selections, the criteria being "artistic and/or technical excellence."

The first major winners were "Nel Blu Dipinto Di Blu (Volare)" (Record and Song of the Year), *The Music From Peter Gunn* (Album of the Year), Perry Como, Ella Fitzgerald, Count Basie, the Kingston Trio, Stan Freberg, and "The Chipmunk Song."

The public perception of the Grammy is mainly that of popular music awards in the fields of rock and roll, country, jazz, blues, classical, and so on. Jay Cocks wrote in *Time* (2/25/91) that "the Grammys have the most unfortunate reputation for often making saccharine choices that toady shamelessly to the marketplace." But Broadway musicals have been a part of the awards ceremonies from the beginning, and the winners have been far from saccharine, though not always uncontroversial.

But unlike the case of some film adaptations, and the Milli Vanilli duo in 1990, the performers on these recordings do their own singing.

1958

The Music Man (Meredith Willson). A Tony winner. See Act One (1958) for details.

1959

A tie:
Redhead (Hague, Fields). A Tony winner. See Act One (1959) for details.
Gypsy (Jule Styne, Stephen Sondheim). Opened May 21, 1959. Cast: Ethel Merman, Jack Klugman, Sandra Church, Lane Bradbury.

Gypsy uses the autobiography of stripper Gypsy Rose Lee to take audiences back to the days of burlesque and vaudeville, with a star turn by Ethel Merman as Rose, the indomitable stage mother who pushes her two daughters into show business. One of the girls, Louise, is destined to become Gypsy Rose Lee, but only after enduring years of vaudeville shows and critical rejections, standing up to her mother, shedding her old image (along with her clothes), and becoming her own woman ("Let Me Entertain You").

Other standout numbers: "Some People," "Small World," "If Mamma Was Married," "Together Wherever We Go," and "Everything's Coming Up Roses."

Even with a great score as competition, it was Merman who got the raves. Brooks Atkinson told *Times* readers that her "personal magnetism electrifies the whole theatre," adding, "[Merman] struts and bawls her way through it triumphantly." Frank Aston of the *World-Telegram* was more subdued: "She proves in her noisy fashion to be a singularly effective dramatic actress with a roaring and turbulent capacity for communication."

Gypsy was nominated for seven Tonys, but it was eligible in 1960 and that was the year of *Fiorello!* and *The Sound of Music* [Act One, 1960].

Original cast: Columbia S 32607. Angela Lansbury's 1973 revival: RCA LBL1-5004. Lansbury's London production toured the U.S. and opened on Broadway in September, 1974; she was presented with a Tony in 1975. Tyne Daly's 1990 revival (she also won a Tony as Mama Rose): Elektra 979239-4.

1960

The Sound of Music (Rodgers and Hammerstein). A Tony winner. See Act One (1961) for details.

1961

How to Succeed in Business Without Really Trying (Frank Loesser). A Tony winner. See Act One (1962) for details.

1962

No Strings (Richard Rodgers). Opened March 15, 1962. Cast: Richard Kiley, Diahann Carroll, Noelle Adam, Bernice Massi.

After long and successful careers writing music to the words of Lorenz Hart and Oscar Hammerstein, Richard Rodgers became both composer and lyricist for this innovative, rule-breaking romance set in Paris.

Kiley is a blocked novelist and Carroll a top fashion model, two Americans footloose and fancy free in the city of love. The interracial love affair, no strings attached, was not the only fresh device Rodgers employed. Taking the title literally, there were no string instruments in the orchestra, and the musicians were not in the pit but behind the scenery with soloists occasionally stepping forward to underscore the action. Even scenery was moved about in full view of the audience.

His gifts for melody never in doubt, Rodgers also proved that he could pen some elegant and witty lyrics as well, with highlights being: "The Sweetest Sounds," "How Sad," "Loads of Love," "Be My Host," "You Don't Tell Me," "Maine," "An Orthodox Fool," and "Eager Beaver."

Calling it "a somber, offbeat affair," John Chapman of the *Daily News* lamented, "I do wish somebody had thought of some jokes." Richard Watts, Jr. of the *Post* agreed that the book by Samuel Taylor was the principle problem: "The evening would have been happier if the book could have been forgotten, and Diahann Carroll and Richard Kiley had gone on singing Mr. Rodgers' beautiful and haunting songs." The *Journal-American*'s John McClain termed

the show "a whopping hit" and Carroll "a perfectly dreamy new
star."

The show was crafted as a star vehicle for Diahann Carroll, and
she shared the leading actress Tony that year with Anna Maria Alberghetti in *Carnival* [Act Two, 1960-1961].

Original cast: Capitol SO 1695.

1963

She Loves Me (Jerry Bock, Sheldon Harnick). Opened April 23,
1963. Cast: Barbara Cook, Daniel Massey, Jack Cassidy, Nathaniel
Frey.

Set in eastern Europe in the early 1930s, this love story of two
coworkers who write love letters to anonymous strangers (who turn
out to be each other, of course) and their many missteps and misunderstandings on the way to love was originally a play by Miklos
Laszlo called *Parfumerie*. Then it was a 1940 movie titled *The Shop
Around the Corner*, starring Margaret Sullivan and James Stewart.
Then it was a 1949 movie musical with Judy Garland and Van Johnson called *In the Good Old Summertime* (the last scene of which has
Judy holding her new baby, Liza Minnelli).

John Chapman of the *Daily News* termed it, "So charming, so
deft, so light, and so right." Norman Nadel of the New York
World-Telegram & Sun also found it "charming," and dubbed it
"a musical play with which everyone can fall in love." Everyone
but Walter Kerr at the *Herald Tribune*, who dismissed the plot as
"pin-sized."

Despite the setting, and the occasional inclusion of violins and
accordions, there are few attempted accents and virtually no ethnicity about the score; it could just as well have been set in Anytown,
America. In addition to the great title song, the show features:
"Days Gone By," "Dear Friend," "Tonight at Eight," "Will He
Like Me?" "Three Letters," "Ice Cream," "A Trip to the Library," "Grand Knowing You," "Perspective" (a number by Frey
on how to keep one's job that harks back to "The Company Way"
in 1961's *How to Succeed in Business Without Really Trying*),

"Ilona," "I Resolve," "I Don't Know His Name," "Where's My Shoe?" and "Tango Tragique." Jack Cassidy won a Tony as a womanizing cad.

Original cast: MGM E (M)/SE (S)-4118 OC (2 records). Reissued by Polydor on CD 0704.

1964

Funny Girl (Jule Styne, Bob Merrill). Opened March 26, 1964. Cast: Barbra Streisand, Sydney Chaplin, Kay Medford.

The role of stage star Fanny Brice (born Fannie Borach) made Streisand an international star and she gives her all as the nonglamorous comic who pushed her way into the Ziegfeld Follies by sheer force of personality and talent. Given equal weight in the show is an early, ill-fated romance with gambler Nicky Arnstein. None of the songs Brice made famous is in the show, but historical inaccuracy is balanced by a standout performance.

Norman Nadel of the New York *World-Telegram* wrote, "Hail to thee, Barbra Streisand; Fanny Brice thou never wert!" Not that he minded: "Miss Streisand prefers to create a 1918 Barbra Streisand, and the justification is that she does it superbly. This young woman is a joy on any stage." For Howard Taubman of the *Times* the show's big flaw was that "part of the time it oozes with a thick helping of sticky sentimentality."

Highlights include: "If a Girl Isn't Pretty," "I'm the Greatest Star," "His Love Makes Me Beautiful," "Sadie, Sadie," "The Music That Makes Me Dance," and the smash hits, "People," "You Are Woman" (sung by costar Sydney Chaplin, son of silent film great Charlie Chaplin), and "Don't Rain on My Parade" (a merry melange of clashing analogies and mixed metaphors adding up to a celebration of self-assertiveness).

Streisand lost the Tony to Carol Channing in *Hello, Dolly!* [Act One, 1964], but won an Oscar for the 1968 film version (a tie with **Katharine Hepburn** in *The Lion In Winter*).

Original cast: Capitol STAO 2059. Film: Columbia BOS-3220.

1965

On a Clear Day You Can See Forever (Alan Jay Lerner, Burton Lane). Opened October 17, 1965. Cast: Barbara Harris, John Cullum, William Daniels, Clifford David, Rae Allen.

During a hypnosis session, Daisy Gamble (Harris) reveals some details of past lives. She also has a tendency to talk plants into growing ("Hurry! It's Lovely Up Here!"). This reincarnation musical moves back and forth between the present day and Daisy's eighteenth-century self, Melinda Wells, before she finally falls for Cullum, the psychiatrist who's been studying her, and chooses to live in the here and now.

While critics gushed over Barbara Harris, notices for the score were mixed. John McClain of the *Journal-American* termed it "a melodious muddle," and Richard Watts, Jr. of the *Post* said "the melancholy fact is that [the songs] aren't very interesting." He also labeled the story "astonishingly heavy, humorless and tedious." Howard Taubman of the *Times*, on the other hand, thought "the most admirable assets of the musical [are] the songs and the leading lady," noting especially the "bright, charming lyrics."

Along with Cullum singing the title song and the dramatic "Come Back to Me" (in a role originally meant for Louis Jourdan), Harris sings "What Did I Have That I Don't Have?" "Tosy and Cosh," and a terrific duet on retirement benefits with William Daniels called "Wait Till We're Sixty-Five." Other highlights: "On the S. S. Bernard Cohn," and "Don't Tamper With My Sister."

Cullum and Harris were nominated for Tonys in 1966 but lost, respectively, to Richard Kiley in *Man of La Mancha* [Act One, 1966] and Angela Lansbury in *Mame* [see next entry].

The 1970 Vincente Minnelli film with Barbra Streisand and Yves Montand left out five perfectly fine songs and added two average ones: "Love With All the Trimmings" and "Go to Sleep."

Original cast: RCA LSOD-2006. Film: Columbia S 30086.

A 1979 reincarnation of the stage show faded after 30 performances.

1966

Mame (Jerry Herman). Opened May 24, 1966. Cast: Angela Lansbury, Bea Arthur, Frankie Michaels (all three of whom won acting Tonys), and Jerry Lanning.

This is the musical version of Patrick Dennis's novel *Auntie Mame* (filmed with Rosalind Russell in 1958), his eccentric aunt who firmly believes in being a glutton at the banquet of life. Her unorthodox methods of raising young Patrick bring down the disapproval of more straight-laced citizens, but free-spirited characters have always played well on stage and film (if not in real life). Mame saves Patrick from a blond bore, steers him right, and takes charge of his subsequent heir.

Douglas Watt of the *Daily News* called it "a show that pulls out all the stops and jams most of them." Walter Kerr noted "the vitamin-depleted form of Beatrice Arthur, a girl who looks like a dragon-fly in mourning," and, continuing the insect metaphor, said of the star, "There is a faintly flyblown delicacy about Miss Lansbury that hints at raffishness while keeping the tea things in order."

Kerr, in the *Herald Tribune*, found a method and a pattern to the composer's ways: "Mr. Herman writes *standard* music, music that sounds like all other music of a reasonably pleasant sort." Norman Nadel at the *World-Journal* thought "almost every measure of music seems familiar," not to mention "mundane," and called the score "an assortment of songs that will please hundreds of thousands, who will be charmed by their ready singability and their essential familiarity."

Songs include: "My Best Girl," "Bosom Buddies," "The Man in the Moon" (sung by star-gazer Bea Arthur), "We Need a Little Christmas," "Open a New Window" (Mame's guiding philosophy), "If He Walked Into My Life," and "That's How Young I Feel."

The 1974 film with Lucille Ball, Bea Arthur, and Robert Preston was an unmitigated, $12 million disaster.

Original cast: Columbia KOL 6600. Reissued on Columbia JST 3000.

1967

Cabaret (Kander and Ebb). A Tony winner. See Act One (1967) for details.

1968

Hair (Galt MacDermot, Gerome Ragni, James Rado). Opened October 17, 1967. Cast: Ronald Dyson, Gerome Ragni, Steve Curry, Lamont Washington, Melba Moore, Lynn Kellogg.

In this "tribal love-rock musical" the good-guy hippies and flower children are known as The Tribe (the play opens with a number of them wearing headbands and loincloths) and the bad-guy cops are the Police-Puppets. Sixties symbols abound: love beads, flowers, drugs, war, peace, free love, and nudity, long hair, race prejudice, protests, four-letter words, chanting. The audience is an accepted presence, alluded to, directly addressed, confronted.

It is not evenhanded, quiet, or contemplative. This is a musical that began Off-Broadway with an attitude, and takes its cue from demonstrators in the streets — it is often a loud, abrasive, in-your-face, antiwar show with the most rudimentary of plots: young Claude is trying to decide whether or not to resist the draft during the Vietnam War.

As a theatrical experience, there was nothing else like it on Broadway before, and its rock score produced some hit singles for a number of popular performers, from Andy Williams to the Rolling Stones, including: "Aquarius," "Frank Mills," "Manchester England," and "Good Morning, Starshine." (For obvious reasons, "Sodomy," a sung list of taboo words, did not get a lot of radio play.) A then-unknown Diane Keaton is part of the all-girl trio singing "Black Boys."

The theme and rock score were guaranteed to polarize critics along generational, political, and philosophical lines. Clive Barnes of the staid *The New York Times* thought it was "likable" with "brilliant lyrics" and "the frankest show in town." Barnes warned his readers that "a great many four-letter words, such as 'love,' are used **very** freely." Others were not so kind.

Writing in the *New York Post*, Richard Watts, Jr. admitted that "Music with a rock beat has a way of sounding the same to me, and there is no number in 'Hair' that stands out in my memory." He also saw the show as "amateurish and a little tiresome . . . its wistful attempt to outrage the peasantry can be irritating because it is unnecessary."

John Chapman of the *Daily News* said, "It is just too damned loud, being insanely electronified like Eddie Fisher." He also complained that "hardly anybody in this twitchy, itchy extravaganza wears shoes and they all kept running up and down the center aisle waving their calluses at me."

The 1979 movie with Treat Williams, John Savage, and Beverly D'Angelo came four years after the war and feels dated, while much of the show's confrontational punch is lost by not being able to interact with the audience, with or without shoes, but the opening "Aquarius" number is visually brilliant.

Original cast: RCA 1150-4-RC. Film: RCA CBL2-3274 (S).

(As late as 1991, *Hair* had not lost its ability to shock. A live performance of the musical in Wichita, Kansas, on January 29, 1991, ended with two cast members being cited by police for violating the city's law against nude dancing in clubs. One of the two, Shannon Conley, had painted the phrase "Freedom of Expression—God Bless America" on her body for all to see. The other actor cited (for mooning the audience) was Mark Wilson. He told reporters, "This is silly. Guys my age are dying in the Middle East, and my butt makes the paper. It's ludicrous.")[1]

1969

Promises, Promises (Burt Bacharach, Hal David). Opened December 1, 1968. Cast: Jerry Orbach, Jill O'Hara, Edward Winter, Marian Mercer, Donna McKechnie.

By 1969 the songwriting team of Bacharach and David virtually owned the pop music charts. Their hits for the younger generation included "What the World Needs Now (Is Love)," "Walk on By," "This Guy's in Love With You," "The Look of Love," "Alfie" (for which Bacharach won his first Grammy as arranger), and "What's New, Pussycat." For their fling at Broadway, Bacharach and David chose a story that had already won an Oscar as Best Picture, *The Apartment*, with a new script by Broadway's comic wizard Neil Simon.

Chuck Baxter (Orbach) is a clerk who, to please his bosses, allows them to use his apartment for illicit amorous pursuits (less tawdry and costly than a motel). He falls for one of the girls who, after being dumped, tries to kill herself in his place. Fran Kubelik (O'Hara) likewise falls for him.

Martin Gottfried of *Women's Wear Daily* went ga-ga over the score: "There are songs and more songs and more songs, one better than the other—tricky rhythm songs, funny songs (not just funny lyrics, but funny MUSIC), fresh harmony songs, lovely little guitar songs . . . the most satisfying and successful musical in a very long time."

The contemporary pop score included: "Upstairs," "You'll Think of Someone," "She Likes Basketball," "Whoever You Are," "I'll Never Fall in Love Again" (a big Dionne Warwick hit that won her a 1970 Grammy), and the title song. Jerry Orbach won a Tony.

Original score: United Artists UAS 9902.

(Jerry Orbach has the distinction of having been in the original cast of the longest running musical, *The Fantasticks* [Act Five], and used that as a springboard for a long and satisfying career on stage, film, and television. His musicals include *Chicago* [Act Five], *42nd Street* [Act One, 1981], and *Carnival* [Act Two, 1960-1961]. He starred on the 1987 CBS detective series *The Law and Harry McGraw*, and his films include *F/X*, *Dirty Dancing*, *Crimes and Misdemeanors*, *Last Exit to Brooklyn*, and *Postcards From the Edge*.)

1970

Company (Sondheim). A Tony winner. See Act One (1971) for details.

1971

Godspell (Stephen Schwartz). Opened Off-Broadway May 17, 1971. Cast: Robin Lamont, Lamar Alford, Peggy Gordon, Gilmer McCormick.

Along with the 1960s' peace movement and its flower children, there came a reflowering of spiritual and religious consciousness that was quite apart from dogma and organized church worship. One musical outgrowth of those years was *Hair*; another was *Godspell*, a rock musical textually based on the Gospel of St. Matthew and featuring a hippie, clown-garbed Jesus wearing a Superman T-shirt and assisted by nine slapstick-prone apostles. They were telling the preachers of the world to lighten up.

A big hit (recorded by The Fifth Dimension) was "Day by Day." Other highlights: "Save the People," "Learn Your Lesson Well," "Bless the Lord," "All for the Best" (done in a 1920s vaudeville style), the bluesy "Turn Back, Old Man," "We Beseech Thee" (complete with a "boom-chicka-boom" chorus), "Alas for You," and "Light of the World."

The show moved to Broadway in June of 1976, at which time Richard Eder of *The New York Times* wrote that *Godspell* "has no bones, but it has many small sinews and darting reflexes," while citing its energy, gaiety, wit, and "inventive variations on the parables of Jesus." On the downside, Eder thought the second half became "sententious."

Original cast: Bell 1102 (S). Reissued on Arista ACB6-8304. Film: Bell 1119 (S).

1972

Don't Bother Me, I Can't Cope (Micki Grant). Opened April 19, 1972. Cast: Micki Grant, Alex Bradford, Hope Clarke, Bobby Hill, Arnold Wilkerson.

Nominated for several Tonys, Micki Grant had the bad timing to put on her musical in the season of Sondheim's *A Little Night Music* [Act One, 1973], which blew away all competition. But that was her only miscalculation.

Cope, as it is known, is a tuneful, rocking, thoughtful joy as Grant portrays the urban black experience in the title number and in "Harlem Streets," "Lookin' Over From Your Side," "You Think I Got Rhythm?" "They Keep Coming," "My Name Is Man," and **"I Gotta Keep Movin'."** There's the foot-tapping gospel influence in "Fighting for Pharoah," a rock sound in "Good Vibrations," a love song called "Thank Heaven for You," and Grant herself sings the contemplative numbers, "Questions," "It Takes a Whole Lot of Human Feeling," and "So Little Time."

A cabaret-styled show with no plot or characters to speak of, *Cope* nonetheless wowed most critics. Richard Watts of the *Post* termed it "lively and infectious entertainment [where] the performers burst into song and dance seemingly at will, and they go about it with a fine zest." *The Wall Street Journal*'s Edwin Wilson wrote: "There is no compromise in the work, no muting of protest," yet the show still managed to have an agreeable message of maintaining joy and humor "amidst the terror, chaos and inhumanity" of modern life.

Saying of the "slickly liberal" show, "it ain't necessarily art," Joseph Mazo of *Women's Wear Daily* wondered if the message was relevant anymore: "It is a slick, loud, joyous commercial, but do we really need to be sold on the idea that black people are human?" *Time*'s T. E. Kalem (5/8/72) said it was "the kind of show at which you want to blow kisses."

Original cast: Polydor PD 6013.

1973

A Little Night Music (Sondheim). A Tony winner. See Act One (1973) for details.

1974

Raisin (Judd Woldin, Robert Brittan). A Tony winner. See Act One (1974) for details.

1975

The Wiz (Charlie Smalls). A Tony winner. See Act One (1975) for details.

1976

Bubbling Brown Sugar (Various composers). Opened March 2, 1976. Cast: **Vernon Washington, Avon Long, Josephine Premice, Vivian Reed, Ethel Beatty, Carolyn Byrd.**

This sparkling revue of music from the heyday of the hot Harlem nightspots featured Washington's rendering of Bill "Bojangles" Robinson's tap style while others brought back fond memories of Duke Ellington, Fats Waller, Eubie Blake, and many more great composers.

There were over forty songs in the show, but only sixteen made it to the cast album, among them: "Honeysuckle Rose," "Swing Low, Sweet Chariot," "Sophisticated Lady," "Stormy Monday Blues," "Stompin' at the Savoy," "It Don't Mean a Thing (if It Ain't Got That Swing)," "His Eye Is on the Sparrow," "God Bless the Child," and "Sweet Georgia Brown."

"There is much that is technically wrong with the musical," opined Martin Gottfried in the *Post*, "but there's one thing that's technically perfect — it's terrific." Clive Barnes of the *Times* noted that "what really gets it bubbling is some of the most likable and lovable music around [and] performances that take off with the noise, speed and dazzle of the Concorde."

Original cast: H&L Records HL-69011. Reissued: Amherst AMH 53310. London's 1977 cast with Billy Daniels and Elaine Delmar: E/Pye NSPD-504 (a double set with more songs than the original, but hard to find).

1977

Annie (Strouse, Charnin). A Tony winner. See Act One (1977) for details.

1978

Ain't Misbehavin' (Waller, Maltby). A Tony winner. See Act One (1978) for details.

1979

Sweeney Todd (Sondheim). A Tony winner. See Act One (1979) for details.

1980

Evita (Webber, Rice). A Tony winner. See Act One (1980) for details.

1981

Lena Horne: The Lady and Her Music Live on Broadway (Various composers). Opened May 12, 1981. Cast: Lena Horne.

More of a retrospective concert than a book musical, the show largely consists of the great Lena Horne singing her repertoire of hit songs and, in between, regaling the audience with stories from her life — most memorable being her battles in Hollywood trying to be taken seriously as an actress (she lost the role of Julie in *Show Boat* to Ava Gardner, whose voice had to be dubbed by someone else).

For anyone of a certain age, the collection of songs is a marvel: "Stormy Weather," "The Lady Is a Tramp," "Push De Button," "Bewitched, Bothered and Bewildered," "Surrey With the Fringe on Top," "From This Moment On," "Where or When," "Copper Colored Gal," "Raisin' the Rent," "I'm Glad There Is You," "I Want to Be Happy," "Can't Help Lovin' Dat Man" and many more provide overwhelming evidence of her vast, underused talent.

As John McClain wrote in his review of her Broadway show *Jamaica* [Act Five] for the New York *Journal-American* (9/1/57), "There are varying degrees of worship for Lena Horne, from the sublime to the ecstatic." This recording shows why.

Original cast: Qwest Records QWE 2Q5 3597.

1982

Dreamgirls (Henry Krieger, Tom Eyen). Opened December 20, 1981. Cast: Sheryl Lee Ralph, Loretta Devine, Jennifer Holliday, Deborah Burrell, Vanessa Bell, Tenita Jordan, Obba Babatunde, Ben Harney, Brenda Pressley, Cleavant Derricks.

This is the story of a Supremes-like girl group called the Dreams (Ralph, Devine, Holliday) as they go from poverty to the top of the charts and the inevitable breakup. *Dreamgirls* is filled with great early-Sixties style rhythm and blues, plus standout performances (Harney, Holliday, and Derricks all won Tonys); *Time* especially

singled out Holliday's "devastating vocal firepower," while praising the trio's "impeccable ensemble precision and delightful brio."
As for the show: "What is palpably dazzling merges imperceptibly
with razzle-dazzle."[2] Tom Eyen's libretto also received a Tony.

The score (not all of which was recorded) includes: "Move
(You're Steppin' on My Heart)," "Fake Your Way to the Top,"
"Steppin' to the Bad Side," "When I First Saw You," "The
Rap," "And I'm Telling You I'm Not Going."

Original cast: Geffen L5 2007.

1983

Cats (Webber, Eliot). A Tony winner. See Act One (1983) for
details.

1984

Sunday in the Park With George (Sondheim). A Circle Award
and Pulitzer Prize winner. See Act Two (1983-1984) for details.

1985

West Side Story (Leonard Bernstein, Stephen Sondheim). Studio
cast: Kiri Te Kanawa, José Carreras, Kurt Ollmann, Tatiana Troy-
anos.

The original *West Side Story* [Act Five] opened 28 years earlier in
1957 and had been recorded many times, both vocally and instrumentally. What made this one unique was the carefully selected
group of opera singers (with actors hired for the spoken parts) and
the participation of Bernstein himself as conductor, the first time he
had ever conducted the score.

While Carreras has the wrong accent for the role of Tony, this
full-length studio recording is in every other way an exciting
achievement. As with *Company* in 1970, a documentary film was
made of the recording sessions, directed by Christopher Swann for
the BBC and titled *Bernstein Conducts West Side Story*. Only when
one hears producer John McClure call for "Take 29" on one number, and "Take 75" on another, does the perfectionism and the
strain of making a recording of a musical become fully comprehen-
sible — and most shows do it in a single day.

After Bernstein's death in 1990, the superlatives rolled in. Michael Walsh wrote in *Time* that he was "the signal musical figure of his age, at once the best, the brightest and the most exasperating," and termed *West Side Story* "still the greatest music-theater piece written by an American."[3] *Newsweek*'s Katrine Ames went even further, calling Bernstein "the greatest figure in the history of American music."[4] History may well settle on his being the greatest conductor — first standing in front of the New York Philharmonic at the age of 25 — and the most charismatic educator of young people. *West Side Story* will certainly remain his finest theatrical legacy.

Studio cast: Deutsche Grammophon 415253-1/4.

1986

Follies in Concert (Sondheim). Performances on September 6 and 7, 1985. Cast: Barbara Cook, Betty Comden, Adolph Green, Lee Remick, Mandy Patinkin, Licia Albanese, George Hearn, Phyllis Newman, Carol Burnett, Elaine Stritch.

Follies was a gloriously brilliant flop when it first appeared in 1971, though its score rated a Tony [Act One, 1972]. It was still so well thought of and talked about more than a decade later, and the people involved with it so disliked the original cast album on Capitol, that the need for a revival and an excuse to rerecord it came together not in a full-scale production but in the atmosphere of a benefit concert. Once it was announced, all 5,500 tickets for its two performances sold out in less than three hours. And it produced, at long last, a full-length album of one of the best scores in Broadway's history.

Concert cast: RCA HBC2-7128. (Also included is Sondheim's background music for the 1974 French film *Stavisky*.)

1987

Les Misérables (Schönberg, Boublil, Knetzmer). A Tony winner. See Act One (1987) for details.

1988

Into the Woods (Sondheim). Its score won a Tony. See Act One (1988) for details.

1989

Jerome Robbins' Broadway (Various composers). A Tony winner. See Act One (1989) for details.

1990

Les Misérables (Schönberg, Boublil, Knetzmer). International studio cast: Gary Morris as Jean Valjean, Philip Quast as Javert, Debbie Byrne as Fantine, Kaho Shimada as Eponine, Michael Ball as Marius, Tracy Shayne as Cosette, Barry James as Thenardier, and Gay Soper as Madame Thenardier.

Neither the London nor the Broadway recordings, long as they are, contain the complete score. Following the worldwide success of the musical, the need for a full recording became obvious but also posed an enormous logistics problem for producer David Caddick.

The Philharmonia Orchestra of London (conducted by Martin Koch) was recorded in London. Then Caddick and his crew, tapes in hand, began a multinational trek to record the stars from a number of *Les Misérables* companies. Morris, for example, had followed Colm Wilkinson for six months on Broadway and, being a country-western singer as well as an opera star, was found in Nashville; others came from Australia and even Tokyo. (Shimada's performance is the most remarkable in that she sings phonetically in a language she cannot speak, yet comes across as being fluent in English.) The result was released on three CDs, three cassettes, or four records, along with a complete libretto booklet.

This recording, as with some previous Grammy winners noted above — *Follies in Concert*, *West Side Story*, and *Lena Horne: The Lady and Her Music* — redefines the term "original cast"; not only did the show's *original* Broadway cast win a Grammy in 1987, but this carefully selected studio cast and orchestra never performed together as a unit, not even in the studio.

(As it won in 1991, the same year that a Grammy went to the late Roy Orbison for a song originally recorded 27 years earlier and for a recording of it made in 1988, it becomes clear that anything is possible at the Grammy Awards.)

The category name for a Broadway Grammy has now evolved to Musical Show Album. Whatever one's definition, this remains an exciting listening experience, and the only complete recording.

Relativity/First Night Records: 88561-1027-4.

REFERENCE NOTES

1. *Newsletter On Intellectual Freedom*, American Library Association. May, 1991 (volume XL, number 3), p. 79.

2. *Time*, January 4, 1982.

3. *Time*, October 29, 1990.

4. *Newsweek*, October 29, 1990.

Act Five:
A Musical World

America's greatest original contribution to the theater is the musical, yet the genre is too often dismissed as escapist entertainment.

—Joanne Gordon[1]

The musicals that follow did not win major awards, though their creators and performers often did. It is not a comprehensive listing, by far. There were thousands to choose from and no book can keep up with the annual influx of new shows.

The musicals in Act Five have been chosen either for their historical importance, their entertainment value, the quality of their performances, their availability, or all of the above. (And a few simply because I like them.) Some are from Off-Broadway. Some are from London's West End. There are book musicals, revues, revivals, sequels, studio casts, an opera, old-fashioned and new-fangled musicals.

There are some flops too, because sometimes, for more reasons than you can wave a baton at, a musical will work better on a home stereo system than it did on the stage. (And vice versa.) They span the entire history of the genre, from Cohan and Kern to Sondheim and Lloyd Webber, from pure escapism to social relevance. All are worth listening to.

[The musical] is a new thing, of course. And I would have to agree with the musical haters that there is much that is awkward, and much that is cheap. . . . But there is no reason why musicals are not suited to "ideas" and to "visions" as well as to 'entertainment.'"

—lyricist Tom Jones[2]

131

The Act (John Kander, Fred Ebb). Opened October 29, 1977. Cast: Liza Minnelli, Roger Minami, Gayle Crofoot.

This is virtually a one-woman show as Liza belts out one show-stopping song after another. There was controversy at the time when it was learned that two of her numbers were prerecorded and lip-synced on stage, but even a dynamo like Minnelli needs a rest now and then. She won a 1978 Tony though the musical played only 233 times.

The songs, revolving around the character of nightclub singer Michelle Craig as she does her show and conjures up memories of her life, loves, and career, include: "Shine It On," "Bobo's," "Turning (Shaker Hymn)," "Arthur in the Afternoon," "City Lights" (a city girl's hilarious response to life on a farm), "Hot Enough for You?" and "My Own Space."

Original cast: DRG Records DRG 6101.

Annie Get Your Gun (Irving Berlin). Opened May 17, 1946. Cast: Ethel Merman, Ray Middleton, John Garth III.

"You Can't Get a Man With a Gun," sings Merman (as sharp-shooter Annie Oakley), and she certainly wasn't making much progress in catching fellow shootist Frank Butler (Middleton) by proclaiming, "Anything You Can Do (I Can Do Better)." But, heck, she was only "Doin' What Comes Natur'lly," and eventually hit the bullseye of his heart.

This is Berlin's best stage musical, with the songs evolving naturally from the characters and story. Other numbers: "I'm an Indian Too," "They Say It's Wonderful," "I Got Lost in His Arms," "I Got the Sun in the Morning," "My Defenses Are Down," "The Girl That I Marry," and that actors' anthem, "(There's No Business Like) Show Business." Rip-roaring fun.

Original cast: Decca DL79018. Studio cast of Kim Criswell and Thomas Hampson (1991): EMI 4DQ54206.

Lincoln Center's 1966 revival with Merman, Bruce Yarnell, Benay Venuta and Jerry Orbach: RCA LSO-1124 RE (this has more songs than the original cast album, including: "Colonel Buffalo Bill," "I'm a Bad, Bad Man," and "An Old Fashioned Wedding").

MGM's 1958 film cast with Betty Hutton and Howard Keel:

MGM E-3227 (M); this includes Berlin's film score for *Easter Parade*.

Anyone Can Whistle (Stephen Sondheim). Opened April 4, 1964. Cast: Angela Lansbury, Harry Guardino, Lee Remick.

Here was a show that looked as if it might run forever. Norman Nadel in the *World-Telegram* found it full of "breath-taking surprises," lyrics that were "more clever than the spoken dialogue," and said he would like to spend a month just hurling roses at the theater to express his thanks. The *Journal-American*'s John McClain thought "the show would seem to be a sure-pop success."

The show closed after nine performances.

Its quick demise was assisted by Howard Taubman's review in the *The New York Times* that berated the creators for "the sloppiness of the book and the lack of laughter in the lines." Blasting the show as "a concept weighed down by its own crudity," Taubman complained, "They have taken an idea with possibilities and have pounded it into a pulp." Richard Watts, Jr. of the *New York Post*, was one of the pallbearers, calling the show "ponderously heavy-handed and clumsily vague," and saying Sondheim's score "suffered from the composer's determination to escape any accusation of giving the audience a good, lively tune."

Though it closed somewhat prematurely, Sondheim's terrific and innovative score is still talked about today. The story had Lansbury, as mayor of a town going bankrupt ("Me and My Town"), luring in tourists by proclaiming a miracle cure took place nearby ("Miracle Song"). Things get complicated when inmates of a local mental home—known as The Cookie Jar—get loose and mingle with the townspeople, with no one able to tell the two groups apart. This inspired a brilliant 13-minute number called "Simple" in which a prospective inmate (Guardino) passes himself off as a visiting psychiatrist and proceeds to shake up everyone's preconceived notions about themselves and life.

Other highlights: "Anyone Can Whistle" (Remick), "Everybody Says Don't" (Guardino), "See What It Gets You" (Remick).

Original cast: Columbia S 32608.

Anything Goes (Cole Porter). Opened November 21, 1934. Cast: Ethel Merman, Jack Whiting, The Foursome, Jeanne Aubert.

Sailing to Europe aboard the ocean liner *S. S. American* are, among others, an exevangelist turned nightclub singer named Reno Sweeney, Public Enemy #13 Moonface Martin and his moll, several upper crust swells, and Billy Crocker, there to break up a romance so he can get the girl. To that end Billy dons a variety of disguises and accents before everyone gets sorted out and celebrity Moonface is ignominiously dumped from the Public Enemy list. Book writers Howard Lindsay and Russel Crouse would go on to win Tonys for *The Sound of Music* [Act One, 1960].

It should be remembered that musical plots of the 1930s made up for their lack of depth by substituting frenzied activity; had there been television in 1934, this would have been a great sitcom. Of the 1987 revival, *Time*'s William A. Henry III (November 27, 1987) called the storyline "sweetly silly" and "still so stale and inane that it wheezes of summer stock." The music is what counts.

This is one of Porter's best scores (it was started before there was a script and finished while sailing to America on the *Ile de France*). It includes the saucy title song, plus: "I Get a Kick Out of You," "All Through the Night," the gospel-flavored "Blow, Gabriel, Blow," "The Gypsy in Me," and "You're the Top."

(The lyric of the latter demonstrates how cultural attitudes change. This sung list of superlatives that ranges from the Mona Lisa's smile to Shakespeare's sonnets includes the phrase "You're Mickey Mouse," seen in 1934 as high praise indeed. By the 1960s, however, to label someone or something with the same name was to imply junky cheapness. Today, with Mickey himself over 50 years of age and his memorabilia worth a great deal of money, the phrase takes on a new, venerable meaning.)

Original cast (taken from various individual recordings over the years and incomplete): Smithsonian American Musical Theater Series DPM1-0284 R007.

Revival cast of 1962 with Hal Linden, Eileen Rodgers, and Kenneth Mars: Epic Footlight Series FLS 15100. The revival interpolated songs from other Porter shows, the best being: "It's Delovely," "Friendship," and "Let's Misbehave." The title tune contains a terrific tap dance routine by the large chorus.

Revival cast of 1987 with Patti LuPone, Howard McGillin, and Bill McCutcheon: RCA 7769-4-RC. McCutcheon won a Tony as featured actor, LuPone and McGillin were nominated, and the show won Best Revival. The score also added Porter's "Easy to Love" from the 1936 film *Born to Dance*. It too has a tap routine during the title tune.

Studio cast of 1989 with Kim Criswell, Cris Groenendaal, Jack Gilford, mezzo-soprano Frederica von Stade: EMI/Angel 4DS 49848. Opera singers who venture into musicals generally overpower the material; they can't sell a song the way Broadway belters can. In this case, they tend to make Porter sound like Gilbert and Sullivan, particularly in the choral arrangements and von Stade's solos. There is no denying the quality of the singing, but would opera lovers want to hear Carol Channing do *Tosca*?

The advantage of this 1989 recording—aside from being the latest and thus most available—is two-fold: It reproduces the original score in its entirety, including the little known "Where Are the Men?" and "What a Joy to Be Young," plus it includes as an appendix three additional songs that were dropped from the original show: "There's No Cure Like Travel," "Waltz Down the Aisle," and the delightfully euphemistic ode to Catharine of Russia, "Kate the Great" (dropped because Ethel Merman refused to sing the double-meaning lyrics). An extra bonus is Criswell's rendering of "Buddy, Beware," a Porterish anthem not unlike Rodgers and Hart's "The Lady Is a Tramp."

The Apple Tree (Jerry Bock, Sheldon Harnick). Opened October 16, 1966. Cast: Barbara Harris, Alan Alda, Larry Blyden.

One can almost hear the TV ads: "Not one, not two, but three, THREE plays in one!" Divided into three parts, *The Apple Tree* does indeed have three entirely unconnected stories to tell, but using the same cast. The sources ranged from Mark Twain (*The Diary of Adam and Eve*), Frank Stockton (*The Lady or the Tiger?*, in which a prisoner must choose his fate behind one of two identical doors, kind of like an early quiz show), and Jules Feiffer (*Passionella*, which modernizes Cinderella by magically turning a female chimney sweep into a rich, sexy movie star—but only in the hours between the Evening News and the Late Late Show).

The versatile Barbara Harris played the temptress in each story. (Said Richard P. Cooke in *The Wall Street Journal*, "Like Woman herself, Miss Harris' personalities and talents seem endless.") Alan Alda, following in his father's musical footsteps [Act One, 1951], does a creditable job with "Eve," "Beautiful, Beautiful World," "It's a Fish" (Adam's first impressions of a baby), "Forbidden Love," and "You Are Not Real." Harris has some crowd pleasers too: "Here in Eden," "Feelings," "What Makes Me Love Him," "Gorgeous," and "Wealth."

Alda was nominated for a Tony while Harris won one as best actress in a musical (1967).

Original cast: Columbia KOS 3020.

Assassins (Stephen Sondheim). Opened Off-Broadway January 27, 1991. Cast: Victor Garber as John Wilkes Booth, Terrence Mann as Leon Czolgosz, Patrick Cassidy as the Balladeer, Jonathan Hadary as Charles Guiteau, Eddie Korbich as Giuseppe Zangara, Greg Germann as John Hinckley, Lee Wilkof as Samuel Byck, Annie Golden as Lynette Fromme, Debra Monk as Sara Jane Moore, and Jace Alexander as Lee Harvey Oswald.

No boy-meets-girl love story for this musical. No stalwart hero or simpering ingénue to touch our hearts. No diverting chorus girls or boys. Absolutely no one to use as a role model. Just warped minds and broken-mirror images of the American political, social, and mental landscape whose shards pierce out collective complacence with each reverberating gunshot.

Assassins is a show that not only turns musical conventions inside out, but also questions our notions of what can and cannot be musicalized. A show that leaps acorss all limiting boundaries (including, some would say, that of good taste and propriety), *Assassins* brings to stunning life a group of successful and would-be killers of presidents to tell their stories. A more pathetic, deranged bunch of life's losers cannot be found on any musical stage.

The cavalcade of criminals runs through the dark underside of the American consciousness like a sewer beneath a great city: Booth, **slayer of Abraham Lincoln**; Czolgosz, who gunned down William McKinley; Guiteau, who killed James Garfield; Oswald, assassin of John F. Kennedy (there are no labyrinthine conspiracy theories here); Zangara, who aimed at Franklin Roosevelt but murdered the mayor of Chicago instead); Byck, would-be killer of Richard Nixon; Moore and Fromme, inept attackers of Gerald Ford; and Hinckley, who thought actress Jodie Foster would love him if he shot Ronald Reagan.

As repugnant as the subject matter appears — and most critics were aghast at it — and despite whatever preconceptions one may have before hearing it, the actuality is entirely unexpected: a lively, tuneful, literate score with lyrics both brilliant and disturbing, its musical motifs encompassing nearly the whole panorama of popular music over the past 125 years, from Civil War folk ballads and Sousa marches to hymns and a soft-rock lament worthy of an acned teenager.

On stage the music was aided and abetted by John Weidman's dark and frequently funny libretto that has the assassins gather first at a carnival's shooting gallery — hit a president, win a prize! Moore and Fromme meet each other in a park and discuss fashion and Charles Manson; Fromme and Hinckley duet on a twisted love song to Manson and Jodie Foster; Booth and the others appear in the Texas School Book Depository to urge Oswald to turn his impotent loser's rage onto Kennedy (a chilling dialogue scene reproduced on the recording).

Musical numbers: "Everybody's Got the Right," "The Ballad of Booth," "How I Saved Roosevelt," "Gun Song," "The Ballad of Czolgosz," "Unworthy of Your Love," "The Ballad of Guiteau," and "Another National Anthem."

It is not enough, of course, to be daring. One also has to accomplish the nearly impossible — to be brilliantly daring — and this Sondheim and Weidman achieved, creating Off-Broadway what may yet come to be viewed as a landmark musical.

At first, the concept was to cover all of history's assassins, back to Brutus, but the final version — with sharper impact — narrowed the focus to America's peculiar stalkers of presidents and the society from which they sprang. It became a musical of American history, as viewed from the unsettling perspective of its most alienated and disaffected villains. From the creaking of Guiteau's body on the gallows to the hum of the electric chair charring Zangara, *Assassins* is a musical like no other; love it or hate it, it is unforgettable.

Original cast: RCA 60737-4-RC. John Weidman's book (with Sondheim's lyrics) is published by Theatre Communications Group.

Babes in Arms (Richard Rodgers, Lorenz Hart). Opened April 14, 1937. Cast: Alfred Drake, Mitzi Green, Robert Rounseville, Wynn Murray, Dan Dailey.

A group of exvaudevillians go on a road tour, leaving their kids behind. These born-in-a-trunk troupers resent it and, to avoid being sent to a work farm, band together to put on their own show, proving that they are no longer babes in arms.

Rodgers and Hart provided Broadway with a fresh, snappy, youth-oriented score that included the lovely "Where or When" (so far, the best déjà vu song ever written), the hilarious "Way Out West," the unabashed "The Lady Is a Tramp," plus "Johnny One Note," "My Funny Valentine," and that back-handed ballad, "I Wish I Were in Love Again."

The original cast did not make a recording.

A superb 1951 studio cast album stars Mary Martin, Jack Cassidy, and Mardi Bayne: Columbia Special Products (reissue) AOS 2570.

A 1990 studio cast of Judy Blazer, Gregg Edelman, Judy Kaye, and Donna Kane with the New Jersey Symphony Orchestra is an equal delight: New World Records NW386-4. This one has the added pleasure of Rodgers' ballet music.

(The 1939 film with Judy Garland and Mickey Rooney used only two of the original songs and ends with an embarrassing blackface number. Meanwhile, it jettisoned from the original a more honest plot line of a would-be producer trying to fire two black performers because they were "too black." The film is a perfect example of the old adage, "If it ain't broke, don't fix it!")

Baby (David Shire, Richard Maltby, Jr.). Opened December 4, 1983. Cast: Liz Callaway, Todd Graff, James Congdon, Catherine Cox, Beth Fowler, Martin Vidnovic.

Love, couples, careers, relationships, marriage, pregnancy, and parenthood in the 1980s, all examined in a lively, funny, contemporary, and contemplative score.

The focus is on three couples. The college-age duo (Callaway and Graff) wonder about the advisability of marriage even with a baby on the way. The somewhat older couple (Cox and Vidnovic) are struggling with infertility, complete with elaborately arranged and cumbersome trysts in hope of finding a solution ("The Plaza Song," "Romance"). The more settled couple (Fowler and Congdon), in their early 40s, already have three grown kids when a fourth unexpectedly starts to develop.

Richard Schickel in *Time* (December 19, 1983) called *Baby* "an entrancing entertainment show," adding that Shire's music "is alive and kicking and often whimsically satirical of what seems to be the entire range of contemporary pop styles. The lyrics by Richard Maltby, Jr. are intricate without being show-offy." The overall effect "succeeds in making you feel good without making you feel stupid."

It was that same feel good aspect that annoyed *Newsweek*'s Jack Kroll (December 19, 1983) who complained the show was "as upbeat as a toddler's grin" and would have benefited from "more guts and grit." The show was nominated for seven Tonys.

Songs include: "What Could Be Better?" "I Want It All," "Fatherhood Blues," "I Chose Right," "The Story Goes On," "The Ladies Singing Their Song" (a delightful look at women discussing their pregnancies), "Patterns," "Easier to Love," "Two People in Love," "And What if We Had Loved Like That?"

Original cast: Polydor 821 593-4 Y-1.

Barnum (Cy Coleman, Michael Stewart). Opened April 30, 1980. Cast: Jim Dale, Glenn Close, Marianne Tatum, Terri White.

The life of master showman, con artist, and politician Phineas Taylor Barnum presented in a circus-like atmosphere complete with a ringmaster, jugglers, clowns, and — not noticeable on the recording — Barnum himself walking a tightrope while singing. This is a lively show that won Jim Dale a Tony as best actor and Close a nomination as his wife (she's one of the few film stars not noted for musicals who actually displays a marvelous singing voice on stage).

Songs: "There Is a Sucker Born Ev'ry Minute," "The Colors of My Life," "I Like Your Style," "Come Follow the Band,"

"Black and White," "The Prince of Humbug," "Join the Circus."

Original cast: CBS JST 36576. London cast with Michael Crawford and Deborah Grant: E/Air Records CDL-1348 (S).

Bells Are Ringing (Jule Styne, Betty Comden, Adolph Green). Opened November 29, 1956. Cast: Judy Holliday, Sydney Chaplin, Jean Stapleton, Eddie Lawrence, George Irving, Peter Gennaro.

Is it a crime, asked the perpetually optimistic Holliday, to start the day with a song? She had audiences answering with a resounding "No way!" after they had seen this tale of an answering service operator (the firm is called Susanswerphone) who not only takes messages (in a variety of voices) but listens in on conversations and helps straighten out the lives of her clients. She finds love with Sydney Chaplin in the bargain.

The big hit was "The Party's Over," but the score also includes: "It's a Perfect Relationship," "On My Own," "It's a Simple Little System," "Is It a Crime?" "I Met a Girl," "I'm Going Back," and "Just in Time." Both stars won Tonys.

The 1960 film, directed by Vincente Minnelli, starred Holliday, Dean Martin, Eddie Foy, Jr., Jean Stapleton, Frank Gorshin, and Fred Clark. The title song and a few others were dropped. New songs included: "Do It Yourself," and "Better Than a Dream."

Original cast: Columbia ST2006. Film: Capitol C4-92060.

Berlin to Broadway With Kurt Weill (Various lyricists include Alan Jay Lerner, Ogden Nash, Marc Blitzstein, Bertold Brecht, Langston Hughes, Ira Gershwin, and Maxwell Anderson.) Opened October 1, 1972. Cast: Margery Cohen, Ken Kercheval, Judy Lander, Jerry Lanning, Hal Watters.

The German-born Weill and his wife Lotte Lenya were forced by the Nazis to flee Berlin in 1933; not only was Weill half Jewish, his shows with Bertold Brecht were suspiciously intellectual (his music was banned in the Reich and the scores were publicly burned). They made it from France to America in 1935 where Weill spent the rest of his life creating original and startling music for the theater.

This loving revue of his music takes selections from *The Threepenny Opera* (including "Mack the Knife"), *Happy End*

("Bilbao Song," "Mandalay Song," "Surabaya Johnny"), *The Rise and Fall of the City of Mahagonny, Johnny Johnson, Street Scene, Knickerbocker Holiday* (in which Walter Huston sang "September Song," and Maxwell Anderson defined his fellow citizens in "How Can You Tell an American?"), *Love Life* ("Progress"), and *One Touch of Venus*, including two of that show's favorites: "That's Him," and perhaps the best love song ever, inspired by a line of Shakespeare's, "Speak Low (When You Speak Love)."
Original cast: Paramount Records (double set) PAS-4000.

The Best Little Whorehouse in Texas (Carol Hall). Opened June 19, 1978. Cast: Carlin Glynn, Delores Hall, Jay Garner, Henderson Forsythe, Susan Mansur, Clint Allman.

> "Larry, Larry, Larry. . . . Do you know the odds against getting a play to Broadway? A million to one. Perhaps more. . . . Dear God. A musical. A musical. A musical. A *musical*!" He moaned and looked stricken and raised his head to regard me with wounded eyes.
>
> —Larry L. King and his agent[3]

This is just as rowdy and raunchy as the title suggests, with a toe-tapping, hand-clapping, country-western score to match. Glynn is Miss Mona, madam of the Chicken Ranch (during the Depression, patrons often paid with poultry). Her establishment ("A Lil' Ole Bitty Pissant Country Place") has come under the glaring lights of a TV muckraker ("Texas Has a Whorehouse in It"). After generations of honest service to the community, political hypocrisy is now going to close her down ("The Sidestep" is a hilarious look at news conferences with Jay Garner as a slippery governor).

Christopher Sharp of *Women's Wear Daily* termed it "more fun than a beer-toting hayride at a Mardi Gras," and a show "located in that vast desert between respectability and profanity." Clive Barnes said it was "a fun new musical," and assured *Post* readers that its "pleasures are surprisingly innocent [and] cheerfully inoffensive." Douglas Watt at the *Daily News* found this bit of bawdry so "genial" in its "cheerful disregard for reality," that "I'm only surprised they didn't sell Girl Scout cookies in the lobby."

Other standout numbers: "20 Fans," "Twenty-Four Hours of

Lovin'," "Doatsy Mae," "The Aggie Song," "The Bus From Amarillo," "No Lies," "Hard Candy Christmas." Glynn and Forsythe both won Tonys as featured performers in a musical.

Also recommended is Larry L. King's book about the show, *The Whorehouse Papers* (Viking Press, 1982).

The 1982 movie version with Burt Reynolds and Dolly Parton was a disaster, dropping many of the songs, rewriting others, and adding new, ineffectual ones composed by Parton. Those who have seen only the movie don't know what a good time they're missing.

Original cast: MCA MCA-3049.

Black and Blue (Various composers). Opened January 26, 1989. Cast: Ruth Brown (a Tony winner), Linda Hopkins, Carrie Smith.

Not quite a book musical but far more than a revue, *Black and Blue* uses classic blues songs as a framework for displaying the song and dance heritage left by some of the greatest black performers in America. The three singing stars are joined by a company of outstanding pit musicians and hoofers — the show required the talents of four choreographers, and all won Tonys.

The vintage songs include: "I'm a Woman," "St. Louis Blues," "After You're Gone," "If I Can't Sell It, I'll Keep Sittin' on It" (the opening verse makes it clear she means an antique chair), "I Want a Big Butter and Egg Man," "Stompin' at the Savoy," "I've Got a Right to Sing the Blues," Duke Ellington's "Black and Tan Fantasy," "Am I Blue?" "Body and Soul," "I Can't Give You Anything But Love," and more.

Original cast: DRG Records SBLC 19001.

Bring Back Birdie (Charles Strouse, Lee Adams). Opened March 5, 1981. Cast: Chita Rivera, Donald O'Connor, Maria Karnilova, Maurice Hines, Marcel Forestieri.

When *Bye Bye Birdie* ended, Albert Peterson proposed to his long-suffering secretary Rose and gave up show business for a career as an English teacher [Act One, 1961].

Now it's twenty years later and Conrad Birdie, who has long since disappeared, is wanted for a TV retrospective. The roar of the greasepaint is loud and soon Albert is on the hunt for the missing rock star, Rose is fit to burst, their daughter has joined a commune, and their son is in a punk rock band. Where Paul Lynde once sang "(What's the Matter with) Kids?" the kids in the sequel sing, "When Will Grown-Ups Grow Up?"

The script is by Michael Stewart; Chita Rivera repeats her role as Rose while O'Connor takes Dick Van Dyke's place as Albert without missing a beat. Forestieri does a splendid Elvis imitation ("You Can Never Go Back"), and the score sparkles with the same energy and style that made the original a smash hit. Chita Rivera was nominated for a Tony.

Other highlights include Rivera's wild country-western number, "A Man Worth Fightin' For," "I Like What I Do," "Twenty Happy Years," "Back in Show Biz Again," "Middle Age Blues," "There's a Brand New Beat in Heaven," "Well, I'm Not!" and "I Love 'Em All" (sung in a 1920s' style by Karnilova as Albert's mother). This book's biggest flop, it played only four times.

Original cast: Original Cast Records OC 8132.

Camelot (Alan Jay Lerner, Frederick Loewe). Opened December 3, 1960. Cast: Richard Burton (Tony winner), Julie Andrews (Tony nominee), Robert Goulet, Roddy McDowall.

This story of King Arthur, Queen Guenevere, Lancelot, Merlin the magician, and the Knights of the Round Table is one of Lerner and Loewe's most memorable scores (though it was not nominated for a Tony as either Best Musical or Best Score).

The songs range from humorous to romantic, lusty to devilish: "I Wonder What the King Is Doing Tonight," "The Simple Joys of Maidenhood," "Follow Me," "The Lusty Month of May," "C'est Moi" (by far the most egocentric lyric ever written for a character), "Then You May Take Me to the Fair," "If Ever I Would Leave You," "The Seven Deadly Virtues," "What Do the Simple Folk Do?" "Fie on Goodness!" and the great narrative number, "Guenevere."

The 1967 film with Vanessa Redgrave and Richard Harris tried to be a fantasy with a gloomy, realistic look. It dropped several good songs but is still enjoyable.

Original cast: Columbia OS 2031. Film: Warner Brothers K-3102 (S).

Can-Can (Cole Porter). Opened May 7, 1953. Cast: Lilo, Peter Cookson, Hans Conried, Gwen Verdon (Tony winner).

Cole Porter loved Paris and it shows in this delightful romp about the efforts of French bluenoses to suppress the infamous can-can dance during the roaring 1890s. "It is nothing more or less than our old friend, sex," reported Richard Watts, Jr. in the *Post*, adding that Porter and company "tossed that prized commodity at the customers with bright, humorous, insistent and commendably frank abandon."

John Chapman of the *Daily News* found that "the greatest joy of last evening was a lissome lass with reddish hair and a docked pony-tail coiffure, Miss Gwen Verdon." She had some strong competition: Brooks Atkinson wrote of her costar, "when Lilo takes charge of a song, she raises the temperature of the theatre perceptibly."

Songs include: "Maidens Typical of France," "Never Give Anything Away," "C'est Magnifique," "Live and Let Live," "Montmart," "It's All Right With Me," "Every Man Is a Stupid Man," and, of course, "I Love Paris."

The 1960 film with Frank Sinatra, Shirley MacLaine, Maurice Chevalier, and Louis Jourdan added "You Do Something to Me," "Let's Do It," and "Just One of Those Things" from other Porter shows.

Original cast: Capitol DW 452. Film: Capitol SM-1301. London revival with Donna McKechnie and Milo O'Shea: Virgin Records 2570.

Chicago (John Kander, Fred Ebb). Opened June 3, 1975. Cast: Gwen Verdon, Chita Rivera, Jerry Orbach, Mary McCarty.

It's the 1920s, a time of Prohibition, gangsters, and "All That Jazz," a time when a would-be vaudeville star like Roxie Hart (Verdon) can shoot her lover and ride the tabloid press to stardom, after serving a brief time in jail ("Cell Block Tango"), where among some other "merry murderesses" she meets Velma Kelly (Rivera).

The jazzy, saucy score includes "All I Care About," "We Both Reached for the Gun," "Roxie," "I Can't Do It Alone," "When Velma Takes the Stand," "Razzle Dazzle," and "Class."

Chicago was nominated for 11 Tonys, and set a record of sorts by losing all of them. (It was the year of *A Chorus Line*.)
Original cast: Arista 9005.

Closer Than Ever (David Shire, Richard Maltby, Jr.). Opened November 6, 1989. Cast: Brent Barrett, Sally Mayes, Richard Muenz, Lynne Wintersteller.
A revue of songs old and new from one of the best contemporary composing teams. Many of the numbers are from their Off-Broadway musicals; several were dropped from *Baby* (see above) and given new life here. Stephen Holden of *The New York Times* wrote that their songs "communicate something rarely found in theatre music nowadays: a rich sweeping sense of lives being lived and people changing over time." Maltby's lyrics make the listener's brain feel alive.
Highlights of this double cassette score: "You Want to Be My Friend?" (a woman railing at the man who just dumped her), "The Bear, the Tiger, the Hamster and the Mole" (a biology lesson on actual reproductive habits), "The Sound of Muzak" (beautifully arranged to sound as syrupy as possible), "One of the Good Guys," "Next Time/I Wouldn't Go Back," "Three Friends," "Another Wedding Song" (composed by Shire for his own wedding), and "Life Story" (sung by an ardent feminist upset because her job applications are now being turned down by women who wouldn't *be* in those positions had it not been for *her* early protesting and sacrificing).
Original cast: RCA 60399-4-RG.

Cole (Cole Porter). Opened in London July 2, 1974. Cast: Ray Cornell, Lucy Fenwick, Peter Gale, Julia McKenzie, Bill Kerr, Rod McLennan, Kenneth Nelson, Elizabeth Power, Angela Richards, Una Stubbs.
In the same class as the Fats Waller show, *Ain't Misbehavin'* [Act One, 1978], or *Berlin to Broadway With Kurt Weill* above, *Cole* is a musical biography of one of Broadway's legendary composer/lyricists. Not only are his best (and some of the most overlooked) songs included in this double set, recorded live with an audience, but a narrative helps tie them all together.

Among the numerous songs: "I Love Paris," "You Don't Know Paree," "Take Me Back to Manhattan," "I'm a Gigolo," "Love for Sale," "Down in the Depths (On the 90th Floor)," "Night and Day," "Anything Goes," "I Get a Kick Out of You," "Begin the Beguine," "You Do Something to Me," "It's Delovely," "Let's Misbehave," "At Long Last Love," "In the Still of the Night," "Make It Another Old-Fashioned, Please," "The Leader of a Big-Time Band," "Please Don't Monkey With Broadway," and a host of others.

Original cast: RCA CRL2-5054.

The Cradle Will Rock (Marc Blitzstein). Opened June 15, 1937. Cast: Will Geer, Howard da Silva, Robert Farnsworth, Olive Stanton, Bert Weston, Jules Schmidt, Charles Niemeyer, Edward Fuller, Peggy Coudray, Blanche Collins.

On January 2, 1938, Marc Blitzstein lamented the state of the musical in *The New York Times*, saying that the only way to write for the American musical theater anymore was to "find a new form, one which will work in a new way and yet manage to offend nobody by its newness." It was not the shock of the new so much as the subject matter that first brought his colloquial labor opera to the front page of the paper.

An antiestablishment, pro-worker, Brechtian opera in a year of violent labor/management clashes and actual steel strikes, *Cradle* has the exploited steel workers of Steeltown fighting for a union against miserly capitalist Mr. Mister, who succeeds in unscrupulously getting the press and powerful "citizen liberty committees" on his side; he even hires thugs to plant bombs and blame it on the workers. Orson Welles directed. The producer was John Houseman. Before its New York opening the play won an annual award by the left-wing New Theatre League, a supporter of what critic Brooks Atkinson termed America's "insurgent theatre."

Songs included: "Oh, What a Filthy Night Court," "Mrs. Mister and Reverend Salvation," "The Freedom of the Press," "The Rich," "Art for Art's Sake" (in which a hypocritical artist and composer — Dauber and Yasha — vie for funds by cozying up to rich patrons), "Nickel Under the Foot" (sung by a streetwalker), "Leaflets," and "Joe Worker."

But what happened off-stage was often more dramatic than the show itself. On a Wednesday night that seems to have foreshadowed the 1990 uproar over federal funding of the arts, the show was set to open at the Maxine Elliott Theatre under the auspices of the WPA Federal Theatre Project. Eighteen thousand advance tickets had already been sold. But word came from Washington that afternoon to shut down the production of all WPA-supported events, including plays, operas, concerts, and art exhibits, until at least July.

The stated reason was a need to restructure the WPA in light of an expected 25%-30% cutback in staff. This explanation was not accepted by everyone, and the story on the front page of *The New York Times* for June 17, 1937, was headed:

STEEL STRIKE OPERA
IS PUT OFF BY WPA
Many Among 600 Gathered for
Preview Charge Censorship
Because of 'Radical' Plot.
OFFICIALS DENY ANY CURB.

Uniformed WPA guards (whom Houseman later termed "Cossacks") locked up the sets and costumes. While star Will Geer stood in front of the theater and sang a couple of songs for the restless crowd, a search began for an empty theater not associated with the WPA. One was found twenty blocks away. Cast and audience then walked to the Venice Theatre, a procession that must have startled onlookers.

There, with no sets and no costumes, and with the actors performing from their seats in the audience to avoid giving an "unauthorized" performance on stage, the show went on. The music was supplied by composer Blitzstein, sitting center stage at a piano. Welles later told reporters the performance was "not a political protest, but an artistic one."

The next day at least four sit-down strikes took place in sympathy with the locked-out show, including one by the WPA project's "Negro unit" that was putting on *The Case of Philip Lawrence* at the Lafayette Theatre. Audience members at a Brahms concert re-

mained in their seats afterwards, joining with forty striking performers elsewhere in the theater. Students and faculty at the WPA
Music Project on Park Avenue also staged a sit-down strike, staying
in their building overnight.

Welles and poet Archibald MacLeish flew to Washington to
plead with WPA administrator Harry Hopkins, but to no avail.

Whether the government would ever have put on the show remains a moot question, for Houseman learned that the WPA had
only leased the rights to the play. He quickly raised $1500 to cover
salary costs for two weeks — the money provided by Helen Deutsch
of the Theatre Guild — and soon the play was under private management and open for business as a commercial venture with the top
ticket price being $1.10 (WPA workers got in for 25 cents).

The actors continued singing from their seats for 19 performances.

In December the musical moved to the Mercury Theatre where,
wrote Atkinson, "*The Cradle Will Rock* rocked a great many
things, including the audience." Calling the show "a stirring success," Atkinson praised the "extraordinary versatility" of Blitzstein's music, as well as the "bitterness of his satire, the savagery
of his music and the ingenuity of his craftsmanship. . . . [he] can
write anything from tribal chant to Tin Pan Alley balladry; the piano
keys scatter scorn, impishness and pathos according to the capri-
cious mood of his story."

The critic also noted that the show provided proof "that a theatre
supported by government funds cannot be a free agent when art has
an insurgent political motive."

One final irony: this pro-union opera was composed by a non-
union man. Once the show went commercial, many of the cast had
to join Actors Equity. Blitzstein, the creator of the show, not only
joined Equity with them, but also the Musicians Union and the
Dramatists Guild; he had not previously been a member of any of
them.[4]

Revival cast (1964) with Jerry Orbach, Lauri Peters, Clifford
David, Rita Gardner, Micki Grant, Hal Buckley, and Nancy Andrews: MGM 4289-2-OC (double album).

London cast (1986) with Patti LuPone: That's Entertainment
Records ZC TED 1105 (complete).

Falsettoland (William Finn). Opened June 28, 1990. Cast: Michael Rupert, Stephen Bogardus, Chip Zien, Faith Prince, Danny Gerard, Heather MacRae, Janet Metz.

This is the third part—and therefore the most readily available—of what is commonly known as The Marvin Trilogy, an Off-Broadway creation of composer/lyricist William Finn and director James Lapine (who also directed *Sunday in the Park With George* and *Into the Woods*). All the plays are short—lasting no longer than 70 minutes, stand on their own, and revolve around the sexual reawakening of Marvin: husband, father, homosexual.

Part One came in 1978 and was titled *In Trousers* (available through Original Cast Records; see Appendix A). That episode introduced Marvin and his family and ended with Marvin discovering his capacity for bisexual love.

Part Two, *March of the Falsettos*, had Marvin (Rupert) being divorced by his wife Trina (Alison Fraser) while starting a relationship with a man named Whizzer (Bogardus). The show adroitly recounted their various therapies with Mendel the psychiatrist (Zien), and how the son Jason (James Kushner) came to grips with his unusual extended family ("My Father's a Homo"). Marvin, however, is left alone at the end as Whizzer leaves and Trina marries Mendel.

So far, the shows were a jolly sitcom-like evening of musical theater, and there the trilogy might have ended as a duet of shows. But then came AIDS, and the devastation it wrought gave Finn a new direction and dimension for his characters, and so was born *Falsettoland*.

Rupert, Bogardus and Zien repeated their roles, with Faith Prince as Trina and Danny Gerard as Jason—now about to have his Bar Mitzvah. Whizzer returns and contracts AIDS (which, the play being set in 1981-1982, does not yet have a name, only victims, and so is referred to with nameless dread in "Something Bad Is Happening"). How will Marvin (and Jason, who has grown fond of his father's lover) handle it? With tears and laughter, for Finn never allows his soap opera plot to get sudsy, using his nimble way with a lyric to blunt the pain while making socially significant (or just funny) points. There is life, love, and passion packed into these short, largely through-composed shows.

When *Falsettoland* opened in mid-1990, completing the long-delayed story with a tragic ending, reviews were mixed. Frank Rich of the *Times* called the play "a kaleidoscopic world of comedy and heartbreak," and "an achingly articulate musical [of] jubilance and courage, not defeat." Clive Barnes admitted to his *Post* readers that he had not liked the first two installments and felt that the third trivialized both AIDS and death, though he conceded that the performances transcended the material: "*Falsettoland* may not be worth doing, but it is being done extraordinarily well."

March of the Falsettos, original cast: DRG Records, SBLC 12581. *Falsettoland*, original cast: DRG Records, 12601. Both scores are available in a double CD package: DRG 22600.

The Fantasticks (Tom Jones, Harvey Schmidt). Opened May 3, 1960, Off-Broadway. Cast: Jerry Orbach, Kenneth Nelson, Rita Gardner, William Larsen, Hugh Thomas.

It nearly closed after one night and often played to audiences as few as four. But through pluck, luck, dedication, word of mouth, sacrifices, penny pinching, and the delightful original cast recording, it became the little musical that could.

Based loosely on Edmund Rostand's *Les Romanesques*, it has played continuously for over 30 years in the same cramped, basement theater where it began (but there's now a *Fantasticks* museum above it). The universality of its youthful love story amid parental interference, the blend of innocence and sophistication, and the stark simplicity of the set have never lost their appeal. Songs include: "Much More," "Metaphor," "It Depends on What You Pay," "Soon It's Gonna Rain," "Round and Round" (in which all the cruelty in the world can be shut out just by donning an imperturbable mask), and "Try to Remember."

Original cast: MGM SE-3872 OC. Also recommended is the book by Donald C. Farber and Robert Viagas, *The Amazing Story of The Fantasticks* (Citadel Press, 1991).

Finian's Rainbow (Burton Lane, E. Y. Harburg). Opened January 10, 1947. Cast: Ella Logan, Donald Richards, David Wayne, Lorenzo Fuller, Delores Martin.

Lyricist Harburg, co-composer with Jay Gorney of "Brother, Can You Spare a Dime?" in 1932, liked to put his social conscience into shows. In this one, an Irishman with a pot of gold stolen from a leprechaun buries it as near to Fort Knox as he can, believing it will multiply. But the land where he plants his bullion is the state of Missitucky, in a county ruled by demagogue Billboard Rawkins (who has his racist views turned upside down when the gold's magic turns his skin black).

But except for "Necessity" (about the burdens of poverty), and "When the Idle Poor Become the Idle Rich," the score is a romantic one: "How Are Things in Glocca Morra?" "Look to the Rainbow," "Something Sort of Grandish," "When I'm Not Near the Girl I Love," and "Old Devil Moon" all cast a magical spell on audiences.

The 1968 film by Francis Ford Coppola is an underrated gem, with a wonderful performance by Fred Astaire (in his last musical). Petula Clark and Don Francks costar; their duet on "Old Devil Moon" is purely bewitching.

Original cast: Columbia OS 2080. Film: Warner Brothers BS 2550. The film score contains Brenda Arnau's heartfelt rendering of "Necessity," though the number does not appear in the film itself—a great loss for moviegoers but a treat for record buyers.

Five Guys Named Moe (Various). Opened in London October 12, 1990. Opened on Broadway in March, 1992. London cast: Kenny Andrews, Clarke Peters, Paul J. Medford, Peter Alex Newton, Omar Okai, Dig Wayne, C. Derricks-Carroll.

A celebration/revue of the songs of Louis Jordan, headliner of the Apollo Theatre, and a rhythm-and-blues singer/composer so popular that he was the first to break the color barrier in Las Vegas hotel showrooms. But this is not a biography. It is a party, a festive one with happy, swinging songs whose only reason for existence was to entertain. A wispy plot has five guys named Moe (Big Moe, Little Moe, Four-Eyed Moe, No Moe, and Eat Moe) using Jordan's catalog of hits to give advice to a broken-hearted suitor. And even that was unnecessary: the songs are their own excuse.

Along with the title song, the show features: "Early in the Morning,'' "Brother Beware," "I Like 'em Fat Like That," "Messy Bessy," "Pettin' and Pokin',", "Life is So Peculiar," "I Know What I've Got," "Azure Te," "Safe, Sane and Single," "Push Ka Pi Shee Pie," "Saturday Night Fish Fry," "What's the Use of Gettin' Sober," "If I Had Any Sense I'd Go Back Home," "Dad Gum Your Hide Boy," "Cal'Donia," "Don't Let the Sun Catch You Crying," "Is You Is or Is You Ain't My Baby?" "Choo Choo Ch'Boogie," and the classic, "There Ain't Nobody Here But Us Chickens."

Original London cast: Relatively/First Night Records 88561-1104-4. Broadway Cast: Columbia, CT 52999.

Flora, the Red Menace (John Kander, Fred Ebb). Opened March 29, 1965. Cast: Liza Minnelli, Bob Dishy, Mary Louise Wilson, Cathryn Damon, Robert Kaye.

A musical look back at the Great Depression, Red-baiting, and blacklisting, an era in which innocent Flora Meszaros (Minnelli) loses her job because of her love for a young, idealistic, stuttering Communist named Harry (Dishy) who convinces her to join the party. Oh, and she also socked a cop at a protest rally, a sure sign of radical tendencies. Love does not quite conquer all, but serves as a learning experience in which Flora becomes willing to fight for workers' rights.

Songs: "Unafraid," "All I Need (Is One Good Break)," "Not Every Day of the Week," "Sign Here," "A Quiet Thing," "Dear Love," "Express Yourself," "Sing Happy," "Hello, Waves" (sung by Dishy with a mouthful of pebbles in an attempt to cure his speech impediment).

Appearing in her first Broadway show, Minnelli won a Tony as best actress in a musical, though the show was an 87 performance flop.

Original cast: RCA CBL1-2760.

Off-Broadway 1987 revival cast with Veanne Cox as Flora and Peter Frechette as Harry: That's Entertainment Records 1159. The revival drops some songs but adds one dumped from the original, **"The Kid Herself,"** plus three new ones: "Keepin' It Hot," "Where Did Everybody Go?" and "The Joke"; composer John Kander is the revival's pianist.

Flower Drum Song (Richard Rodgers, Oscar Hammerstein). Opened December 1, 1958. Cast: Miyoshi Umeki, Larry Blyden, Juanita Hall, Ed Kenney, Keye Luke, Pat Suzuki, Jack Soo.

Life in San Francisco's Chinatown is a constant cultural clash as the China-born older generation grows perplexed with the modern attitudes of their American-born offspring. This is especially jarring when a Chinese mail order bride with Old Country values is smuggled in to be the wife of hep-cat Sammy Fong (Blyden). Gene Kelly directed. Blyden and Umeki were nominated for Tonys but lost to their only competitors, Richard Kiley and Gwen Verdon, both in *Redhead* [Act One, 1959].

The easygoing, tuneful score features, "You Are Beautiful," "A Hundred Million Miracles," "I Am Going to Like It Here," "Like a God," "Grant Avenue," "Chop Suey," "Don't Marry Me," "Love Look Away," "Gliding Through My Memories" (sung by Jack Soo, later a costar on TV's *Barney Miller*), and the show's biggest hit, "I Enjoy Being a Girl."

The 1961 film starring Nancy Kwan, James Shigeta, Umeki, Soo, and Hall, was leisurely paced and quite enjoyable; though Kwan's voice was dubbed by B. J. Baker, the riveting and leggy dance routine for "I Enjoy Being a Girl" was all hers.

Original cast: Columbia OL 5350. Film: MCA 37089 (S).

Forbidden Broadway (Various composers). Opened January 15, 1982. Cast: Gerard Alessandrini, Nora Mae Lyng, Fred Barton, Chloe Webb, Bill Carmichael.

This Off-Broadway revue was the brainchild of Gerard Alessandrini and can be wickedly funny as it does not satirize Broadway so much as it skewers it like a shish kebab. Being a long-running, topical revue, the cast and songs are in a constant state of change, making the 1984 and 1990 recordings audio photographs of a few moments in time. But what moments!

Songs on the first cast album include takeoffs on *Evita*, *Fiddler On the Roof*, *Nine*, and *Hello, Dolly!*, parodies of songs by Cole Porter and Gilbert and Sullivan, and perfect impressions of Mary Martin, Ethel Merman, Angela Lansbury, Patti LuPone, Carol Channing and other stars.

Off-Broadway Cast: DRG Records SBLC 12585.

The volume two edition, 1990, is on DRG 12599 featuring a new cast lampooning Stephen Sondheim, Andrew Lloyd Webber, Liza Minnelli, Bob Fosse, Patti LuPone, Chita Rivera, Rita Moreno, George M. Cohan, and *Les Misérables*, among other targets.

George M! (George M. Cohan). Opened April 10, 1968. Cast: Joel Grey, Betty Ann Grove, Jill O'Hara, Bernadette Peters, Loni Ackerman, Jonelle Allen.

The life of George M. Cohan made a star of Joel Grey and briefly revived an interest in the songs that helped create the musical comedy form. It also demonstrated how much Broadway had changed since Cohan's day, for this was the season of *Hair*.

Songs (and snippets of songs) include: "Give My Regards to Broadway," "Forty-Five Minutes From Broadway," "Mary (Mary's a Grand Old Name)," "Yankee Doodle Dandy," "Over There," "Harrigan," "You're a Grand Old Flag," "Musical Comedy Man," "All Aboard for Broadway," "The Belle of the Barber's Ball," "Nellie Kelly I Love You," and "I'd Rather Be Right."

Grey was nominated for a Tony but lost to Jerry Orbach in *Promises, Promises* [Act Four, 1969].

Original cast: Columbia KOS-3200.

Girl Crazy (George and Ira Gershwin). Opened October 14, 1930. Cast: Ethel Merman (her first Broadway show), Ginger Rogers (not yet discovered by Hollywood), Allen Kearns, William Kent, Willie Howard.

The original production made a star of Merman, and playing in the pit orchestra were soon-to-be superstars of swing Gene Krupa, Glenn Miller, and Benny Goodman. What a night of music that must have been!

The boy-meets-girl-while-out-of-his-element story was formulaic but serviceable for the wonderful Gershwin score. A New York playboy (Kearns) is packed off to the family's womanless Arizona ranch — he covers the distance by taxi — to dry out and there meets a cowgirl/postmistress (Rogers), imports some showgirls, and turns the homestead into a dude ranch, complete with gambling and a floorshow headed by brassy Ethel Merman as Frisco Kate. There are the usual romantic complications before various couples get sorted out, and the cab driver (Howard) ends up being elected sheriff.

The 1943 film starring Judy Garland and Mickey Rooney is one of the better adaptations of a Broadway show, though some plot lines were considerably changed.

Songs include: "Bidin' My Time," "Could You Use Me?" "Bronco Busters," "Embraceable You," "Sam and Delilah," "I Got Rhythm," "Boy! What Love Has Done to Me," "Cactus Time," and "But Not for Me."

The original cast was not recorded. An excellent 1951 studio cast is headed by Mary Martin, Louise Carlyle, and Eddie Chappel: Columbia Special Products COS 2560.

The first complete recording of the score—a project of the Library of Congress and Roxbury Recordings—was released in November 1990 and stars Lorna Luft, David Carroll, Judy Blazer, David Garrison, Vicki Lewis, and Frank Gorshin as cabbie Gieber Goldfarb; the CD version comes with a 100-page booklet: Elektra Nonsuch 79250-4.

A lavish 1992 revival dropped ten songs, added other Gershwin hits, and featured a new book and title: *Crazy For You*, which won a Tony. [See Appendix D.]

Golden Boy (Charles Strouse, Lee Adams). Opened October 20, 1964. Cast: Sammy Davis, Jr. (Tony nominee), Paula Wayne, Roy Glenn, Johnny Brown, Billy Daniels, Kenneth Tobey, Louis Gossett.

The musical version of Clifford Odets' 1937 play of a concert violinist who turns to boxing for financial reasons, this update gives young Joe Wellington (Davis) the chance to get out of Harlem's poverty by using his fists. The show chronicles his rise and fall— the latter brought about by unscrupulous management and his misplaced love of a woman (rejection and disillusion cause him to furiously kill a man in the ring, after which the dazed Joe is himself killed in a car wreck).

The songs, both powerful and poignant, include: "Night Song," "Gimme Some," "Stick Around," "Don't Forget 127th Street" (a block party production number, with Davis and Brown ironically enumerating the joys of ghetto living along with their neighbors), "Lorna's Here," "This Is the Life," "While the City Sleeps," "Colorful" (in which Joe explains that while he has been green with inexperience, yellow with fright, and sadly blue, black suits him best), "Can't You See It?" and "No More."

Original cast: Capitol SVAS-2124.

Grease (Jim Jacobs, Warren Casey). Opened February 14, 1972. Cast: Barry Bostwick, Adrienne Barbeau, Carole Demas.

Nominated for seven Tonys, this 1950s-styled rock score was supposed to be a parody, but it sounded so authentic, brought back such nostalgic feelings, that audiences loved it. The show played and played and played until, late in 1979, it broke *Fiddler on the Roof*'s then-record for endurance with 3,243 performances (it finally closed after show number 3,388).

The plot of a boy and girl from opposite sides of the track finding common ground and love was far from new, but the happy, funny, rocking score was a triumph: "Summer Nights," "Those Magic Changes," "Greased Lightnin'" (a rock and roll love song to a souped-up car), "Look at Me, I'm Sandra Dee," "Born to Hand-Jive," and "Beauty School Dropout" all brought back a sound and an era.

The 1978 film starred John Travolta, Olivia Newton-John, Eve Arden, Sid Caesar, Jeff Conaway, and Stockard Channing and filled out the score with some vintage songs, including "Tears On My Pillow," "Hound Dog," and Rodgers and Hart's "Blue Moon."

Original cast: MGM 1SE-34. Film: RSO RS2-4002.

I Can Get It for You Wholesale (Harold Rome). Opened March 22, 1962. Cast: Elliott Gould, Marilyn Cooper, Lillian Roth, Harold Lang, Jack Kruschen, Sheree North, Barbra Streisand.

Based on Jerome Weidman's first novel (1937), the musical tells the story of brash, ambitious shipping clerk Harry Bogen (Gould) who begins his ruthless climb to the top in New York's garment district by selling out his striking coworkers. In time he manages to cheat on his loving girlfriend with a showgirl, betrays his partner, robs his own growing company, and alienates all who ever stood by him. This was not your average musical comedy hero.

The wit, humanity, and luscious melodies of Rome's score helped soften Harry's crookedness, the same way Rodgers and Hart's score for *Pal Joey* helped make a louse palatable [Act Two, 1951-1952].

The songs include: "The Way Things Are," "When Gemini Meets Capricorn," "Momma, Momma," "The Sound of Money," "The Family Way," "Ballad of the Garment Trade," "A Gift Today" (a Bar Mitzvah celebration), "A Funny Thing Happened (on My Way to Love)," and "What's in It for Me?" Newcomer Streisand, as a put-upon secretary, belted out one classic comedy number called "Miss Marmelstein," soared to dramatic heights with the finale, "What Are They Doing to Us Now?" and earned a Tony nomination.

Original cast: Columbia AKOS-2180.

(The book was filmed in 1951 as a nonmusical vehicle for Susan Hayward. To accommodate the star, the character of Harry Bogen was changed to Harriet Boyd, an ambitious dress designer. As a sop to the sensibilities of movie audiences, the scheming Harriet reformed at the end and chose true love and homemaking over greed.)

I Do! I Do! (Tom Jones, Harvey Schmidt). Opened December 5, 1966. Cast: Robert Preston, Mary Martin.

A two character musical based on Jan de Hartog's 1952 Tony-winning play, *The Four Poster*, a big brass bed serving as the centerpiece of both shows. The plot follows the course of a long marriage from the honeymoon ("Goodnight") through spats ("Nobody's Perfect"), parenthood ("Something Has Happened," "Love Isn't Everything," "When the Kids Get Married"), an affair ("The Honeymoon Is Over"), nostalgia ("Where Are the Snows of Yesteryear?"), and an ever-deepening mutual love ("My Cup Runneth Over").

Other memorable songs: "I Love My Wife," "A Well-Known Fact," "Flaming Agnes," "The Father of the Bride," and "What Is a Woman?" Preston won a Tony; Martin lost to Barbara Harris in *The Apple Tree* [see above]. "It is a happy show," wrote Norman

Nadel in the *World Journal Tribune*, "generous with charm and lavish with love."

Original cast: RCA LSO-1128 (reissued on CD and tape in 1990).

I Love My Wife (Cy Coleman, Michael Stewart). Opened April 17, 1977. Cast: Lenny Baker (Tony winner), James Naughton, Ilene Graff, Joanna Gleason.

Mate swapping in the suburbs of Trenton (which, as the score points out, isn't exactly Gomorrah but, hey, they try). The funny foibles of two bored couples discovering that they really are not cut out to be swingers and that they love their spouses after all comes equipped with four onstage musicians and a fantastic musical score that runs the gamut of styles from country-western and jazz to ragtime and good ol' show tunes, with lyrics romantic and tender, raunchy and satiric.

Newsweek (May 2, 1977) dubbed it "an impudent little show," while *Time* (May 2, 1977) called it "a twinkling piece of innocent bawdry" with "thoroughly beguiling tunes and saucily intelligent lyrics."

Songs include: "We're Still Friends," "By Threes," "Love Revolution," "A Mover's Life," "Someone Wonderful I Missed," "Sexually Free," "Lovers on Christmas Eve," "Scream," "Ev'rybody Today Is Turning On" (a brilliantly punny satire on contemporary life), "Married Couple Seeks Married Couple," and "Hey There, Good Times."

Coleman was nominated for a Tony as composer; Michael Stewart was nominated as lyricist and writer; Gene Saks won a Tony as director.

Original cast: Atlantic SD 19107.

(Both Gleason and Naughton would eventually win Tonys, she for *Into the Woods* in 1988, he for *City of Angels* in 1990.)

I'm Getting My Act Together and Taking It on the Road (Gretchen Cryer, Nancy Ford). Opened December 16, 1978. Cast: Gretchen Cryer, Margot Rose, Betty Aberlin, Don Scardino.

Singer/composer Heather Jones (Cryer) is divorced, an ex-soap opera star, and has just turned 39. This chronological milepost, and an upcoming road tour with her band, triggers memories of her past, from being daddy's smiling little girl ("Smile") to an empty-headed bride ("Dear Tom"). Now she's her own woman, one who refuses to be "Put in a Package and Sold."

Songs: "Old Friend," "Strong Woman Number," "Lonely Lady," "Natural High," "Miss America," and "In a Simple Way I Love You."

Original cast: CBS X-14885.

Irma La Douce (Marguerite Monnot, Alexandre Breffort, lyrics translated and adapted by Julian More, David Heneker, Monty Norman). Opened September 29, 1969. Cast: Elizabeth Seal, Keith Michell, Clive Revill.

This unlikely love story of a Paris prostitute and a law student gives to the seedy backstreets off Pigalle the same romantic glow Comden and Green cast over Manhattan. The jealous but unemployed student can't handle the idea of his girl continuing her trade in order to support them and dons a disguise to become her only customer, an exhausting predicament, particularly when he becomes even more jealous of his other self and ends up in jail for having done away with the nonexistent lover. He escapes on a raft, clears his name, and Irma gives up her career.

The score includes: "Valse Milieu," "Our Language of Love," "She's Got the Lot," "Le Grisbi Is le Root of le Evil in Men," "The Wreck of a Mec," "That's a Crime," "From a Prison Cell," and "There Is Only One Paris for That."

None of the songs were in the 1963 nonmusical movie with Shirley MacLaine and Jack Lemmon, except instrumentally as background music. A great waste.

Original cast: Columbia OS 2029.

Jacques Brel Is Alive and Well and Living in Paris (Jacques Brel, with English translations by Eric Blau and Mort Shuman). Opened January 22, 1968. Cast: Elly Stone, Mort Shuman, Shawn Elliott, Alice Whitfield.

For those who like ideas and thinking with their music, this show is crammed with them. There is no story, no libretto. Each song could well be a self-contained one act play. All of them have something to say about the world in which we live, often about war and peace, politics and hypocrisy, love and death. Brel's lyrics are often angry and bitter. The original played over a thousand performances at New York's Village Gate, and productions of it can crop up almost anywhere in the world.

The score includes: "Marathon," "Madelene," "The Statue" (a brilliant look at hypocrisy as a slain soldier returns to ridicule the heroic statue erected in his name), "Jackie," "Alone," "Old Folks," "Timid Frieda," "Bachelor's Dance," "Next," "The Bulls," "Amsterdam," "Middle Class," "Carousel," "Song for Old Lovers," and "If We Only Have Love," among others.

The 1975 film starred Stone, Shuman, Joe Masiell and Brel.

Original cast: Columbia D2S-779. Film: Atlantic SD2-1000.

(The title has, inevitably, become a misnomer: Since late 1978 Brel has been dead and buried on the French Polynesian island of Hiva-Oa. His songs live on.)

Jamaica (Harold Arlen, E. Y. Harburg). Opened October 31, 1957. Cast: Lena Horne, Ricardo Montalban, Ossie Davis, Josephine Premice, Adelaide Hall.

Perhaps *Newsweek* best described the show in the headline of a review (November 11, 1957): "Calypso con Corny." The story was "an underdressed idyll about pearls, mackerel, hurricanes, and the love of a simple fisherman for a fancy dressmaker named Savannah." This "so-so planter's punch" turned into a hit on the strength of Lena Horne, in her first starring role, and the songs of Arlen and Harburg.

Walter Kerr of the *Herald Tribune* said *Jamaica* "is the kind of musical that leads you to wonder whether it was produced simply because all concerned had such high, happy hopes for the original-cast album." If so, the real winners are record collectors.

The numbers include: "Push de Button" (about all the modern conveniences in far-off America), "Little Biscuit," "Cocoanut Sweet," "Hooray for de Yankee Dollar," "Monkey in the Mango Tree," "Take It Slow, Joe," "Ain't It the Truth," "Leave the Atom Alone," "Incompatibility," and the satiric "Napoleon" (which takes note of how great historical figures end up as brand names on products, as in Napoleon brandy and pastry, Cleopatra cigars, DuBarry lipstick, Gladstone bags, Hoover vacuums, and Bismark herring, among others).

Original cast: RCA LSO (S)-1103.

(Though considered a musical genius by his peers, Harold Arlen managed to compose songs for just nine Broadway shows in 30 years, few of them big hits. He is best known for popular tunes such as "Blues in the Night," "It's Only a Paper Moon," and "I've Got a Right to Sing the Blues." His Hollywood songs such as "Get Happy," "The Man That Got Away," and most notably the ones in *The Wizard of Oz* — "Over the Rainbow" won an Oscar — kept him away from Broadway.)

Jerry's Girls (Jerry Herman). Opened February 28, 1984. Cast: Carol Channing, Leslie Uggams, Andrea McArdle, Suzanne Ishee, Diana Myron, Ellyn Arons.

A tuneful revue of songs from Jerry Herman's long Broadway career with numbers taken from *Hello, Dolly! Mame, Mack and Mabel, Parade, Milk and Honey* (a musical about the founding of modern Israel), *Dear World, A Day in Hollywood/A Night in the Ukraine,* and *La Cage aux Folles.*

When the originals are not available, a revue is the next best thing, and, thanks to the cast and Herman's talent for composing songs that hold up outside the context of a show, this is better than most. Channing, with the most unique voice on Broadway, reprises her signature songs from *Dolly!.* Uggams brings sheer beauty to the ballads "If He Walked Into My Life," "It Only Takes a Moment," and "I Am What I Am." McArdle, who starred in *Annie* seven years earlier [Act One, 1977], proved she was more than just a cute kid with a big voice, nearly stealing the show from the veterans with "Show Tune," "Wherever He Ain't," "So Long, Dearie," and "Look What Happened to Mabel."

Other songs: "Put on Your Sunday Clothes," "We Need a Little Christmas," "Tap Your Troubles Away," "Bosom Buddies," "Shalom," "Milk and Honey," "Movies Were Movies," "Time Heals Everything," "Song on the Sand." Composer Herman joins the cast in singing the finale.

Original cast: Polydor 820 207-4 Y-2 (double cassette).

(When the club show first moved to Broadway on December 18,

1985, the cast was made up of Dorothy Louden, Tony nominee Chita Rivera, and Leslie Uggams.)

Jesus Christ, Superstar (Andrew Lloyd Webber, Tim Rice). Opened October 12, 1971. Cast: Ben Vereen, Barry Dennen, Yvonne Elliman, Bob Bingham, Samuel Wright.

The rock-opera life and death of Jesus with a superior set of lyrics, contemporary rock music stylings, and fine performances. Vereen is Judas, who is less of a villain than a disillusioned social activist.

Tim Rice's original idea was to tell the story through the eyes of Judas, a personage he felt to be "somewhat maligned at times"[5] — which is what prompted protesters to parade in front of the theater calling the show blasphemous.

With this show Webber and Rice pioneered the use of releasing a studio cast album to test public reaction before trying to mount an expensive musical. The *original* cast, in the studio, featured Murray Head as Judas, Ian Gillan as Jesus, Elliman as Mary Magdalene, and Mike D'Abo as a wickedly funny Herod. Their version sold 2.5 million copies before the show opened on Broadway. Then came the Broadway cast, and then the idiosyncratic film by Norman Jewison in 1973 in which ancient Jerusalem has modern tanks and other startling visual images, turning the movie into a 103-minute music video.

Of the stage production, Douglas Watt of the *Daily News* called Ben Vereen "simply magnificent" as Judas.

Highlights include Elliman's "I Don't Know How to Love Him" and "Everything's Alright," the biggest hits from the show, along with: "Heaven on Their Minds," "This Jesus Must Die," "Hosanna," "Pilate's Dream," "Damned for All Time/Blood Money," and "King Herod's Song" (a startling and effective music hall turn).

Original studio cast: Decca DXSA 7206. Broadway cast: Decca 75103. Film cast: MCA 11000 (S).

Joy (Oscar Brown, Jr., Sivuca, Luiz Henrique). Opened January 27, 1970. Cast: Oscar Brown, Jr., Jean Pace, Sivuca, Norman Shobey.

Billed as "A Musical Come-Together," this is a difficult show to categorize. There is no book to speak of, yet it is more than a revue, more than a musical soapbox despite its message of brotherhood, peace, and love. The songs—as one expects from jazzman Brown—are eloquent, lovely, angry, funny, and political, charged with energy, emotion, and meaning. On record, this is a thoughtful entertainment not hurt by its dated references to Richard Nixon and Spiro Agnew, Vietnam, and the racial integration of television commercials.

Jean Pace brings her beautiful voice to bear on "Brown Baby," "Funny Feelin'," "Afro Blue," "Under the Sun," and "If I Only Had." Sivuca, a Brazilian accordionist, plays and sings along on "Mother Africa's Day," "Sky and Sea," and "What Is a Friend?" Brown handles "Time," "Wimmen's Ways" (a comic retelling of the Adam and Eve story), and the talking blues number that ends the show, "Funky World."

Original cast: RCA LSO-1166.

Let 'em Eat Cake (George Gershwin, Ira Gershwin). Opened October 21, 1933. Cast: Victor Moore, William Gaxton, Lois Moran.

The sequel to the Pulitzer Prize musical *Of Thee I Sing* [Act Three, 1932] was, if anything, a satire with a sharper bite and stronger opinions. Of course, it was coauthor George S. Kaufman who once said that satire is what closes on Saturday night. He may have had this show in mind for it barely lasted twelve weeks.

In the sequel, the party voted into power on the theme "Love Is Sweeping the Country" is voted out to the tune of "Tweedledee for President." The two ousted leaders, President Wintergreen and Vice President Throttlebottom, decide to overthrow the government by force of arms ("Comes the Revolution"), using blue shirts as their peoples' uniform ("Shirts by the Millions").

When matters come to a head, they decide to settle things with a baseball game between representatives from the League of Nations ("The League of Nations: No Comprenez, No Capish, No Versteh") and the justices of the Supreme Court ("Up and at 'Em," "I Know a Foul Ball"). Anarchy with blood in the streets looms before ex-First Lady Mary Wintergreen starts a counterrevolution among America's women who rebel not because of politics, but against the new order's drab uniforms ("Fashion Show").

The original cast was not recorded. Until recently, despite a 1978 revival, the score was lost to record buyers. A great 1987 studio cast is now available (usually with *Of Thee I Sing* on a second cassette) starring Maureen McGovern, Larry Kert, and Jack Gilford, conducted by Michael Tilson-Thomas: CBS SMT42639.

Meet Me in St. Louis (Hugh Martin, Ralph Blane). Opened November 2, 1989. Cast: Donna Kane, Betty Garrett, Jason Workman, George Hearn, Charlotte Moore, Milo O'Shea.

Every so often a hit musical film finds its way onto Broadway. In this case, it took 45 years for the Vincente Minnelli-Judy Garland classic to make the transition. The story, from a Sally Benson novel, follows the Smith family during the year 1903, the year of the great St. Louis World's Fair and Exposition. Esther Smith (Garland in the film, Kane on stage) falls for "The Boy Next Door" (Tom Drake/Jason Workman), while father (Leon Ames/George Hearn) has to decide whether to move the family from St. Louis to New York.

It was the performances and songs that carried this flimsy bit of nostalgia on film, and the same held true for the play—and hearing them again is always a fresh delight: "The Trolley Song," "Have Yourself a Merry Little Christmas," the title song, and "Under the Bamboo Tree" (composed by Bob Cole).

For the stage version, the two 75-year-old composers came out of retirement to add more songs, all very much in the same spirit as the originals, including: "Be Anything but a Girl," "A Touch of the Irish," "Raving Beauty," "A Day in New York," "Diamonds in the Starlight," "Irish Jig," and "Paging Mr. Sousa."

"If the show doesn't charm you," Howard Kissel told his *Daily News* readers, "your heart must be even harder than a theater critic's." He may have had the *Times* critic, Frank Rich, in mind, for Rich wrote that the show combined "insipid acting, an inane book, and a complete lack of originality."

Original cast: DRG Records SBLC 19002.

Miss Saigon (Alain Boublil, Claude-Michel Schönberg, Richard Maltby, Jr.). Opened in London September 20, 1989; New York opening, April 11, 1991. Broadway cast: Lea Salonga, Jonathan Pryce, Willy Falk, Hinton Battle, Liz Callaway.

Along with the debris of wrecked helicopters and planes, sand-bagged bunkers, hills of rusting beer and soda cans, and acres of gravestones, the American forces that evacuated Vietnam in April 1975 also left behind — as have soldiers throughout history — a battalion of children. Fathered by GIs and raised by their Vietnamese mothers, these Amerasian children provided the initial inspiration for *Miss Saigon*. The basic plot is an updated variation of Puccini's opera, *Madame Butterfly*.

In the modern version, a U.S. Marine named Chris (Falk), is about to be shipped home when he falls in love with Kim (Salonga), a new arrival at a Saigon bordello — the opening number is quite raw and realistic in its language, both from the whores and the men craving them. (The scene essentially turns the romance of Rodgers and Hammerstein's "Some Enchanted Evening" on its head, the two strangers who fall in love across a crowded room doing so in a brothel and not at a cocktail party.)

They marry, but are quickly separated when the city falls to the North Vietnamese and Chris is airlifted away amid the chaos. He does not know Kim is pregnant. He returns to Saigon three years later — with his American wife (Callaway). There, through the machinations of Kim's sleazy, opportunistic, one-time pimp (Pryce), he learns he has a son just as Kim sacrifices herself by suicide so that the boy will have a better life in America.

The music in this powerful, through-composed drama is equal to the stunning stage effects which include a helicopter taking off and landing during the fall of Saigon. The effects helped make this the most expensive musical ever — it required an initial investment of $10 million before the first curtain went up, and the top ticket price in New York was set at $100.

While one may quibble about adhering too close to *Butterfly*'s tragic ending, the music is first rate: "The Heat Is on in Saigon," "The Movie in My Mind," "Why God Why?" "The Last Night of the World," "The Morning of the Dragon," "I Still Believe," "If You Want to Die in Bed," "I'd Give My Life for You," "What a Waste," and "The American Dream" all grow brilliantly out of the characters and story.

Miss Saigon created a furor in America long before it opened in New York. Responding to protests by its Asian members, Actors Equity denied permission for Jonathan Pryce to perform on Broadway, and insisted that producer Cameron Mackintosh replace his star with an Asian actor. Pryce, a past Tony winner in the 1977 drama *Comedians*, had already won an Olivier Award as Best Actor in London for the role of the Engineer, but some saw the casting of a Welshman as a Eurasian as discriminatory.

Mackintosh saw the issue as one of artistic freedom and abruptly canceled the Broadway opening, offering to refund all of the record-setting $25 million in advance ticket sales. It also meant losing 29 jobs for Asian-American actors.

Opinions on the concept of "non-traditional casting" flew from all sides over the ensuing weeks. Equity head Colleen Dewhurst found an analogy in the image of white stage performers donning blackface and charged *Miss Saigon* with being no better than a yellowface minstrel show.[6] Some even argued that Lea Salonga, a Filipino, was not Asian enough for the title role.

Tempers were hot on both sides. By August 16, after stormy protests by a large number of Equity members, the union reversed itself, saying, "The council determined that, indeed, Mr. Pryce qualifies as a star in accordance with the criteria established in the agreement between Equity and the League of American Theaters and Producers."[7] After more meetings to iron out details, the Broadway opening came off on April 11, 1991, with Pryce and Salonga repeating their roles.

The result?

Critical reaction in New York was mixed. The cost, the London success, and the negative publicity of the casting battle perhaps made some critics resistant to the musical (opening night protesters had shifted their target from the casting to the show's depiction of Asian women as hookers and sex objects; the only aspect of the show that went unprotested appears to have been the use of the term "Miss" in the title instead of "Ms").

Frank Rich of the *Times* called the big helicopter finale an "inane" stunt, and found parts of the show "simplistic, derivative and, at odd instances, laughable." Yet Rich applauded the overall effort as "a gripping entertainment of the old school" with "lush melodies" and "spectacular performances." Pryce was termed "electrifying."

At the opposite end was Michael Feingold who lacerated the show in *The Village Voice* (April 23, 1991) as "garbage," suggested the creators commit ritual suicide for exploiting the issue of Amerasian children, and labeled the score "amplified pop swill." Feingold attacked Pryce as "a scrawny, balding, middle-aged Welsh ham [who] looks exactly as silly as Carol Channing would playing the life of Lena Horne." For taking the role, Pryce was dubbed "a sleazier whore than any bar girl in the history of Saigon." Feingold saw the helicopter sequence as the equivalent of "a techno-update of the midget clown car in a circus."

A later review in the *Times* by David Richards (April 21, 1991) credited Pryce with a "galvanizing mixture of ferocity and subservience . . . biting into lyrics that can actually lay claim to some bite of their own." The helicopter finale was listed as being "Among the astounding stage effects of the late-20th-century musical," and the show itself one that would "amaze a lot of people for years to come."

Newsweek's Jack Kroll (April 22, 1991) saw it as "an eclectic pop musical [that's] accessible to audiences from Broadway to Budapest to Tokyo," singling out Salonga's "sweetness and gallantry" and the "Brechtian brilliance" of Pryce.

In *Time* (April 22, 1991), William A. Henry III called *Miss Saigon* "a cracking good show," and said Salonga was "incandescently in command of the stage." In *The New Yorker* (April 29, 1991), Mimi Kramer dismissed Salonga as not looking enough like a war waif and said her singing was a "strained, high-pitched belt, somewhere between a yelp and a whine," while knocking the show as a "dramatic vacuum [that] has no real characters, no ironies, no ideas."

It won the Outer Critics Circle Award as Best Musical. Nominated for 11 Tonys in a year when many people predicted a backlash against big, imported musicals (and not helped by the Equity controversy), it won three, all for the performances of Pryce, Salonga, and Battle. (In his acceptance speech, Hinton Battle pointedly thanked the producer for being "color-blind" in his casting.) It lost Best Musical and Best Original Score to the homegrown *The Will Rogers Follies* [Act One, 1991].

Original London cast with Salonga, Pryce, Simon Bowman, and Peter Polycarpou: Geffen M5G 24271. At press time, there were no plans to record the Broadway cast.

Also recommended is a picture-filled book by Edward Behr and Mark Steyn titled *The Story of Miss Saigon* (Arcade, 1991).

My One and Only (George and Ira Gershwin). Opened May 1, 1983. Cast: Tommy Tune, Twiggy, Charles "Honi" Coles.

This freely adapted version of Gershwin's *Funny Face* very nearly died during out-of-town tryouts. By the time it staggered onto Broadway, the show had gone through at least two writers, five directors, and dozens of "show doctors" trying to breathe life into it, Mike Nichols and Michael Bennett among them. It had also run up a production cost of $4.5 million. Then, against all odds, the show became a smooth, delightful hit.

The plot of the 1927 original, and of the 1957 film — Fred Astaire was in both — were tossed aside (showing just how comfortably adaptable old scores could be). The new story had aviator Billy Buck Chandler (Tune) falling for channel swimmer turned aquacade star Edith Herbert (Twiggy) as they globetrot from Harlem to Morocco, all the while beset by — in the words of *Newsweek*'s reviewer — "various dippy troubles."

John Beaufort in *The Christian Science Monitor* termed it "a skylarking entertainment," and even Frank Rich of the *Times*, with some reservations, admitted "it's the only new or old musical of the season that sends us home on air."

The one thing it had in common with the original was a great score, with some extras taken from other Gershwin shows (what *Time* called "divine pilferage"): "I Can't Be Bothered Now," "Blah Blah Blah," "Soon," "Kickin' the Clouds Around," "Sweet 'n Low Down," "Strike Up the Band," "He Loves and She Loves," "'S Wonderful" (sung on stage by Tune and Twiggy while splashing about in a shallow pool; though there is no splashing on the recording, there is plenty of tap dancing), "Nice Work if You Can Get It," "Little Jazz Bird," "Funny Face," "How Long Has This Been Going On?" and "My One and Only."

Time (May 16, 1983) called it a "goofy cardboard comedy romance," and compared the 6'6" Tune and the waif-like Twiggy to "a skyscraper and swizzle-stick song-and-dance duo." Coles and Tune won Tonys, the skyscraper becoming the first person to have won in four categories during his career — as actor, featured actor, choreographer, and director.

What secret formula turned the near flop into a hit? *Time* quoted Mike Nichols as saying: "What it needed was to be commercialized, yes, vulgarized — if that's Broadwayizing, then so be it."

Original cast: Atlantic 80110-2.

(Tommy Tune and Twiggy also teamed up for the 1971 Ken Russell film, *The Boy Friend*, a 1920s-styled doo-wacka-doo musical based on the Sandy Wilson stage hit.)

Now Is the Time for All Good Men (Gretchen Cryer, Nancy Ford). Opened September 26, 1967, Off-Broadway. Cast: David Cryer, Sally Niven (stage name of Gretchen Cryer), Art Wallace, Anne Kaye, Steve Skiles.

It opened about a month before *Hair* [Act Four, 1968] and could thereby be considered the first antiVietnam War musical. That it was lost in the debate over *Hair*'s nudity, profanity, and rock music is a pity because this is arguably the better, more thoughtful, of the two.

It is the story of ex-soldier Mike Butler (Cryer), once jailed for having belated conscientious objections to the war after he was in uniform. Now released from prison, Mike tries to settle as a teacher in Bloomdale, Indiana, only to find himself in the midst of a right wing, love-it-or-leave-it kind of town ("Good Enough for Grandpa"). The local teaching philosophy concerning pupils is to just "Keep 'em Busy" and out of trouble; thinking for yourself is cause for suspicion. Mike's presence and feelings begin to change the lives of some of his students ("Down Through History," "All Alone"), and of Sarah Larkin (Niven/Cryer), the music teacher. But soon his prison term is made public and one patriotic citizen takes a shot at him.

Other good songs include: "Tea in the Rain," "Halloween Hay-ride/Katydid," "See Everything New," and one man's premature eulogy for the son he's proud to be sending to Vietnam, "A Star on the Monument." Gretchen Cryer thought the score to be "very much in the Rodgers and Hammerstein vein . . . though the show had a very gritty story, it had a very romantic score."[8]

Original cast: Columbia OS 3130.

Nunsense (Dan Goggin). Opened December 12, 1985. Cast: Christine Anderson, Edwina Lewis, Semina De Laurentis, Marilyn Farina, Suzi Winson.

The scene is the auditorium of the Mount St. Helen's School, which is run by the Little Sisters of Hoboken. There was once a thriving convent here but, as luck would have it, Sister Julia mistak-enly served up some tainted *vichyssoise* and killed all but a handful of the nuns. Now the remaining five sisters have to put on a variety show to raise money for the mass burial.

From this incredibly thin—and hilariously tasteless—plot, Dan Goggin created a riotous (perhaps even heavenly) Off-Broadway show with an amazing abundance of puns on the words "habits" and "nun" (ads for the show in 1991 proclaimed, "Nun Better!") and a delightful score as the sisters vie for the star spot in their musical revue, belting out numbers such as "Turn Up the Spot-light," "Tackle That Temptation With a Time-Step," "So You Want to Be a Nun," "Growing Up Catholic," "We've Got to Clean Out the Freezer," "Just a Coupl'a Sisters," and "Nunsense Is Habit-Forming."

The emotional high point comes when Sister Mary Amnesia gets her memory back right in the middle of singing "I Could've Gone to Nashville."

Original cast: DRG Records, SBLC 12589.

Oh, Coward! (Noël Coward). Opened Off-Broadway October 4, 1972. Cast: Barbara Cason, Jamie Ross, Roderick Cook.

This delightfully witty and tuneful collection of songs by Noël Coward, England's lyrical answer to Cole Porter, is loosely con-structed around his life. But, mostly, this is just a great song fest, with such classics as: "Mad Dogs and Englishmen," "Dance Little

Lady," "Something to Do With Spring," "Poor Little Rich Girl,"
"If Love Were All," "Ziegeuner," and "Sail Away."

Also included are the purely fun songs, like the one of failed
missionary "Uncle Harry," and "Why Do the Wrong People Travel?" "The End of the News" (a middle class British couple keeping their chins up while waiting for a bus), "Nina" (the girl who
hated to dance and refused to begin the beguine), "Mrs. Worthing-
ton," and "Let's Do It" (Cole Porter's song with some new lyrics
by Coward).

"Extraordinary," Coward once observed, "how potent cheap
music is."[9] He and his audiences delighted in proving it time and
time again.

Original cast (double set): Bell 9001.

Oh, Kay! (George Gershwin, Ira Gershwin). Opened November
8, 1926. Cast: Gertrude Lawrence, Victor Moore, Oscar Shaw.

A tale of socialites foiling the agents of Prohibition, the slight
plot rendered excusable by the richness of the Gershwin score:
"Clap Yo' Hands," "Do, Do, Do," "Someone to Watch Over
Me," "Fidgety Feet," "Heaven on Earth," and "Dear Little
Girl."

The original cast was not recorded. A fine studio cast from 1957
starred Barbara Ruick, Jack Cassidy, and Allen Case: Columbia
Special Products ACL1050. A 1960 revival with Marti Stevens,
Linda Lavin, and Penny Fuller: DRG 15017 (CD); as a bonus, this
also contains the 1959 revival of Jerome Kern's *Leave It to Jane*
with Kathleen Murray, Art Matthews, Monroe Arnold, and George
Segal. (An all black 1990 revival of *Oh, Kay!* set in Harlem was not
a success and a recording, regrettably, has not been released.)

Oklahoma! (Richard Rodgers, Oscar Hammerstein). Opened
March 31, 1943. Cast: Alfred Drake, Joan Roberts, Celeste Holm,
Lee Dixon.

A landmark masterpiece, *Oklahoma!* was the first teaming of
Rodgers and Hammerstein, the first hit musical to include a ballet
(by Agnes de Mille in her Broadway debut), the first to exclude
leggy chorus girls, the first to rely solely on plot and character for

the musical interludes, and the first to produce what would become a state song.

It was a simple, folklorish story from a play by Lynn Riggs called *Green Grow the Lilacs*. (The original play was something of a musical in that it employed a large number of folk songs popular during Oklahoma's frontier days.) No one in the show was a star (though most rose quickly after opening night).

Hammerstein's gift for romance and affecting lyrics was perfectly in sync with farmer Laurie's love for cowboy Curly and her near fatal flirtation with hired hand Jud Fry. Contrary to the revealed wisdom of starting a show with a rousing, center stage number, Hammerstein had Alfred Drake standing in the wings singing the languid "Oh, What a Beautiful Morning," followed it with a courting song, "The Surrey With the Fringe on Top," and then had comic Lee Dixon sing of the wonders of "Kansas City" (where they've built skyscrapers seven stories high!). The rousing title song came at the very end.

Other well-known favorites: "I Cain't Say No," "People Will Say We're in Love," "Many a New Day."

Wolcott Gibbs dubbed it "completely enchanting [and] equipped with some of the best music and dancing in a long time." *Newsweek* (April 12, 1943) praised the ballet numbers and found the show to be "thoroughly refreshing without being oppressively rustic" (though Laurie's long tease of Curly was labeled "a perversity of female behavior pretty glaring even for musicomedy").

Even without chorus girls, the *World-Telegram*'s Burton Rascoe found something to ogle, declaring that "old-fashioned lace drawers can be more seductive than a G-string."

Though it did not win the Pulitzer Prize for drama, the award committee gave *Oklahoma!* a special citation for excellence.

The 1955 movie starred Gordon MacRae, Shirley Jones, Gloria Grahame, Gene Nelson, James Whitmore, Charlotte Greenwood, and, as the evil Jud, Rod Steiger. The film soundtrack also includes "The Farmer and the Cowman."

Original cast: MCA-2030. Film: Capitol SWAO 595.

On the Town (Leonard Bernstein, Betty Comden, Adolph Green). Opened December 28, 1944. Cast: John Battles, Cris Alexander, Betty Comden, Adolph Green, Nancy Walker, George Gaynes.

When this story of three happy-go-lucky sailors on a 24-hour liberty in New York opened on Broadway (based on Bernstein's earlier ballet show, *Fancy Free*), the world was still at war; Berlin would not fall for five more months. As fast, jaunty escapism, it couldn't be beat.

Gabey (Battles) falls for a poster of Miss Turnstiles (Sono Osato) in the subway, then spends his leave tracking her down while his buddies find romance in, of all places, a taxi and a museum. Nancy Walker, who in later years won fame in nonsinging TV roles (and as a huckster for paper towels), is Hildegarde Esterhazy, a love-starved cab driver ("Come Up to My Place"). Comden is an anthropologist fascinated with Green's prehistoric looks ("Carried Away"). If so many people can fall in love in such a short time, it can only happen on the musical stage.

Like *Oklahoma!* the year before, *On the Town* featured ballet — with subway riders, not cowboys. Other sparkling tunes: "Lonely Town," "I Can Cook Too," "Lucky to Be Me," "Some Other Time."

The wonderful 1949 film starred Gene Kelly, Frank Sinatra, Ann Miller, Betty Garrett, Vera-Ellen, and Jules Munshin. Added songs included "Prehistoric Man," "When You Walk Down Main Street with Me," and a title number.

Original cast (reassembled in a studio in 1960, and with John Reardon doing Battles' role): Columbia S 31005.

On Your Toes (Richard Rodgers and Lorenz Hart). Opened November 30, 1936. Cast: Ray Bolger, Doris Carson, Luella Gear, Monty Woolley, Tamara Geva.

Oklahoma! integrated ballet into its storyline, but Rodgers experimented with it seven years earlier in this show where the floundering finances of a ballet troupe are central to the plot. Bolger is a jazz composer who saves a Russian ballet company with a modern composition called "Slaughter on Tenth Avenue" (as gangsters are mistakenly after his head, the title goes a long way toward explaining his state of mind).

Before that big finale, there are songs: "It's Gotta Be Love" (in which Hart again backhands the ballad by comparing the symptoms of love to those of various diseases), "The Heart Is Quicker Than the Eye," "Glad to Be Unhappy," "There's a Small Hotel," "Quiet Night," and the snobbish "Too Good for the Average Man."

The original cast was not recorded. A 1952 studio cast starred Jack Cassidy, Portia Nelson, Ray Hyson, and Laurel Shelby: Columbia Special Products COS2590.

The 1983 revival cast (which won a Tony) will do in a pinch. Not that the performances flagged, but the engineering on the album is appalling — as with a rock album, the music is at the same level as the voices, which makes most of Hart's delicious lyrics indecipherable. It does, however, include the "Princess Zenobia Ballet" music: Polydor 813 667-1 Y-1.

Once on This Island (Lynn Ahrens, Stephen Flaherty). Opened October 18, 1990. Cast: La Chanze, Jerry Dixon, Sheila Gibbs, Kecia Lewis-Evans, Andrea Frierson, Milton Craig Nealy, Eric Riley, Ellis E. Williams.

Calypso music was not new to Broadway when this show opened in 1990 [see *Jamaica*, above]. But those who thought calypso was limited to Harry Belafonte singing "Day-O" discovered that the form could also be used dramatically to great effect.

Once on This Island, based on Rosa Guy's novel *My Love, My Love*, is a cautionary tale of class differences and the power of love as told by the island's Storytellers during a bad storm. This is a tale of gods, goddesses, devils, love, and tragedy. An orphan of a storm turned pawn of the gods, Ti Moune (La Chanze) is a young peasant girl so in love with an upper-class young man that she risks her life to prove the power of love over death, only to learn that peasant girls in this "jewel of the Antilles" do not marry above their station. Even when her love is spurned, the anguished Ti Moune does not waver, proving to the gods that love is stronger than death. For her devotion, she is transformed into a sheltering tree whose spirit will one day find happiness with the son of her love.

Calling the show an "effervescent achievement," Frank Rich of the *Times* wrote that "the audience feels the otherworldly thrill of discovering the fabric of its own lives in an enchanted tapestry from a distant shore.'' Howard Kissel of the *Daily News* was not impressed, saying the musical "aims for folk and comes out fake.'' *Newsday*'s Jan Stuart said "its simplicity arrives like a refreshing tropical breeze to blow away the stale spectacles of Andrew Lloyd Webber.''

Kecia Lewis-Evans as Asaka, Mother of the Earth, and Adrea Frierson as Erzulie, Goddess of Love, practically steal the recording and make believers out of the most cynical of listeners, while Eric Riley is a sinister Papa Ge, the Demon of Death, waiting ominously for the lovers to face reality.

Song highlights: "Waiting for Life,'' "Rain,'' "Mama Will Provide,'' "Some Say,'' "The Human Heart,'' "We Dance,'' "One Small Girl,'' "Forever Yours,'' "Ti Moune,'' "Why We Tell the Story.''

Original cast: RCA 60595-4-RC.

110 in the Shade (Tom Jones, Harvey Schmidt). Opened October 24, 1963. Cast: Robert Horton, Inga Swenson, Stephen Douglass, Will Geer, Lesley Warren.

N. Richard Nash's *The Rainmaker* was a hit play and then a hit 1956 movie (with Katharine Hepburn and Burt Lancaster). The musical's storyline is not unlike that of *The Music Man*. A charming con artist comes to an out-of-the-way town bent on selling the yokels a bill of goods—a boy's band in one, rain in the other. In both, it is the town spinster who sees through the con and, at first, attempts to expose him, then falls in love.

At the end, Starbuck the rainmaker (Horton) is as much surprised to see rain as Professor Harold Hill was to hear music from his band. The main difference comes at the final curtain: Marian the librarian's only suitor was Harold Hill, but Lizzie Curry (Swenson) has two suitors and chooses to stay with the down-to-earth Sheriff File (Douglass) rather than ride off with the dreamer Starbuck.

The creators of *The Fantasticks* [above] delivered another fine score in their first Broadway venture that came right from the hearts of the characters: "Lizzie's Coming Home,'' "Love, Don't Turn Away,'' "Poker Polka,'' "The Rain Song,'' "You're Not Foolin' Me,'' "Raunchy,'' "A Man and a Woman,'' "Melisande,'' "Wonderful Music,'' "Everything Beautiful Happens at Night.''

Geer and Swenson were nominated for Tonys, losing, respectively, to Jack Cassidy in *She Loves Me* [Act Four, 1963] and Carol Channing in *Hello, Dolly!* [Act One, 1964].

Original cast: RCA LSO 1085. Reissued on tape and CD in 1990 on RCA 1085-2-RG.

Over Here! (Richard M. Sherman, Robert B. Sherman). Opened March 6, 1974. Cast: Janie Sell (Tony winner), Patty Andrews, Maxene Andrews, Samuel E. Wright, John Travolta, Phyllis Somerville, Douglass Watson.

The time is the early 1940s and America is at war. But that's over there, over there (as George M. Cohan once sang), and this is over here, over here. On a cross-country train, to be exact, where two singers (Patty and Maxene Andrews) find themselves in a trio with a Nazi spy (Sell). She's found out in the end, of course, but who cares when you have such great big band music to listen to?

The brothers Sherman (composers of the film *Mary Poppins*) beautifully recreate the music of an era, from ballads ("Wartime Wedding," "Where Did the Good Times Go?") to big band boogie ("We Got It!" "The Big Beat"), public service jingles ("Buy a Victory Bond"), and even a song tailor made for a certain type of army training film ("The Good Time Girl"). Samuel E. Wright (later known as the voice of Sebastian the crab in *The Little Mermaid*) does a terrific jive tune called "Don't Shoot the Hooey to Me, Louie," and a then-unknown John Travolta does "Dream Drummin'" (wishing he were Gene Krupa).

Original cast: Columbia KS 32961.

Paint Your Wagon (Alan Jay Lerner, Frederick Loewe). Opened November 12, 1951. Cast: Robert Penn, Olga San Juan, Tony Bavaar, Rufus Smith, James Barton.

Jennifer Rumson (San Juan) is the only woman in a California gold rush town of 1853. Her father Ben (Barton) has his hands full keeping the hoards of lusty miners at bay, and the one who slips past him is a young Mexican named Julio. Ben, meanwhile, takes up with a polygamous Mormon's cast-off wife. Jennifer is sent off to school and returns to be reunited with Julio just before her father's tragic, and penniless, death.

The 1969 movie plot was considerably different. In that, Ben (Lee Marvin) and his new Pardner (Clint Eastwood) become cohusbands to an auctioned-off Mormon wife named Elizabeth (Jean Seberg). They do most of their prospecting under the town's many saloons where gold dust falls through the floorboards. Their tunnels (and a runaway bull) bring about a collapse of the town. Ben and the miners move on while Pardner stays with Elizabeth to take up farming.

The scores were somewhat different too, making two separate recordings advisable. The songs they have in common are: "I Talk to the Trees," "I'm on My Way," "They Call the Wind Maria," "I Still See Elisa," "Whoop-Ti-Ay," "Hand Me Down That Can o' Beans," "Wand'rin' Star," and "There's a Coach Comin' In" (expanded to over twice its original length in the film).

The Broadway cast album includes: "Rumson," "What's Going on Here?" (sung by Olga San Juan, known in her film days as The Puerto Rican Pepperpot), "How Can I Wait?" "In Between" (in which Ben proposes marriage by denigrating himself à la Shakespeare's Henry V), "Carnio Mio," "All for Him," and "Another Autumn."

The film's score, with Lerner's new lyrics set to music by Andre Previn, added: "The First Thing You Know," "A Million Miles Away Behind the Door" (Anita Gordon singing for Seberg), "The Gospel of No-Name City," "Best Things," and "Gold Fever."

The movie was such an expensive flop when it first opened that a short version, minus most of the songs, quickly replaced the original in theaters. The uncut film, however, is quite excellent (despite Eastwood's thin and uncertain singing voice).

Original cast: RCA LOC-1006. Reissue: RCA 60243-4-RG. Film: Paramount PMS 1001.

Peter Pan (Mark Charlap, Jule Styne, Carolyn Leigh, Betty Comden, Adolph Green). Opened October 20, 1954. Cast: Mary Martin, Cyril Ritchard, Kathy Nolan.

Sir James M. Barrie's 1904 classic tale of Peter Pan, the boy who refused to grow up (Martin), Wendy (Nolan), Captain Hook (Ritchard), and the Lost Boys came magically to life in this musical rendering. Hook roars and Peter soars — with the aid of wires. Martin and Ritchard won Tonys. When Martin died late in 1990, it was this, her third Tony-winning role, that drew the fondest remembrances.

Reviews of the score were mixed, but everyone loved the star, their praises typified by Robert Coleman's *Daily Mirror* column in which he proclaimed Mary Martin to be "nothing less than magnificent."

Martin's limited 16-week engagement (after playing first in Los Angeles and San Francisco) was sold out in New York before it opened. But it wasn't long before the whole country — or those who could afford that newfangled invention, the television — got to see the show televised live on March 7, 1955, and a tape was rerun on January 9, 1956, then put away on a shelf until 1990 when it was rerun again and then released on home video.

The songs are uniformly enjoyable: "I've Gotta Crow," "Never Never Land," "I'm Flying," "Hook's Tango," "Indians," "Wendy," "Tarantella" (by Hook and the Pirates), "Oh My Mysterious Lady," "Ugg-a-Wugg," "Distant Melody," "Hook's Waltz."

Original cast: RCA LSO-1019(e) RE.

Though the best remembered, Martin's was not Peter Pan's first musical outing. Maude Adams sang the role in an unrecorded 1905 Broadway production. And film star Jean Arthur took flight in a semimusical (five songs by Leonard Bernstein and lots of background music) in 1950, with Boris Karloff as a memorable Captain Hook. Jean Arthur did not sing, the songs being taken mainly by Marcia Henderson as Wendy, and Karloff. John Chapman of the *Daily News* thought that Arthur "in her short haircut, looks like a small Burgess Meredith," while Richard Watts, Jr. of the *Post* was more prophetic in noting: "Jean Arthur, looking and sounding pleasantly like Mary Martin, is boyish and engaging." That short score, along with a lot of dialogue and narration, is available on Columbia's Chart-Buster label, JST 4312.

Ex-gymnast Cathy Rigby took to the boards and wires in a 1991 production nominated for a Tony as Best Revival.

Pins and Needles (Harold Rome). Opened November 27, 1937. Cast: Members of the Ladies Garment Workers Union, including Al Levy, Nettie Harary, Millie Weitz, Ruth Rubinstein, Ruth Elbaum.

Where *The Cradle Will Rock* [above] used the conflict between workers and bosses as the basis for a dramatic opera, Harold Rome took those same sentiments—again from the perspective of the workers—and turned it into a political musical comedy revue and then into a Broadway hit, and he did it using a cast of actual garment workers.

The key number is "Sing Me a Song With Social Significance," a splendid anthem which tells the audience exactly what's coming. There were the expected pro-union numbers such as, "It's Better With a Union Man," "Not Cricket to Picket," "One Big Union for Two" (a love song with union analogies), and "Chain Store Daisy." There were also political satires such as "Doing the Reactionary," "Sitting on Your Status Quo," and "Four Little Angels of Peace" (an ironic number featuring Hitler, Mussolini, England's Anthony Eden, and a generic Japanese official). There were noncontroversial songs as well: "Sunday in the Park," "What Good Is Love?" "Nobody Makes a Pass at Me," and "I've Got the Nerve to Be in Love."

The original cast was not recorded. An excellent 25th anniversary studio cast featured Jack Carroll, Rose Marie Jun, Barbra Streisand, and composer Rome (singing the Biblical "Mene, Mene, Tekel," and of the joys of being a G-Man in "When I Grow Up"): Columbia OS-2210.

Porgy and Bess (George Gershwin, Ira Gershwin, Du Bose Heyward). Opened October 10, 1935. Cast: Todd Duncan, Anne Brown, John Bubbles, Edward Matthews.

Seven years after the book by Du Bose and Dorothy Heyward had been a nonmusical stage hit, the Gershwin version appeared and has overshadowed the original ever since.

Billed as a "folk opera," the story centers on a black ghetto area of shacks known as Catfish Row. Here a poor cripple named Porgy falls in love with a fallen woman named Bess. She takes up with him just to hide out from the police while her main man Crown is being sought for murder. By the time Crown returns, Bess has grown to love Porgy but is also being torn apart by an addiction to "Happy Dust" sold by a pusher named Sportin' Life. Porgy kills Crown in a struggle, but Bess is lured to the bright lights of New York by Sportin' Life and his cocaine. At the end, Porgy gets on his goat-driven cart and sets off to find Bess and bring her back. No one who sees the show doubts that he'll succeed.

The score contained sung dialogue and lots of great songs (indeed, many critics at the time rejected the term "opera" and referred to it as a lot of Broadway show tunes with sung dialogue between them). In the decades since its premiere, *Porgy and Bess* has been played by opera companies internationally and has proven itself to be the most lasting musical stage legacy of the Gershwin brothers.

The songs include: "A Woman Is a Sometime Thing," "My Man's Gone Now," "I Got Plenty o' Nuttin'," "Bess, You Is My Woman," "A Red-Headed Woman," "Oh, Doctor Jesus," "It Ain't Necessarily So," "I Loves You, Porgy," "There's a Boat Dat's Leavin' Soon for New York," and "I'm on My Way."

Though the show was not a commercial success, initial reviews were generally good, with *Time* (October 21, 1935) praising the music as "frequently inspired" and the choruses as "richly eloquent."

Respect for the opera seems to gain with each new production. The 1953 revival with Leontyne Price, William Warfield and Cab Calloway, for example, landed on Broadway only after a triumphant tour of Paris, London, and Vienna, at which time Brooks Atkinson wrote in the *Times*, "George Gershwin, if he were alive today, would feel thoroughly vindicated." The score, said Atkinson, was "a major work of art—a tumultuous evocation of life among some high-spirited, poignant, admirable human beings. It is all Gershwin and it is gold."

The 1959 film version was directed by Otto Preminger with a heavy hand and probably holds some sort of record for stars lip-syncing to other peoples' voices: Robert McFerrin sings for Sidney Poitier, Adele Addison sings for Dorothy Dandridge, Loulie Jean Norman—a French-English white woman—sings for Diahann Carroll, Inez Matthews sings for Ruth Attaway, and, because of contract conflicts, Cab Calloway sings on the recording in place of Sammy Davis, Jr.

There are numerous recordings of this great show from which to choose. Because of its length, the recordings are nearly always selections of key songs.

The complete score was stunningly presented in 1977 by the Houston Opera Company with Clamma Dale (a Tony nominee) and Donnie Ray Albert: RCA ARL 3-2109.

A 1986 full-length recording featuring Willard White, Cynthia Haymon, Damon Evans, and Bruce Hubbard: EMI/Angel 49568.

The two original stars, Duncan and Brown, recorded excerpts in 1942, available on MCA: MCA-2035.

The original Sportin' Life was one-time vaudeville hoofer John Bubbles, and his performance remains the best — his Sportin' Life is savage and evil, scary to listen to. He can be heard with the 1963 studio cast of Leontyne Price and William Warfield on RCA LSC-2679.

A 1951 studio cast with Lawrence Winters, Camilla Williams, and Avon Long was given a Grammy Hall of Fame award in 1976: Columbia OSL-162.

Several studio casts bear mentioning. Harry Belafonte and Lena Horne on RCA LSO(S)-1507; Ella Fitzgerald and Louis Armstrong's 1957 recording for Verve, VE-2-2507; Cleo Laine and Ray Charles do an excellent jazz/blues version on RCA CPL2-1831.

Also recommended is Hollis Alpert's book, *The Life and Times of Porgy and Bess: The Story of an American Classic* (Knopf, 1990).

Pump Boys and Dinettes — On Broadway (score composed by the cast members, principally Jim Wann). Opened July 10, 1981. Cast: John Foley, Mark Hardwick, John Schimmel, Debra Monk, Jim Wann, Cass Morgan.

An unusual show in that cast members contributed to the music and lyrics, all of which are in a country-western style. The action centers around a gas station and roadside diner called The Double Cupp (run by the Cupp sisters, Prudie and Rhetta) and the people who work in them. The plot, according to Gerald Clarke in *Time* (March 1, 1982), "is as thin as a dime tip," but overall the musical was "as cheery, relaxed and amiable as the first really warm day of spring."

Songs include: "Highway 57," "Taking It Slow," "Serve Yourself," "Menu Song," "The Best Man," "Mona," "Pump Boys," "Tips," and "The Night Dolly Parton Was Almost Mine."

Original cast: CBS FM-37790 (S). Reissued on CD in 1989 as CBS MK 37790.

The Rink (John Kander, Fred Ebb). Opened February 9, 1984. Cast: Chita Rivera (Tony winner), Liza Minnelli, Scott Holmes.

The setting is a roller-skating rink on the verge of being torn down. After a seven-year estrangement, wandering hippie daughter Angel (Minnelli) comes calling on her mother Anna Antonelli (Rivera). They thrash over old times, bad times and good, good men and bad, and grow to like each other more than when the show started.

A wobbly vehicle to show off the talents of its two superstars but, as far as the recording goes, that is a good enough excuse. The numbers include: "Chief Cook and Bottle Washer" (Rivera declaring her own emancipation), "Don't Ah, Ma Me" (the first argument between mother and daughter, both hilarious and scatological), "Blue Crystal," "We Can Make It," "After All These Years," "Angel's Rink and Social Center," "What Happened to the Old Days?" "The Apple Doesn't Fall," "Marry Me," and the dramatic "Mrs. A."

Reviews were generally mixed, with high praise for veteran Chita Rivera (who had to endure a dance routine of a gang rape by three hoods) and critical raspberries for the Terrance McNally story. Richard Corliss in *Time* (February 20, 1984) lauded Rivera's "high-voltage presence and performance," and noted that at age 51 she "could by now sell a song to the deaf."

Original cast: Polydor 823 125-4 Y-1.

The Roar of the Greasepaint—The Smell of the Crowd (Leslie Bricusse, Anthony Newley). Opened May 16, 1965. Cast: Anthony Newley, Cyril Ritchard, Gilbert Price, Joyce Jillson.

An allegory of life in which Sir (Ritchard) dominates Cocky (Newley) because . . . well, because he can. It's the "haves" against the "have-nots" of the world and how the "haves" maintain control and dominance by continually changing the rules on the "have-nots." Cocky eventually rebels, Sir backs down, and a new bond of mutual dependence is forged. Newley was nominated for a Tony as director, Ritchard for acting.

The score contains: "A Wonderful Day Like Today," "This Dream," "Where Would You Be Without Me?" "Look at That Face," "The Joker," "Who Can I Turn to (When Nobody Needs Me)," "What a Man!" "Feeling Good" (an excellent solo of freedom by Price), and "Nothing Can Stop Me Now!"

Original cast: RCA LSO-1109.

The Rothschilds (Jerry Bock, Sheldon Harnick). Opened October 19, 1970. Cast: Hal Linden (Tony winner), Paul Hecht, Keene Curtis (in a number of roles), Leila Martin, Jill Clayburgh.

This story of how Mayer Rothschild and his five sons rose from the walled-in Jewish ghetto of the Frankfurt of 1772 to become advisors to kings and a titled family all in the space of Mayer's lifetime is the story of industriousness, intelligence, fortitude, and the overcoming of prejudice and oppression.

Everyone had high praise for Hal Linden, but opinions on the overall production were mixed. Clive Barnes told *Times* readers the show "will give a lot of pleasure to a lot of people." One of whom was not Martin Gottfried of *Women's Wear Daily*, who labeled the show a "vulgarization of musical theatre."

The composers of *Fiddler on the Roof* (which opened in 1964 and was still playing) again tapped their musical roots (both the ethnic and Broadway roots) and produced a strong story of struggle, love, and survival against all odds. The songs include: "He Tossed a Coin," "Everything," "Sons," "Rothschild and Sons," "This Amazing London Town," "They Say," "I'm in Love, I'm in Love" (a duet between Hecht and Clayburgh), and "In My Own Lifetime." Following his Tony award, Linden went on to star on TV as New York cop *Barney Miller* for seven hilarious years.

Original cast: Columbia S-30337.

The Secret Garden (Marsha Norman, Lucy Simon). Opened: April 25, 1991. Cast: Daisy Eagan, John Babcock, Mandy Patinkin, John

Cameron Mitchell, Robert Westenberg, Rebecca Luker, Tom Toner, Alison Fraser.

The source for this 1991 musical was a 1911 novel by Frances Hodgson Burnett, the same author responsible for *Little Lord Fauntleroy*.

In this tale, an orphan named Mary Lennox (Eagan), having lost both parents in an Indian cholera epidemic, is packed off to live in England with her withdrawn, hunchbacked uncle, Archibald Craven (Patinkin). Also in residence, though bedridden, is her unbearable cousin Colin (Babcock). Phantoms from their past cohabit the stage, including Mary's parents, Craven's dead wife, and various apparitions from India (even though life there for the neglected child was not exactly crumpets and tea).

Virtually all of the living characters are among life's walking wounded, emotional basket cases, including the disagreeable children. What changes them, giving each a fresh vigor and love of life, is Mary's discovery of an untended garden behind the house and the Yorkshire peasant boy Dickon (Mitchell) who helps her bring the garden, herself, and her still-breathing relatives back to the land of the living.

A book beloved by girls, it was fitting that the musical took shape under a group of talented women led by producer/designer Heidi Landesman, director Susan H. Schulman, composer Lucy Simon (older sister of pop singer/composer Carly Simon), and writer/lyricist Marsha Norman, the latter best known at the time for her brilliant 1983 Pulitzer Prize-winning drama, *'night, Mother*.

Calling the group "very much Sondheim's daughters," the *New Yorker*'s Mimi Kramer (May 13, 1991) hailed the musical as "quiet, charming, subtle, intelligent, and wholly literary in its approach to adaptation." *Newsweek*'s Jack Kroll (May 6, 1991) thought the phantoms and dream scenes overdone, disagreed with delaying the audience's view of the garden until the end, and felt that the touching simplicity of the source material was smothered "with a stifling sophistication," and by the $6.2 million budget.

At *Time* (May 6, 1991), William A. Henry III had no hesitation in his praise: "Vibrant and thought provoking to look at, melodic and poignant to hear, movingly acted and blessed with a dazzling

11-year-old star, this is the best American musical of the Broadway season."

Highlights include: "There's a Girl," "Wick," "The Girl I Mean to Be," "I Heard Someone Crying," "It's a Maze," "Winter's on the Wing," "If I Had a Fine White Horse," "A Bit of Earth," "Show Me the Key," "Quartet," "Race You to the Top of the Morning," "Hold On," "Where in the World," "How Could I Ever Know," and "Lily's Eyes." The atmospheric recording features a lot of dialogue setting up the musical numbers.

Tonys went to Daisy Eagan as Featured Actress, Marsha Norman for the book, and Heidi Landesman for scenic design.

Original cast: Columbia/Sony CT 48817.

Show Boat (Jerome Kern, Oscar Hammerstein, P. G. Wodehouse). Opened December 27, 1927. Cast: Howard Marsh, Norma Terris, Helen Morgan, Charles Winninger, Edna May Oliver, Jules Bledsoe.

After *Show Boat*, the American stage musical was changed forever. This landmark show's score grew naturally out of the characters and situations, and what characters!

While Joe (Bledsoe) and other black stevedores sing of hard work and no play, the somewhat dishonest riverboat gambler Gaylord Ravenal (Marsh) enlists as an actor on the showboat *Cotton Blossom* after its two stars Steve and Julie (Ellis and Morgan) are forced by the laws of segregation to leave the troupe. Cap'n Andy's daughter Magnolia (Terris) falls for the shady Gaylord; he marries and then deserts her and their daughter after running up a lot of debts. Julie becomes an alcoholic nightclub singer who secretly helps Magnolia break into show business. Twenty years after he disembarked, Gaylord returns and makes up with his wife and daughter.

It sounds like pure soap opera, but in its day *Show Boat* was dynamite stuff, bringing a heretofore unknown depth to the musical stage. The unforgettable songs include: "Make Believe," "Can't Help Lovin' Dat Man," "I Might Fall Back on You," "Ol' Man River," "You Are Love," "Life Upon the Wicked Stage," and "Bill" (lyric by P. G. Wodehouse).

As with *Porgy and Bess*, there are a lot of versions of *Show Boat* to choose from, though the original cast was not recorded. The first full recording of the score was by a 1972 London cast featuring Cleo Laine, Thomas Carey, Lorna Dallas, Kenneth Nelson, Andrew Jobin, and Ena Cabayo: Stanyan Records 10048.

A 1988 studio cast contains virtually the entire show, including dialogue, and features opera singers Frederica von Stade, Teresa Stratas, Jerry Hadley, Paige O'Hara, David Garrison (then playing the yuppy neighbor Steve Rhoades on Fox TV's *Married . . . With Children*), and Bruce Hubbard as Joe. Hubbard played the role earlier with the Houston Opera and went on to play it again on the London stage. The recording concludes with about 45 minutes of music written for various revivals of the show but never used: EMI/ Angel A4-49108 (3 CDs, plus libretto booklet). EMI/Angel also has a highlights version on 4DS-49847.

Excerpts from 1932 cast members Helen Morgan and Paul Robeson are on RCA AVM1-1741.

A 1962 studio cast of John Raitt, Barbara Cook, and William Warfield is on Columbia PS 2220.

Side by Side by Sondheim (Stephen Sondheim). Opened in London May 4, 1976; in New York April 18, 1977. Cast: Millicent Martin, Julia McKenzie, David Kernan.

Despite the high critical regard for Sondheim's genius, most of his shows have lost money. His uncompromising dedication to the story and characters, and his unwillingness to toss in a few potential song hits, not to mention his ahead-of-his-time originality, all combine to create a gulf between the composer and the mass audience.

Side by Side was an attempt to reach that audience by separating the songs from the shows and presenting them in a revue format. It was a great success and finally brought Sondheim's name out in front of the footlights.

There are 31 songs on the double album, including: "Comedy Tonight," "The Little Things You Do Together," "Another Hundred People," "You Could Drive a Person Crazy," "Everybody Says Don't," "Send in the Clowns," "We're Gonna Be All Right" (with some lyrics that were cut from the original in *Do I Hear a Waltz?*), "Losing My Mind," "If Momma Was Married," and Martin's thrilling rendition of "I'm Still Here."

Original cast: RCA CBL2-1851.

Silk Stockings (Cole Porter). Opened February 24, 1955. Cast: Don Ameche, Hildegarde Neff, Gretchen Wyler, George Tobias, Julie Newmar.

"A saucy, sexy, satiric saturnalia," gushed Robert Coleman in the *Daily Mirror*. "Brash, tuneful and immensely funny. It moves like a rocket bent on reaching the moon in a hurry."

Based on the Greta Garbo film *Ninotchka*, this was Cole Porter's last Broadway show, and by no means his least. Ameche plays Steve Canfield, an American talent agent in Paris trying to talk a Soviet composer into writing for the movies. A stern, humorless Comrade Ninotchka (Neff) is sent to retrieve the composer and a trio of capitalistic-minded comrades, but ends up being seduced by Paris and Canfield both.

Brooks Atkinson told readers of the *Times* it "represents the best goods in the American musical comedy emporium," adding, "this is one of Gotham's memorable shows, on a level with *Guys and Dolls*."

The songs include: "Paris Loves Lovers," "Stereophonic Sound" (a satire on contemporary movie gimmicks such as Technicolor and Cinemascope), "It's a Chemical Reaction, That's All," "All of You," the hilarious "Siberia," and the risqué "Satin and Silk."

The 1957 film featured Fred Astaire and Cyd Charisse (using the singing voice of Carol Richards), and added "Fated to Be Mated" and "The Ritz Roll and Rock." (The lyrics to "Stereophonic Sound" were also cleaned up a bit, dropping references to Marilyn Monroe's backside and Ava Gardner playing Lady Godiva.)

Original cast: RCA LOC-1016. Film: MGM 3542.

So Long, 174th Street (Stan Daniels). Opened April 27, 1976. Cast: Robert Morse, Loni Ackerman, George S. Irving.

A 16 performance flop, but a hugely comic and enjoyable one to listen to nonetheless. Based on Carl Reiner's play *Enter Laughing*, the musical is set in the Bronx, circa 1935, where young David Kolowitz (Morse) dreams of someday being a world famous actor. His mother, however, wants him to be a druggist and lays some hilarious guilt trips on him with "My Son, the Druggist" and "If

You Want to Break Your Mother's Heart." Naturally, David finds both love and a way out of the Bronx by show's end.

Most of the songs reveal David's inner fantasies of wealth, fame, and beautiful girls, including: "David Kolowitz, the Actor," "It's Like," "I'm Undressing Girls With My Eyes," "Bolero On Rye," "You" (which uses snatches of classic lyrics from Porter, Hart, and Berlin, among others), "He Touched Me," "Men," and the wickedly risque number, "The Butler's Song," in which David imagines himself bedding all of Hollywood's screen sirens, from Garbo to Maria Montez, while his butler takes reservations.

The original cast was not recorded. A studio cast reassembled most of them, with the inclusion of Kaye Ballard as David's mother: Original Cast Records OC 8131.

Sophisticated Ladies (Duke Ellington and friends). Opened March 1, 1981. Cast: Gregory Hines, Hinton Battle, Judith Jamison, Phyllis Hyman, P. J. Benjamin, Mercedes Ellington, Gregg Burge.

If the original Ellington sides are not available, this glorious revue of his career is the next best thing. Songs include: "Perdido," "It Don't Mean a Thing," "Take the 'A' Train," "Solitude," "Don't Get Around Much Anymore," "Caravan," "Drop Me Off in Harlem," "In a Sentimental Mood," "I'm Beginning to See the Light," "Do Nothing 'Til You Hear From Me," "Mood Indigo," "I Got It Bad and That Ain't Good," and "Sophisticated Lady," plus lesser known tunes such as "Hit Me With a Hot Note and Watch Me Bounce," "Fat and Forte," and "Cotton Tail."

Battle won a Tony; Hines and Hayman were nominated, as was the show.

Original cast: RCA CBL2-4053 (double set).

Stop the World, I Want to Get Off (Leslie Bricusse, Anthony Newley). Opened in London July 20, 1961; in New York October 3, 1962. Cast: Anthony Newley, Anna Quayle.

Littlechap (Newley) is an ambitious sort ("I Wanna Be Rich") and a flagrant womanizer who gets his "Typically English" girlfriend Evie (Quayle) pregnant and has to marry her ("Lumbered" he is, and not afraid to sing about it). On a business trip to

Russia ("Glorious Russian") he also gets himself lumbered by Anya (also played by Quayle). Later he is equally compromised by a maid from Germany (Quayle again), who is "Typische Deutsche." A success as a businessman (who, nonetheless, gets so confused by his life that at any moment he is apt to yell, "Stop the world!"), Littlechap next gets involved with an American airhead named Ginny (yup, Quayle), and goes into politics ("Mumbo Jumbo"). Once in retirement, he begins to realize that the only person he ever really loved was himself ("What Kind of Fool Am I?").

Other notable songs: "Once in a Lifetime," "Gonna Build a Mountain," "Someone Nice Like You," "Meilinki Meilchick," "All American," and "Family Fugue." For her multiple incarnations, Quayle won a Tony. She should have won four.

The 1966 movie with Tony Tanner and Millicent Martin was filmed just as if it were being presented on a stage and is quite good. The 1978 stage revival with Sammy Davis, Jr., and Marian Mercer included a new song, "Life Is a Woman."

Original cast: London 88001. Film: Warners 1643. Revival: Warners HS 3214.

Strike Up the Band (George and Ira Gershwin). Opened January 14, 1930. Cast: Bobby Clark, Paul McCullough, Dudley Clements, Blanche Ring, Doris Carson.

Despite initial and enthusiastic praise from out-of-town critics, the original 1927 version of this sharp satire bombed, never arriving on Broadway. It was decided that the public just wasn't ready for a barbed musical attack on rapacious capitalists, jingoistic masses, and corrupt politicians as sketched by the acid pen of George S. Kaufman. The plot had a businessman manipulating the United States into a war with Switzerland in order to protect the profits from his firm's inferior cheese. Talk about protectionist trade policies!

A major rewrite followed, with Morrie Ryskind tailoring a new script to suit the comic antics of Clark and McCullough (the cheese controversy was changed to chocolate). The Gershwins also had to rewrite songs and compose new ones. The new version was a Broadway hit in 1930, paving the way for more political musicals like *Of Thee I Sing* [Act Three, 1932].

Neither cast was recorded and the scores were lost to the public until 1991 when they were again brought to life by a talented studio cast. The 1927 score features Brent Barrett, Don Chastain, Rebecca Luker, Jason Graae, Beth Fowler, Charles Goff, and Juliet Lambert. Songs include: "Fletcher's American Cheese Choral Society," "17 and 21," "Typical Self-Made American," "The Man I Love," "Yankee Doodle Rhythm," "Strike Up the Band," "Oh This is Such a Lovely War," "Hoping That Someday You'd Care," and "The War That Ended War."

Studio cast: Elektra Nonsuch/Roxbury Recordings 79273-4. Double set. The complete 1930 score has also been recorded and is scheduled for release in the Spring of 1993.

Sweet Charity (Cy Coleman, Dorothy Fields). Opened January 29, 1966. Cast: Gwen Verdon, John McMartin, Thelma Oliver, Helen Gallagher, Ruth Buzzi.

Based on the Fellini film *Nights of Cabiria*, *Sweet Charity* tells the story of dancehall hostess Charity Hope Valentine (Verdon), frequent doormat for uncaring guys. She is determined to make something of herself, fall in love, and live happily ever after (maybe she thinks she's in a musical). She meets Oscar Linquist (McMartin) in a stalled elevator and they very nearly get married — until Oscar balks after learning what she does for a living and dumps her (this made more sense in the movie where Cabiria/Charity was a streetwalker).

There were nine Tony nominations, with director Bob Fosse winning one as choreographer.

The Coleman/Fields score is a classic, with such songs as "Big Spender," "There's Gotta Be Something Better Than This," "If My Friends Could See Me Now," "Baby Dream Your Dream," "Where Am I Going?" "I'm a Brass Band," "The Rhythm of Life," and "I Love to Cry at Weddings."

Those titles represent some of the most memorable show tunes in the history of Broadway, yet at least one opening night critic, Stanley Kauffmann of *The New York Times*, proclaimed the next morning that there were "no tunes that can be remembered. There is not even a tune that one would *want* to remember."

Feelings ran decidedly different when the show was revived in

1986. Then, Douglas Watt of the *Daily News* called it "Cy Coleman's most exuberant score, fitted out with smart lyrics by the late Dorothy Fields," and *The Wall Street Journal*'s Edwin Wilson backed him up: "Cy Coleman's driving, upbeat score is probably his best [and] Dorothy Fields' witty, inventive lyrics remain top-drawer."

The revival starred Tony nominee Debbie Allen (of TV's *Fame*); Tonys were won by supporting players Bebe Neuwirth (of TV's *Cheers*) and Michael Rupert (the star of *Falsettoland*, above). The show itself was named Best Revival, outdoing the original.

The 1969 movie starred Shirley MacLaine, Chita Rivera, Paula Kelly, John McMartin, Stubby Kaye, and, doing "The Rhythm of Life," Sammy Davis, Jr. The film dropped "Baby Dream Your Dream," adding "My Personal Property" and "It's a Nice Face."

Original cast: Columbia KOS-2900. Film: Decca DL 71502. Revival: EMI 4XT 517196.

They're Playing Our Song (Marvin Hamlisch, Carole Bayer Sager). Opened February 11, 1979. Cast: Robert Klein, Lucie Arnaz.

Two diametrically opposed songwriters (he a disciplined neat-freak, she a scatterbrained kook) are teamed together to write songs. They fall in love, break up, then get back together again for a big finale. What it lacked in original concept it made up for with a funny Neil Simon script and some exciting, contemporary songs, including: "Fallin'," "Workin' It Out," "Right," "Just for Tonight," "When You're in My Arms," and "I Still Believe in Love." Hamlisch's instrumental music for the second act overture, the "Entre Act," is super.

Original cast: Casablanca NBLP-7141.

Threepenny Opera (Kurt Weill, Bertolt Brecht). Opened on Broadway April 13, 1933. Cast (1954 Off-Broadway revival): Lotte Lenya, Scott Merrill, Jo Sullivan, Beatrice Arthur.

Based on John Gay's 1728 play *The Beggar's Opera*, Brecht's version is a scathing (and sometimes repulsive) look at modern life and the corruption that permeated Germany in the 1920s, told as a chronicle of the unsavory adventures of a gang of London thieves in

Victorian times headed by the murderous (and much-married) Macheath. His downfall proves that there is no honor among thieves, or, by extension, women and the police either. His last minute rescue from the gallows and subsequent peerage and pension says a lot about politics.

It was a smash hit in Germany in 1928 but flopped when it came to America — the 1933 production was greeted with much critical resistance and many took it to be thinly disguised propaganda for socialism. If anything, it was ahead of its time, and the 1954 revival (newly translated by Marc Blitzstein) ran Off-Broadway for over 2,700 performances.

Songs include: "The Ballad of Mack the Knife" (popular renditions by Louis Armstrong and Bobby Darin were an enormous boost for the revival), "The Ballad of Sexual Dependency," "Pirate Jenny," "The Perpendicular Song," "The Ballad of What Keeps a Man Alive," "The Uncertainty of Human Condition," "Memories Tango Ballad," "Ballad of Pleasant Living," "Solomon Song," and "Jealousy Duet."

Revival cast of 1954 featuring Scott Merrill, Martin Wolfson, Lotte Lenya, Jo Sullivan, Charlotte Rae (best known to TV viewers for playing Edna Garrett on *The Facts of Life* for eight years), Gerald Price, George Tyne, and Beatrice Arthur as Lucy Brown: Polydor 820260-4 Y-1. (Future television comic John Astin can be heard leading the chorus in the "Wedding Song.")

New York Shakespeare Festival's 1976 revival cast of Raul Julia, Blair Brown, C. K. Alexander, Elizabeth Wilson, Ellen Greene, and Caroline Kava: Columbia PS-34326. (Brown and Kava fling unexpurgated curses at one another in the "Jealousy Duet.")

The 1989 film was titled *Mack the Knife* and starred Raul Julia, Richard Harris, Julia Migenes (whose career dates back to playing Zero Mostel's daughter Hodel in the original *Fiddler on the Roof* in 1965), rock star Roger Daltry, and Julie Waters; Elizabeth Seal, the star of *Irma La Douce*, has a nonsinging role as Molly: CBS SMT-45630.

The Unsinkable Molly Brown (Meredith Willson). Opened November 3, 1960. Cast: Tammy Grimes (Tony winner), Harve Presnell, Cameron Prud'homme.

If there was a spunkiness contest between heroines of musicals, Little Orphan Annie, Auntie Mame, Fannie Brice, Sally Bowles, Eliza Doolittle, Charity Hope Valentine, and others would be just so many runners-up to Molly Brown, who defiantly sings "I Ain't Down Yet" not once, not twice, but three times (just in case anybody doubted her resolve).

An orphan found drifting down a river in a basket, Molly grows up poor but determined to be rich. And nobody better tell her she can't (or she might reprise her big number). She does get rich, of course, and breaks into high society thanks to marrying Leadville Johnny Brown (Presnell), a man with a knack for finding lucrative silver deposits. They go through more than one fortune and Molly survives the sinking of the Titanic as a heroine before living happily ever after.

Other songs: "Belly Up to the Bar, Boys," "My Own Brass Bed," "I'll Never Say No," "Bea-u-ti-ful People of Denver," "Are You Sure?" (a revivalist number), "Bon Jour (The Language Song)," and "Dolce Far Niente" (the attempt by a Count to seduce Molly).

The 1964 movie starred Presnell, Debbie Reynolds, and Ed Begley.

Original cast: Capitol SWAO (S)-1509. 1989 reissue: Capitol C4-92054. Film: MGM SE (S)-4232 ST.

West Side Story (Leonard Bernstein, Stephen Sondheim). Opened September 26, 1957. Cast: Larry Kert, Carol Lawrence, Chita Rivera, Marilyn Cooper, Grover Dale, Eddie Roll.

"A venturesome forward step," said John Chapman in the *Daily News*, "a bold new kind of musical theatre — a juke-box Manhattan opera . . . extraordinarily exciting." To John McClain of the New York *Journal-American* it was "an entirely new form. There are arias, duets, choral numbers; there is ballet and jive, and there is an appealing libretto. It is the most exciting thing that has come to town since 'My Fair Lady.'"

It was *Romeo and Juliet* with songs, dances, and New York street gangs battling for turf, principally between the white Jets and the Puerto Rican Sharks. The pulse-pounding Bernstein music in "The Dance at the Gym," "The Rumble," "Jet Song," and "Cool" is matched by Sondheim's satiric lyrics to "America" and "Gee, Officer Krupke!" Other standouts: "Something's Coming," "Maria," "Tonight," "I Feel Pretty," and "A Boy Like That." The original idea came from choreographer Jerome Robbins, who won a Tony for his brilliant work.

Robert Coleman told *Daily Mirror* readers, "It moves with the speed of a switchblade knife thrust," while Chita Rivera "lights up like a handful of Fourth-of-July sparklers." Brooks Atkinson admired it as "a profoundly moving show that is as ugly as the city jungles and also pathetic, tender and forgiving."

The 1961 movie won an Oscar as Best Picture and Oscars for its supporting players, George Chakiris and Rita Moreno.

Original cast: Columbia S 32603. Film: Columbia OS-2070 (Marni Nixon sings for Natalie Wood and Jim Bryant for Richard Beymer). Also see Act Four's 1985 Grammy Award.

Working (Stephen Schwartz, Micki Grant, Mary Rodgers, James Taylor, Susan Birkenhead, Craig Carnelia). Opened May 14, 1978. Cast: Bob Gunton, David Patrick Kelly, Joe Mantegna, Lynne Thigpen, David Langston Smyrl, Susan Bigelow, Robin Lamont, Lenora Nemetz.

Studs Terkel, the Chicago-based master of the interview, conducted a series of talks with people in all walks of life, recording their attitudes toward their jobs, and published the collection in a book called *Working*. Where most people just saw interviews, no matter how fascinating, Stephen Schwartz saw one act plays, some of them musicals. He assigned selected interviews to a variety of composers and *Working* is the result, a kind of musical revue about jobs, tied together with Schwartz's opening, "All the Livelong Day" (utilizing some lines from Walt Whitman).

There are songs about a parking lot attendant ("Lovin' Al"), a paperboy ("Neat to Be a Newsboy"), a teacher ("Nobody Tells Me How"), a housewife ("Just a Housewife"), a waitress ("It's an Art," a song about being proud of what you do and how you do it, whatever it may be), and a trucker ("Brother Trucker"). Two of **Micki Grant's songs** are special standouts, one on blocked opportunities ("If I Could Have Been") and one on domestic work ("Cleaning Women").

Original cast: Columbia JS-35411. It did not fare well as a musical, lasting just 25 performances, but the recording stands as an excellent concept album of related songs.

REFERENCE NOTES

1. Joanne Gordon, *Art Isn't Easy: The Achievement of Stephen Sondheim* (Carbondale: Southern Illinois University Press, 1990), p. 1.

2. *The New York Times*, May 30, 1965.

3. Larry L. King, *The Whorehouse Papers* (New York: Viking, 1982), p. 31.

4. *The New York Times*, June 17-20, 1937; June 27, 1937; December 6, 1937 (review).

In his autobiography, *Run-Through* (Simon & Schuster, 1972, p. 25), John Houseman related how the dissolution of the WPA Arts Projects was inevitable as the economy improved following the great Depression, especially since "there were those, in and out of Congress, who had never ceased to feel that relief workers were bums . . . and who regarded the Arts Projects as a particularly dangerous form of Trojan horse, loaded with screwballs and Reds."

5. Al Kasha and Joel Hirschhorn, *Notes on Broadway* (New York: Simon and Schuster, 1985), p. 233.

6. *The Village Voice*, August 21, 1990.

7. El Paso *Times*, August 17, 1990.

8. Ibid., p. 77.

9. *Oxford Dictionary of Quotations* (New York: Oxford University Press, 1979), p. 163.

Coda: Appendixes

APPENDIX A
The Search

In collecting anything, from art to antiques, the hunt itself is very often the most exciting and satisfying part of the process.

For librarians, the best places to start are local radio stations, particularly the ones that have been around a long time; they just might have a storeroom or closet containing old, used, original cast albums that are not needed anymore and that they might be willing to donate. Letters to regular book donors might also turn up some music gifts.

The next and easiest step is to visit local record stores. After checking the in-store stock, browse through the bargain bins and catalogs. (Stores, however, will usually order only shows that are in print. The out-of-print recordings are the real challenge.)

The quarterly Opus edition of the *Schwann Catalog* is a good investment for knowing what is available. While its listings are mostly of classical music, they often list 20 or more pages of stage, film, and TV soundtracks. An added bonus is that there are usually ads inside from companies that can find virtually anything listed. For subscription information, or to buy single copies, write: Schwann Opus Publications, P.O. Box 41094, Nashville, TN 37204.

Show Music, published under the auspices of the Goodspeed Opera House, is a unique and invaluable quarterly magazine for musical fans that reviews new original cast recordings as well as film scores, videos, foreign stage productions, and books about the theater. Editor Max O. Preeo is also the librarian for Goodspeed's impressive theater arts collections and an excellent source of information. Write: SHOW MUSIC, Box 466, Goodspeed Landing, East Haddam, CT 06423.

Subscriptions to theater magazines will also keep the collector up to date on new shows. Three worth reading are: *TheaterWeek* (28 W. 25th St., 4th Floor, New York, NY 10010), *Playbill* (71 Vanderbilt Avenue, New York, NY 10169), and *American Theatre* (Theatre Communications Group, 355 Lexington Ave., New York, NY 10164-0217).

For those with large budgets there is *The New York Theatre Critics Reviews*, a biweekly (except between seasons) that reprints a collection of raves and pans for the major shows each year. The 1991 cost was $110 a year. Write: Critics Theatre Reviews, Inc., Four Park Avenue, Suite 21D, New York, NY 10016.

Writing directly to the record companies sometimes works, though they prefer dealing with established commercial outlets.

A look in the phone directories of major cities such as New York, Los Angeles, and Chicago will produce the names of companies that specialize in stocking or finding musicals, used or in mint condition. Three places to start: A-1 Record Finders, P.O. Box 75071, Los Angeles, CA 90075; The Record Hunter, 507 5th Avenue, New York, NY 10017; Footlight Records, 113 E. 12th St., New York, NY 10003.

Bruce and Doris Yeko are a collector's dream come true. They not only run a catalog service for hard to find shows but started their own record label to preserve those musicals passed over by the major recording companies. They call it Original Cast Records. Two of their personal productions are in this book: *Bring Back Birdie* and *So Long, 174th Street*. Their catalog of available shows is very useful. Write: Broadway/Hollywood Recordings, attention Bruce Yeko, Box 496, Georgetown, CT 06829.

With imagination, time, the perseverance of a true searcher, and a proper budget, every show in this book can be obtained in one or more formats. Good hunting!

APPENDIX B

Reference Material

Once a listener gets hooked on musicals, it is only natural for that person to go in search of further information. There are numerous histories of the musical genre as well as biographies of major composers that are immensely helpful in supplying both historical and critical information. A basic list follows.

Histories

Bordman, Gerald. 1978. *American Musical Theatre: A Chronicle*. New York: Oxford University Press. Bordman lists every musical show from 1866 through 1978, providing basic information and frequently barbed comments on each.

Ewen, David. 1977. *All the Years of American Popular Music*. New York: Prentice-Hall. Musicologist Ewen covers the full spectrum of the nation's musical heritage, from colonial days through rock and roll, with a good emphasis on theater and film music.

Ewen, David. 1959. *The Complete Book of the American Musical Theater*. New York: Henry Holt.

Goldman, William. 1969. *The Season: A Candid Look at Broadway*. New York: Harcourt, Brace, and World.

Gottfried, Martin. 1979. *Broadway Musicals*. New York: Harry N. Abrams.

Green, Stanley. 1974. *The World of Musical Comedy*. New York: A. S. Barnes and Company. Green covers the history of the musical by devoting each chapter to a principal composer.

Morrow, Lee Alan. 1987. *The Tony Award Book: Four Decades of Great American Theater*. New York: Abbeville Press.

Biographies

Adler, Richard, and Lee Davis. 1990. *You Gotta Have Heart*, Adler's autobiography. New York: Donald I. Fine, Inc.

Bergreen, Laurence. 1990. *As Thousands Cheer: The Life of Irving Berlin*. New York: Viking.

Bernstein, Leonard. 1982. *Findings*. New York: Simon and Schuster.

Bordman, Gerald. 1980. *Jerome Kern: His Life and Music*. New York: Oxford University Press.

Eells, George. 1967. *The Life That Late He Led*, biography of Cole Porter. New York: Putnam.

Gordon, Joanne. 1990. *Art Isn't Easy: The Achievement of Stephen Sondheim*. Carbondale: Southern Illinois University Press.

Gruen, John. 1978. *Menotti: A Biography*. New York: Macmillan.

Guernsey, Otis. 1964. *Playwrights, Lyricists, Composers on Theater*. New York: Dodd, Mead.

Hart, Dorothy. 1976. *Thou Swell, Thou Witty: The Life and Lyrics of Lorenz Hart*. New York: Harper and Row.

Jablonski, Edward. 1987. *Gershwin*. New York: Doubleday.

Kasha, Al, and Joel Hirschhorn. 1985. *Notes on Broadway, Intimate Conversations With Broadway's Greatest Songwriters*. New York: Simon and Schuster (a Fireside Theatre book).

Lees, Gene. 1990. *Inventing Champagne: The Worlds of Lerner and Loewe*. New York: St. Martin's Press.

Lerner, Alan Jay. 1978. *The Street Where I Live*. New York: W. W. Norton.

Mandelbaum, Ken. 1989. *A Chorus Line and the Musicals of Michael Bennett*. New York: St. Martin's Press.

Peyser, Joan. 1987. *Bernstein: A Biography*. New York: Beech Tree Books/William Morrow.

Rodgers, Richard. 1975. *Musical Stages*. New York: Random House.

Schwartz, Charles. 1977. *Cole Porter: A Biography*. New York: Dial Press.

Shapiro, Doris. 1990. *We Danced All Night: My Life Behind the Scenes With Alan Jay Lerner*. New York: Morrow.

Taylor, Deems. 1953. *Some Enchanted Evenings: The Story of Rodgers and Hammerstein*. New York: Harper.

Walsh, Michael. 1989. *Andrew Lloyd Webber, His Life and Works*. New York: Harry N. Abrams.

Zadan, Craig. 1989. *Sondheim & Co*. New York: Harper & Row, 2nd updated edition.

Books on Recordings

DeBus, Allen G. 1989. *The Complete Entertainment Discography*. New York: DaCapo Press.

Harris, Steve. 1988. *Film, Television and Stage Music on Phonograph Records*. Jefferson, North Carolina: McFarland.

Hummel, David. 1984. *The Collector's Guide to the American Musical Theatre*, 2 volumes. Metuchen, New Jersey: The Scarecrow Press. Comprehensive and indispensable.

Lynch, Richard Chigley. 1987. *Broadway on Record*. Westport Connecticut: Greenwood Press.

Raymond, Jack. 1982. *Show Music on Record*. New York: Frederick Unger Publishing Co.

APPENDIX C

Recorded Anthologies

To supplement an original cast collection, particularly in the case of the pioneer Broadway composers whose best works predated the era of the cast album (and whose songs were often meant to stand on their own outside the context of a show), there are collections of songs by a variety of popular artists. A collector should always be on the lookout for such anthologies. A brief list follows.

Bennett/Berlin. Tony Bennett. Columbia PCT 44029, 1987.

Bobby Short Celebrates Rodgers and Hart. Bobby Short. Atlantic SD 2-610, 1975.

Bobby Short Is K-Ra-Zy for Gershwin. Bobby Short. Atlantic SD 2-608, 1973. Double set.

Bobby Short Loves Cole Porter. Bobby Short. Atlantic SD 2-606, 1971. Double set.

The Broadway Album. Barbra Streisand (mostly songs by Sondheim). Columbia OCT 40092, 1985.

Broadway Baby. Dorothy Loudon. A mix of memorable melodies from Sondheim, Rodgers and Hart, Berlin, Kander and Ebb, and others. DRG Records SLC 5203.

Classic Gershwin. Cleo Laine. Columbia FMT 42516.

Cleo Sings Sondheim. Cleo Laine. RCA 7702-4-RC, 1988. A veteran of several London productions of Sondheim shows, jazz singer Cleo Laine is fast becoming his principle pop music interpreter and this recording is a delight from beginning to end.

Cole. Cole Porter sings selections from his 1935 show *Jubilee*. The flip side has selections from Mary Martin, Danny Kaye, and Ethel Merman. Columbia, KS 31456, 1973.

The Cole Porter Songbook. Ella Fitzgerald. Verve VE-2-2511, 1956, reissued 1976. Double set. Elegance personified.

Dionne Warwick Sings Cole Porter. Arista AC8573.

The George and Ira Gershwin Songbook. Ella Fitzgerald. Verve VE-2-2525, 1959, reissued 1978. Double set.

The George and Ira Gershwin Songbook. Various artists, with Julie Andrews, Perry Como, Della Reese, Eartha Kitt, Dinah Shore and others. RCA 9613-4-R.

The Harold Arlen Songbook. Ella Fitzgerald. Verve 817 526-1, 1961, reissued 1984. Double set.

Ira Gershwin Loves to Rhyme. Ira Gershwin, Harold Arlen. Mark 56 records 721, 1975.

Ira Gershwin Lyrics. Rosemary Clooney. Concord CJ-112.

The Irving Berlin Songbook. Ella Fitzgerald. Verve 2683 027, 1958. Double set.

The Jerome Kern Songbook. Ella Fitzgerald. Verve 825 669-2.

Julie Wilson Sings the Kurt Weill Songbook. DRG CDSL 5207.

Julie Wilson Sings Stephen Sondheim. DRG CDRG 5206.

Mary Martin Sings, Richard Rodgers Plays. BMG Classics 60558-4-RG.

Michael Feinstein Sings the Burton Lane Songbook, Vol. 1. Elektra/Nonesuch 79243-4.

Music of Harold Arlen. Rosemary Clooney. Concord CJ-220.

Music of Irving Berlin. Rosemary Clooney. Concord CJ-255.

Naughty Baby. Maureen McGovern sings Gershwin. CBS FMT 44995, 1990.

Night and Day: The Cole Porter Songbook. Various artists, including Dinah Washington, Louis Armstrong, Sarah Vaughn, Fred Astaire, Ella Fitzgerald, Billy Eckstine, and Mel Torme. PolyGram 847 202-4.

Pure Gershwin. Michael Feinstein. Elektra, E4-60742, 1987.

Remember: Michael Feinstein Sings Irving Berlin. Michael Feinstein. Elektra, E4 60744, 1987.

The Rodgers and Hart Songbook. Ella Fitzgerald. Verve VE-2-2519, 1956, reissued 1977. Double set.

The Rodgers and Hart Songbook. Various artists, including Julie Andrews, Perry Como, Vic Damone, Eddie Fisher, Tony Mar-

tin, Ann-Margret, Nancy Walker, Dinah Shore, Morgana King, and Anthony Newley. RCA 8590-2-R.
Rosemary Clooney Sings Ira Gershwin Lyrics. Concord CJ-112.
Rosemary Clooney Sings the Music of Harold Arlen. Concord CJ-210.
Rosemary Clooney Sings the Music of Cole Porter. Rosemary Clooney. Concord CJ-185.

APPENDIX D

As We Went to Press . . . .

The 1991-1992 musical season began inauspiciously with the early demise of *Nick & Nora* (Strouse/Maltby) after nine performances, but the season turned out to be one of the best in years; all should produce fine original cast recordings.

Tony nominees: *Crazy for You*, with its wonderful patchwork Gershwin score and story loosely based on *Girl Crazy* [Act Five]; *Falsettos*, a combining of two Off-Broadway hits, *March of the Falsettos* and *Falsettoland* [Act Five]; the British import *Five Guys Named Moe* [Act Five]; and *Jelly's Last Jam*, using the music of Jelly Roll Morton and Luther Henderson, lyrics by Susan Birkenhead, starring Tony winners Gregory Hines and Tonya Pinkins.

The Tony winner: *Crazy for You*, with Harry Groener, Jodie Benson, and Michele Pawk (Angel, 4DQ 54618). Best Original Score: *Falsettos*, music and lyrics by William Finn.

Best revival was *Guys and Dolls* (RCA) with Peter Gallagher, Nathan Lane, Josie de Guzman, and Tony winner Faith Prince.

The New York Drama Critics Circle did not give out a Best Musical award, deciding there was nothing new or original enough.

Late releases: *The Most Happy Fella* (RCA), a two-piano version transplanted from the Goodspeed Opera House starring Spiro Malas, Sophie Hayden, and Tony winner Scott Waara; *Putting It Together*, a London revue of Stephen Sondheim's work (First Night Records); *Grand Hotel* (RCA); a studio cast of *The King and I* with Julie Andrews and Ben Kingsley (Phillips Records); and, yes, even *Nick & Nora* (That's Entertainment Records).

The 1992-1993 season looked mainly to Hollywood and the past for material to musicalize: *My Favorite Year, The Goodbye Girl,* and *Kiss of the Spider Woman* were films that became stage musicals with excellent recordings, while *Tommy* metamorphosed from a 1969 album and 1975 movie into a 1993 smash Broadway hit. Even *Anna Karenina* hit the boards singing.

The Circle and Tony winner for the 1992-1993 season was by veterans John Kander, Fred Ebb, and Terrence McNally: *Kiss of the Spider Woman: The Musical* (RCA/BMG 09026 61579-4). They each won Tonys, as did their three star performers, Brent Carver, Anthony Crivello, and the indestructible Chita Rivera. Best Musical nominees: British import *Blood Brothers* by Willy Russell (RCA/BMG); the Marvin Hamlisch and David Zippel adaptation of Neil Simon's *The Goodbye Girl* (Columbia CT 53761), starring Martin Short and Bernadette Peters; and *The Who's Tommy* (RCA), composer Peter Townshend sharing Best Original Score with Kander and Ebb. *My Favorite Year* (RCA/BMG 09026 61617-4) was an early flop, yet produced a terrific recording with Tim Curry, Lainie Kazan, and Tony winner Andrea Martin.

To update the Grammy Awards, *The Will Rogers Follies* and the revival of *Guys and Dolls* are the most recent winners, with *The Who's Tommy* the next likely winner.

Bibliography

Most of the information in this volume came from material supplied with various original cast recordings. Appendix B contains a list of general books on the subject of musical theater in America; most were invaluable in nailing down specific dates or for confirming plot twists, number of performances, and biographical information. Newspaper and magazine review sources are noted in the text. The most frequently consulted reference sources were:

Bordman, Gerald. 1978. *American Musical Theatre*. New York: Oxford University Press.

Eells, George. 1967. *The Life That Late He Led* (biography of Cole Porter). New York: Putnam.

Ewen, David. 1977. *All the Years of American Popular Music*. New York: Prentice-Hall.

Green, Stanley. 1974. *The World of Musical Comedy*. New York: A. S. Barnes and Company.

Hummel, David. 1984. *The Collector's Guide to the American Musical Theatre*. Metuchen, New Jersey: The Scarecrow Press.

Jablonski, Edward. 1981. *The Encyclopedia of American Music*. Garden City, New York: Doubleday.

Jablonski, Edward. 1973. *The Gershwin Years*. New York: Doubleday.

Maltin, Leonard. 1989. *Leonard Maltin's TV Movies and Video Guide*. New York: Signet/New American Library.

Raymond, Jack. 1982. *Show Music on Record — From the 1890s to the 1980s*. New York: Frederick Ungar Publishing.

Stevenson, Isabelle, ed. 1987. *The Tony Awards*. New York: Crown.

Webster's American Biographies. 1975. Charles Van Doren, ed. Springfield, Massachusetts: G. & C. Merriam Company.

Zadan, Craig. 1989. *Sondheim & Co.* New York: Harper & Row, 2nd updated edition.

General Index

Song Index